THE SHAPING OF
TESS OF THE D'URBERVILLES

Liza ~~~

Tess

~~A Daughter~~ of the D'Urbervilles.

Book First.

~~Her Education~~ The maiden

Chapter I.

On an evening in the latter part of May a middle-aged man
was ~~riding~~ home, walking ∧ ~~town~~ from Stourcastle ~~market~~ by a lane which
led into the recesses of the neighbouring Vale of Blakemore ∧ or Blackmoor.
The pair of legs ~~that carried him were feeble~~ were rickety, and there was a bias
in his ∧ gait that inclined him to the left of a straight line ∧ somewhat.
He occasionally gave a smart nod, as if in confirmation of ~~the~~ some opinion,
∧ he was not ~~thinking~~ of anything in particular. An empty ~~b~~
egg-basket was slung upon his arm. ~~Presently~~ and the nap of his hat was ruffled,
∧ grey ∧ Presently He was met by an elderly parson astride on a
~~bl~~ mare, who, as he rode, hummed a wandering tune.

"Good-night," said the ~~pedestrian~~ with the basket.

"Good-night, Sir John," said the parson.

The man with the basket, after another pace or two, halted, & turning
round ∧ called to the last speaker.

"Now, Sir, begging your pardon, & ∧ not knowing your name, we ∧ well as I know 'ee by sight,
met last market-day on this road about this time, & I said 'Good-
night', & you made reply 'Good-night, Sir John', as now."

∧ and a patch worn away at the brim where he seized it to take it off.

British Museum Additional MS. 38182, fol. 1

THE SHAPING OF
TESS OF THE D'URBERVILLES

J. T. LAIRD

OXFORD
AT THE CLARENDON PRESS
1975

Oxford University Press, Ely House, London W. 1

GLASGOW NEW YORK TORONTO MELBOURNE WELLINGTON
CAPE TOWN IBADAN NAIROBI DAR ES SALAAM LUSAKA ADDIS ABABA
DELHI BOMBAY CALCUTTA MADRAS KARACHI LAHORE DACCA
KUALA LUMPUR SINGAPORE HONG KONG TOKYO

ISBN 0 19 812060 5

*Printed in Great Britain
at the University Press, Oxford
by Vivian Ridler
Printer to the University*

PREFACE

THE first two chapters of this book are devoted to bibliographical matters which provide the foundation for the structure of critical analysis that follows. Chapter I deals mainly with the line of transmission of the text of *Tess of the d'Urbervilles* and with the circumstances surrounding its composition and publication. In chapter II interest focuses on the manuscript of the novel, and, more specifically, on the evidence furnished by foliation and naming of characters in the task of identifying the Ur-text and the five main layers of manuscript material.

The identification of the Ur-text makes possible a partial reconstruction of Hardy's Ur-novel; consequently, in chapters III and IV I am concerned with analysing the distinctive features of this early version of *Tess*, in terms of its plot, themes, and imagery. Changes made in the manuscript during the later stages of its composition are discussed in the following three chapters (V–VII), where attention is directed towards new developments in moral tone, themes, imagery, and characterization.

In chapters VIII and IX the subject of inquiry is the continuing evolution of the novel in its various printed forms—beginning with the serial version published in the *Graphic* during the second half of 1891 and the 'episodic sketches' published in the *Fortnightly Review* and the *National Observer* of the same year and continuing with the key editions of 1891, 1892, 1895, 1902, and 1912.

I should like to acknowledge my debt of gratitude to the Trustees of the Thomas Hardy Memorial Collection for permission to quote from the manuscript of *Tess of the d'Urbervilles* and from manuscript material deposited in the Thomas Hardy Memorial Collection in the Dorset County Museum, Dorchester; to the same Trustees and the British Museum for permission to reproduce two pages from the manuscript of *Tess*; and to Macmillan London Ltd. for permission to quote from the published texts of Hardy's novel. My thanks are also due to the staff of the British

Museum, the Dorset County Museum, and the Bodleian Library, Oxford, who together with the staffs of numerous other libraries have given me valuable help in obtaining access to the material on which this book is based. Finally, I wish to express my appreciation to Mr. Paul Turner of Linacre College, Oxford, Professor G. K. W. Johnston of the Faculty of Military Studies, University of New South Wales, at Duntroon, and Professor Richard Little Purdy of New Haven, Connecticut, for helpful advice, and to my wife and family for unfailing tolerance and moral support during the preparation and writing of this book.

J. T. L.

June 1974

CONTENTS

List of Plates   viii

Abbreviations   ix

Note on Method of Transcribing Manuscript Passages   xi

PART ONE. BIBLIOGRAPHICAL PROBLEMS

    I. The Line of Transmission   3

    II. The Manuscript   21

PART TWO. THE UR-NOVEL

    III. Plot and Themes   31

    IV. Imagery (Symbolism and Myth)   52

PART THREE. DEVELOPMENTS IN THE MANUSCRIPT

    V. Bowdlerization and Themes   71

    VI. Images and Motifs   87

    VII. Characterization   118

PART FOUR. DEVELOPMENTS IN THE PRINTED VERSIONS

    VIII. Earlier Printed Versions (to the First Edition)   149

    IX. Later Printed Versions (to the edition of 1912)   174

PART FIVE. CONCLUSION   187

Appendix   193

LIST OF PLATES

Folio 1 of the manuscript of *Tess of the d'Urbervilles*
(B.M. Add. MS. 38182)   frontispiece

Folio 280 (folio 319 in Hardy's final foliation system)
of the manuscript of *Tess of the d'Urbervilles*
(B.M. Add. MS. 38182)   facing page 15

ABBREVIATIONS

RELATING TO VERSIONS OF *TESS*

B.M. MS.   The manuscript of *Tess of the d'Urbervilles* (British Museum Additional Manuscript 38182).

F.R.   *Fortnightly Review*, no. 293 (New Series), 1 May 1891.

G.   *Graphic*, xliv (July–December), 1891.

N.O.   *National Observer*, vi (New Series), no. 156, 14 November 1891.

X   *Tess of the d'Urbervilles* ('Fifth Edition'), Osgood, McIlvaine, London, 1892.

Y   *Tess of the d'Urbervilles* ('Wessex Novels' edition), Osgood, McIlvaine, London, 1895.

Z   *Tess of the d'Urbervilles* (Uniform Edition), Macmillan, London, 1902.

OTHER ABBREVIATIONS

C.P.   Thomas Hardy, *The Collected Poems of Thomas Hardy*, Macmillan, London (Fourth Edition), 1930.

DCM   Dorset County Museum, Dorchester, England.

Early Life   See *Life*.

Gregor   Ian Gregor and Brian Nicholas, *The Moral and the Story*, Faber, London, 1962.

Guerard   Albert J. Guerard, *Thomas Hardy*, Harvard University Press, Cambridge, Mass., 1949.

Later Years   See *Life*.

Life   Florence Emily Hardy, *The Life of Thomas Hardy*, Macmillan, London, 1962. (Includes *The Early Life of Thomas Hardy, 1840–1891* (1928), and *The Later Years of Thomas Hardy, 1892–1928* (1930).)

M138   *Macmillan Archive: Correspondence and Papers of the Publishing Firm of Macmillan and Co., 19th and 20th Centuries*, vol. cxxxviii (British Museum Additional Manuscript 54923).

M139   *Macmillan Archive: Correspondence and Papers of the Publishing Firm of Macmillan and Co., 19th and 20th Centuries*, vol. cxxxix (British Museum Additional Manuscript 54924).

Millgate   Michael Millgate, *Thomas Hardy: His Career as a Novelist*, Bodley Head, London, 1971.

Paris   Bernard J. Paris, 'A Confusion of Many Standards', *Nineteenth-Century Fiction*, xxiv, 1969.

Paterson   John Paterson, *The Making of 'The Return of the Native'*, University of California, Berkeley, 1960.

Purdy   Richard Little Purdy, *Thomas Hardy: A Bibliographical Study*, Clarendon Press, Oxford, 1954.

NOTE ON METHOD OF TRANSCRIBING MANUSCRIPT PASSAGES

Words cancelled in the manuscript are run through thus: ~~discovered~~

If the cancelled word is indecipherable, a line is drawn thus: ——

If the cancelled word is difficult to decipher, the word is followed by a question mark thus: ~~discovered~~ [?]

A substitution made immediately after the original reading and written on the same line is shown thus: ~~discovered~~ found (italics are not used).

Any interlinear amendment (whether a substitution or interpolation) is shown in italics, above either the cancelled word or the caret mark ($_\wedge$).

Any later addition at the end of a line is treated as if it were an interlinear interpolation.

Any amendment in the margin of the manuscript leaf is enclosed in pointed brackets and appears in italics thus: ⟨*as he afterwards discovered*⟩.

Broken underlining in Hardy's manuscript is retained and indicates 'stet'.

Double lines in Hardy's manuscript under lower-case letters are retained and indicate that capitalization was required by Hardy.

All material on the verso of a leaf is transcribed in the same way as material on the recto.

In all quoted passages, from both manuscript and printed sources, all italics may be assumed to be mine, except for titles and other words normally italicized, or unless specifically attributed to the original author.

PART ONE
BIBLIOGRAPHICAL PROBLEMS

I

THE LINE OF TRANSMISSION

I

M Y main concern in the following pages is to trace the gradual evolution of Thomas Hardy's famous novel, *Tess of the d'Urbervilles*, from the earliest stage of its composition in manuscript form, dating from at least as early as October 1888, until the publication of the quasi-definitive version of the text in the Macmillan 'Wessex Edition' of 1912.[1]

Most of the attention will be given to the many changes in plot, themes, imagery, and characterization introduced into the novel during this period of approximately twenty-three and a half years. Some of the changes were forced on Hardy by the moral attitudes of editors and publishers of magazines and newspapers, whose opinions, in turn, were often no more than typical expressions of

---

[1] The Agreement to publish the novel that later became *Tess of the d'Urbervilles* was originally signed on 29 June 1887, between Thomas Hardy and William Frederic Tillotson, proprietor of the *Bolton Weekly Journal*. According to this Agreement, Hardy was to receive one thousand guineas for 'the exclusive serial right of Publication together with the right of supply to America of Advance Sheets', and, in return, he agreed to deliver 'Four instalments, on or before the Thirtieth day of June 1889; and the remainder by weekly instalments, until completed' ('Tillotson Fiction Agreements, 1885-1887', Bodleian Library MS., Eng. Misc. f. 395/1, pp. 152-61). There is no evidence that Hardy immediately began the composition of his novel, which at this stage was untitled; and the earliest indication that the novel had been begun is found in an entry in the *Early Life*, dated 30 September 1888 (see also p. 9 below).

The Macmillan Wessex Edition of *Tess*, published in 1912, is the last edition to have been thoroughly revised by Hardy and to embody textual changes of sufficient substance to be of interest to the literary critic. It is not, however, the definitive text of the novel. This title must be reserved for the 1920 reprint of the Wessex Edition, which incorporates in addition to its own small group of trifling revisions a few equally trifling amendments which had first appeared during 1919 in the sumptuous Mellstock Edition. The trivial nature of Hardy's amendments in the Mellstock Edition of *Tess* may be illustrated by the following (italicized) insertion in chapter 18: 'The conventional farm-folk of his imagination —personified *in the newspaper-press* by the pitiable dummy known as Hodge—were obliterated after a few days' residence' (vol. 1, p. 157). Moreover, as his letters to Macmillan during 1919 show, Hardy did not check the proofs of *Tess* in the Mellstock Edition (*M139*, pp. 114, 122). The nine pages of 'corrections' submitted for the Mellstock Edition and the 1920 reprint of the Wessex Edition are still extant and are held at DCM.

the general spirit of Grundyism still abroad in genteel society of the day; while others arose quite naturally from the creative process itself. Even the enforced changes were usually handled by Hardy with genuine creative artistry: the stimulus may have been external and censorious but most of the author's ultimate alterations were imaginative and vivifying. This was so despite the fact that, in the short term, Hardy showed that he was prepared, however reluctantly, to mutilate a small number of key scenes in the manuscript, solely to secure serial publication in the *Graphic* newspaper, such mutilations being purely temporary in their influence on the novel's line of transmission. Occasionally, also, the changes led to effects that were sentimental, melodramatic, or improbable. For the most part, however, the evolutionary process turns out to have been one of amelioration; and in tracing the various stages in the development of this novel it will become apparent that we are witnessing the gradual transformation of a relatively crude tale about the seduction of a relatively commonplace heroine, with its aftermath of purely personal sorrow, into a richly imaginative and genuinely tragic exploration of a number of significant themes—all revolving around the general concept of the fate of natural innocence adrift in a world without order or justice.

The genetic approach adopted in this study possesses three important advantages over the more traditional, impressionistic approach to the text of Hardy's novel. First, by affording the reader the opportunity of studying the author's creative processes it eventually leads to a surer and deeper understanding of the meaning of the definitive text. Secondly, it throws considerable light on the reasons for the uneven quality of the writing in the definitive text, helping the reader to perceive the causes of both strengths and weaknesses in a novel which, in spite of its deserved reputation as Hardy's masterpiece, remains a singular mixture of artistry and clumsiness. Thirdly, the approach reveals the existence of a significant dichotomy between Hardy the novelist and Hardy the exegetical writer—between the noble desire for candour and sincerity which characterizes Hardy's literary aspirations and achievements in *Tess* and the obfuscations and inaccuracies to be found among his comments on the circumstances surrounding its composition and publication. Hardy's misleading statements appear mainly in the *Early Life of Thomas Hardy* and in the various prefaces to the novel, and are far more numerous than has hitherto been suspected; for, while earlier textual critics such as Mary Ellen Chase and Richard Little Purdy[2] were able to identify some of the inaccuracies in Hardy's published statements about *Tess*, they were not in a position to be aware of the nature and degree of others, which only a study of the present kind can detect. It is, indeed, no exaggeration to say that by a combination of untruths, half-truths, and vague assertions Hardy, sometimes deliberately, offered his readers an account of events that was less than frank, and this has had the effect of obscuring, over the years, a complete understanding of the publishing problems he faced and the measures he took to overcome them.

I I

It will be best to begin with a brief outline of the main line of transmission of the text of *Tess of the d'Urbervilles*, which is based on seven different versions of the novel.

The earliest extant version of the complete novel is the author's holograph manuscript deposited in the British Museum in 1911. This version, which may be termed the B.M. MS., contains material dating from October 1888, or even earlier, until the autumn of 1891, although Hardy's statement in the *Early Life* that he was 'putting the finishing touches to *Tess*' in March 1891[3] suggests that he had virtually completed work on the manuscript draft of the novel in the spring of that year. The B.M. MS. is a bound volume, consisting of 525 unruled leaves, measuring $8\frac{1}{4}'' \times 10\frac{1}{8}''$ and with the text usually limited to the recto, although insertions occasionally appear on the verso. Forty leaves are unaccountably missing and one is incomplete.[4] As will be demonstrated later, the 525

---

[2] See Mary Ellen Chase, *Thomas Hardy from Serial to Novel*, Minneapolis, Minn., 1927, pp. 69, 71, 93, 101, 102, 107, 108; and Purdy, pp. 71–3.

[3] *Life*, p. 234.

[4] '39 (scattered through the first 180) are missing and 1 is incomplete' (Purdy, p. 70). The incomplete leaf is fol. 69, of which more than half has been cut away. The 39 leaves obviously missing are those bearing the following foliation numbers: 8, 9, 15, 16, 17, 21, 23, 31, 32, 33, 40, 41, 48, 55, 56, 57, 58, 63, 66, 71, 100, 101, 109, 114, 115, 116, 120, 121,

B

extant leaves contain five well-defined chronological layers of material. The two earliest layers, detectable on 232 of the leaves, constitute what may properly be termed an Ur-text: this, in turn, denotes the existence of an Ur-novel during the period from at least as early as October 1888 until November 1889, the latter date being established by evidence analysed in the next section of this chapter and in chapter II. Examination of the B.M. MS. also shows that during 1890 Hardy concentrated on the preparation of a special serial manuscript of approximately 518 leaves, which constituted a shortened and expurgated version of the novel, suitable for publication in a family magazine or newspaper of the day. The B.M. MS., with its foliation running from 1 to 565, was not assembled until after the serial manuscript had been returned to Hardy by the printers of the *Graphic*, the weekly newspaper in which the novel first achieved publication in England; for only then was it practical for Hardy to restore to their places the forty-seven omitted leaves and a small number of leaves that had been temporarily rewritten for serial purposes.

The second important chronological version of the novel is the printed serial text, as it appeared in the *Graphic*, in twenty-four weekly instalments, from 4 July until 26 December 1891 (the exceptions being the issues of 11 July and 7 November). Next comes the English First Edition, which differs considerably, in certain respects, from both the *Graphic* version and the B.M. MS. Divided into seven 'Phases', instead of the six 'Books' of the *Graphic* version, the First Edition was published in three volumes by Osgood, McIlvaine and Company about the last day of November 1891. A few minor errors in spelling, usage, and type-setting were corrected in the second impression, published about the beginning of February 1892.

The next distinctive version is the so-called 'Fifth Edition', the first of the one-volume editions of *Tess*, which appeared from the

---

122, 124, 125, 126, 134, 138, 139, 144, 145, 146, 179 (in Hardy's final foliation system). But Purdy does not seem to have taken account of the missing fol. 157. The leaf bearing the double number 157/158 must in fact have been originally fol. 158, on the evidence of material found in the *Graphic* and First Edition text but missing from the MS. (The material deals with Tess's recognition of Angel Clare in the cow barton at Talbothays farm.) The length of this section in the printed texts would be sufficient to fill a leaf of the MS.

same publishing house on 30 September 1892 and incorporated a surprisingly large number of important changes, affecting plot, themes, and dialect. Then followed the Osgood, McIlvaine and Company's 'Wessex Novels' edition of *Tess*, published in 1895 as the first volume of what was originally a sixteen-volume Uniform Edition of Hardy's prose fiction (which ultimately developed into a twenty-volume Collected Edition of the prose and poetry). Although this 1895 edition of *Tess* made use of the plates of the 'Fifth Edition', it included a number of minor revisions, cunningly inserted to require the minimum amount of type resetting but affecting even the original wording of the Preface of 1892. A few additional revisions, affecting mainly chapters 45 and 46, were made in the autumn of 1902, when Macmillan and Company published the novel in their new Uniform Edition of Hardy's works.

The last significant version in the direct line of transmission is the Macmillan 'Wessex Edition' of *Tess*. Containing one major textual alteration and a large number of minor ones designed mostly to modify the heroine's use of dialect or to achieve greater precision of style, it was published on 30 April 1912 as the first volume in what eventually developed into a twenty-four-volume edition of the author's Collected Writings. In addition to its own Preface dated March 1912, it contains the author's 'General Preface to the Novels and Poems', dated October 1911.

Three other publications require passing notice. The first, the American serial version of the novel as published in *Harper's Bazar* from 18 July to 26 December 1891, is substantially the same as the *Graphic* version, despite a number of departures in the second half. Although providing the text for the American First Edition of *Tess*, published at the end of January 1892 by Harper and Brothers, and continuing to influence subsequent American editions for some time, it had no influence on editions published in England and may thus be passed by without further discussion. More relevant to our purpose are two short pieces, extracted from the manuscript before it was prepared for submission to the *Graphic*. These were published independently as separate sketches, with the original name of the heroine suppressed and new material incorporated. Hardy, himself, refers to these sketches in his 'Explanatory Note to the First Edition' of *Tess*, dated November 1891: 'The main portion of the following story appeared —with slight modifications—in the *Graphic* newspaper; other chapters, more especially addressed to adult readers, in the *Fortnightly Review* and the *National Observer*, as episodic sketches. My thanks are tendered to the editors and proprietors of those periodicals for enabling me now to piece the trunk and limbs of the novel together, and print it complete, as originally written two years ago.' Of the two sketches mentioned, that published in the *Fortnightly Review* of May 1891, under the title 'The Midnight Baptism', is the more important, bibliographically, in its relationship to *Tess*, its influence being stronger even than that of the manuscript on the second part of chapter 14 in the First Edition (and, consequently, in all subsequent editions as well). The sketch published in the *National Observer* of 14 November 1891, under the title 'Saturday Night in Arcady', is of little bibliographic significance, its influence on the First Edition being limited to a small number of mostly unimportant readings in chapter 11.

III

The circumstances surrounding the composition and publication of *Tess of the d'Urbervilles* must now be examined in greater detail. In particular, attention needs to be given to the complicated history of the manuscript, which was directly influenced by Hardy's determination to achieve serial publication before publication in volume form, and to Hardy's methods in preparing the texts of the serial version, the First Edition, and the editions of 1902 and 1912. An understanding of these matters is essential before the following chapters can be readily assimilated by the reader. However, even more fundamental is the need to rediscover a number of truths that lie behind certain untruths, half-truths, and vague assertions offered by Hardy in the *Early Life* and the Prefaces to *Tess*, which for too long have hampered attempts to understand the effect exerted on the novel by unusual circumstances. Consequently, an examination of the details surrounding the composition and publication of *Tess* must concern itself, at times, with the misleading nature of some of Hardy's claims on these matters.

That Hardy was giving thought to the planning and writing of *Tess* by 30 September 1888 is indicated by the following entry in the *Early Life*, a volume ostensibly written by the second wife, Florence Emily, but in fact Hardy's own account of his life during the years 1840–91:

'September 30. "The Valley of the Great Dairies"—Froom.
'"The Valley of the Little Dairies"—Blackmoor.
'In the afternoon by train to Evershot. Walked to Woolcombe, a property once owned by a—I think the senior—branch of the Hardys. Woolcombe House was to the left of where the dairy now is. On by the lane and path to Bubb-Down. Looking east you see High Stoy and the escarpment below it. The Vale of Blackmoor is almost entirely green, every hedge being studded with trees. On the left you see to an immense distance, including Shaftesbury.
'The decline and fall of the Hardys much in evidence hereabout.'[5]

As Hardy's bibliographer, Richard Little Purdy, was the first to reveal, the novel, under an earlier title, *Too Late Beloved* (or *Too Late, Beloved!*), was 'designed from the first for Tillotson and Son of Bolton and their newspaper syndicate' and was 'well under way' by February 1889, serial publication being due to begin 'before the end of the year'.[6] Hardy's own earliest report on the progress of the novel states that at the end of July 1889 he and his wife returned from a holiday in London to his home in Dorchester, 'where during August Hardy settled down daily to writing the new story he had conceived, which was *Tess of the d'Urbervilles*, though it had not yet been christened'.[7] On 9 September 1889, according to Purdy, Hardy wrote to Tillotsons that he was forwarding to them 'a portion of the MS. of "Too Late Beloved"—equal to about one-half, I think . . . The remainder to follow as per agreement'; Tillotsons, however, were, in Purdy's words, 'distinctly taken aback' by 'the nature of the story', and asked 'that the story should be recast and certain scenes and incidents deleted entirely'. Hardy would not agree to this suggestion, with the result that the agreement was

[5] *Life*, p. 214.   [6] Purdy, pp. 71, 72.   [7] *Life*, p. 221.

cancelled, although 'with no ill feeling on either side'. On 25 September Tillotsons wrote to tell Hardy that they had returned 'whole of proofs and copy to the point we had in type, being up to chapter 16 [Book 1, as printed in the *Graphic*, or Phase the First and Phase the Second], and now send the remaining manuscript which our printers have not seen'.[8]

What became of the Tillotson proofs is not known, but Hardy's next step was to send as much of his manuscript as he had written to the editor of *Murray's Magazine*, Edward Arnold, who, in reply to an inquiry from Hardy, had expressed interest in the novel in a letter dated 7 October. On 15 November Arnold, after consulting Murray, rejected the novel as 'not, in our opinion, well adapted for publication in this Magazine', and went on to give his reasons:

> When I had the pleasure of seeing you here some time ago, I told you my views about publishing stories where the plot involves frequent and detailed reference to immoral situations; I know well enough that these tragedies are being played out every day in our midst, but I believe the less publicity they have the better, and that it is quite possible and very desirable for women to grow up & pass through life without the knowledge of them. I know your views are different, and I honour your motive which is, as you told me, to spare many girls the misery of unhappy marriages made in ignorance of how wicked men can be. But since I dissent from that view, I feel bound to take my own course in regard to the Magazine.[9]

Following Arnold's return of the manuscript, Hardy immediately sent it off to the next editor on his list, Mowbray Morris, editor of *Macmillan's Magazine*. Morris took less than ten days to come to his decision, which was similar to Arnold's, that 'it would be unwise for me to publish it in my magazine'. Morris's letter, dated 25 November, is a crucial document in the study of the early history of the evolution of *Tess of the d'Urbervilles* and for that reason needs to be quoted in full:

> I have now read your manuscript—read it always with interest and often with pleasure. The rural scenes seem to me particularly good—more so than the 'entirely modern bearings' &c. I cannot think there

---

8 Purdy, p. 72. A note, written in red ink, on the first page of the original Agreement between Hardy and William Frederic Tillotson states that Hardy's letter cancelling the Agreement was dated 24 September 1889.

9 MS. held at DCM. Printed in Millgate, pp. 283-4.

should be any theological offence in it. The amateur baptism might perhaps startle some good souls; but there is nothing that can in reason be called irreverent, for poor Tess was obviously in very sober earnestness.

But there are other things which might give offence, &, as I must frankly own to think, not altogether unreasonably. Of course, you will understand that I write only of the fitness of the story for my magazine, beyond which I have neither the right nor the wish to go. My objection is of the same nature as I found myself obliged, you may remember, to make occasionally to the Woodlanders. It is not easy for me to frame it in precise words, as it is general rather than particular. Perhaps an instance or two may explain my meaning. It is obvious from the first page what is to be Tess's fate at Trantridge; it is apparently obvious also to the mother, who does not seem to mind, consoling herself with the somewhat cynical reflection that she may be made a lady *after* if not *before*. All the first part therefore is a sort of prologue to the girl's seduction which is hardly ever, & can hardly ever be out of the reader's mind. Even Angel Clare, who seems inclined to 'make an honest woman' of Tess, has not as yet got beyond a purely sensuous admiration for her person. Tess herself does not appear to have any feelings of this sort about her; but her capacity for stirring & by implication for gratifying these feelings for others is pressed rather more frequently & elaborately than strikes me as altogether convenient, at any rate for my magazine. You use the word *succulent* more than once to describe the general appearance & condition of the Frome Valley. Perhaps I might say that the general impression left on me by reading your story—so far as it has gone—is one of rather too much succulence. All this, I know, makes the story 'entirely modern', & will therefore, I have no doubt, bring it plenty of praise. I must confess, however, to being rather too old-fashioned—as I suppose I must call it—to quite relish the entirely modern style of fiction.

There is one other criticism I am tempted to make. It seems to me that a story dealing almost entirely with country life & people is the better served by being written in as simple, clear, straightforward a style as possible. There are some passages in your manuscript where neither the thought nor the language is very clear to me; & words sometimes of which I am not sure that I understand the meaning. This you will doubtless say, & possibly with justice, is my stupidity. But you also sometimes use words which do not seem to me English at all. *Venust*, for example, on p. 214. The meaning is clear enough, of course; but surely the word is no English one. Surely one might as well say of a brave man that he was *fort*, or of a learned man that he was *doct*, as of a pretty woman that she was *venust*.

I hope that I shall not seem to have said too much, or to have said it discourteously. You asked for my frank opinion, & I have tried to give it with no unnecessary frankness, but yet to give it.

I make no doubt that your story will find many admirers, & certainly no one can deny its cleverness; but I have also no doubt that it would be unwise for me to publish it in my magazine.[10]

It was this letter of Morris's which finally convinced Hardy that, in its present form, his novel had no chance of publication in any of the family-type magazines which alone could afford to pay him the amount of money he believed appropriate to his artistic skill and reputation. From Edward Arnold, for example, he had demanded £50 a month, to which Arnold had replied, 'I won't conceal from you that £50 a month is more than we are in the habit of paying.'[11] Hardy now found himself facing an acute critical decision: should he complete the novel without substantially altering the part already written and publish the work in volume form only, thus forfeiting the returns from the lucrative periodical market? Or should he first revise the completed section, taking into account the moralistic objections of Tillotsons, Arnold, and Morris, before finishing the novel, and thus reap, as was his desire and custom, the rewards of both kinds of publication? As the present study will show, it was the latter course that he pursued.

Hardy's own account in the *Early Life* of this dilemma and the solution he found represents an attempt to disguise a number of facts, but especially the full extent of the changes made to the manuscript during the period that followed his receipt of Mowbray Morris's letter. Hardy implies, indeed, that these changes were limited to temporary omissions and modifications, such as would affect only the serial text. His version of events, which occurs among his entries for November 1889, needs to be quoted in full, before further comment can be offered:

However, the business immediately in hand was the new story *Tess of the d'Urbervilles*, for the serial use of which Hardy had three requests, if not more, on his list; and in October as much of it as was written was

---

[10] MS. held at DCM. Partially printed in the present author's article, 'The Manuscript of Hardy's "Tess of the d'Urbervilles" and What It Tells Us', *AUMLA* (Journal of the Australasian Universities Language and Literature Association), xxv, 1966, 69-70. Later printed in full in Millgate, pp. 284-6. The italics are Morris's.

[11] Arnold to Hardy (7 Oct. 1889), DCM.

offered to the first who had asked for it, the editor of *Murray's Magazine*. It was declined and returned to him in the middle of November virtually on the score of its improper explicitness. It was at once sent on to the second, the editor of *Macmillan's Magazine*, and on the 25th was declined by him for practically the same reason. Hardy would now have much preferred to finish the story and bring it out in volume form only, but there were reasons why he could not afford to do this; and he adopted a plan till then, it is believed, unprecedented in the annals of fiction. This was not to offer the novel intact to the third editor on his list (his experience with the first two editors having taught him that it would be useless to send it to the third as it stood), but to send it up with some chapters or parts of chapters cut out, and instead of destroying these to publish them, or much of them, elsewhere, if practicable, as episodic adventures of anonymous personages (which in fact was done, with the omission of a few paragraphs); till they could be put back in their places at the printing of the whole in volume form. In addition several passages were modified. Hardy carried out this unceremonious concession to conventionality with cynical amusement, knowing the novel was moral enough and to spare. But the work was sheer drudgery, the modified passages having to be written in coloured ink, that the originals might be easily restored, and he frequently asserted that it would have been almost easier for him to write a new story altogether. Hence the labour brought no profit. He resolved to get away from the supply of family fiction to magazines as soon as he conveniently could do so.

However, the treatment was a complete success, and the mutilated novel was accepted by the editor of the *Graphic*, the third editor on Hardy's list, and an arrangement come to for beginning it in the pages of that paper in July 1891. It may be mentioned that no complaint of impropriety in its cut-down form was made by readers, except by one gentleman with a family of daughters, who thought the blood-stain on the ceiling indecent—Hardy could never understand why.[12]

It will be recalled that in a previous entry in the *Early Life* Hardy had misleadingly claimed that his novel had 'not yet been christened' in August 1889, although Purdy was later to reveal the fact that it already bore at that time the title *Too Late Beloved*. Purdy was also responsible for publicizing the details of Hardy's negotiations with Tillotson and Son of Bolton, which are not even mentioned in the account of events given in the above extract, where the assertion is made that the editor of *Murray's Magazine* was 'the first' editor to ask for and receive a copy of the manuscript of the novel. It is

[12] *Life*, pp. 221–2.

true that there exists another published statement by Hardy in which Tillotsons are mentioned in connection with *Tess*. This takes the form of a letter in the *Westminster Gazette* of 10 May 1893, in which Hardy defended himself against the possibility of plagiarism by revealing that certain chapters of *Tess* 'were in the hands of Messrs. Tillotson and Sons, the syndicate-publishers of Bolton, so early as September 1889, and were partly put into type by their printers at that date'.[13] But in the *Early Life* this information is not recorded, and the reader of the passage is left with the final impression that only three periodicals—*Murray's*, *Macmillan's*, and the *Graphic*—were involved in the negotiations for Hardy's novel.

Even more disturbing is the explanation Hardy gives to his readers of the 'plan' he adopted after the editor of *Macmillan's Magazine* had declined the novel. As will become obvious, Hardy's explanation of this 'unprecedented' plan represents little more than a travesty of the actual plan he put into effect between 25 November 1889 and the date when he eventually submitted his completed manuscript to the *Graphic*. Hardy asks us, in effect, to believe that all the alterations made during this period were bowdlerizations dictated by the need to appease the next strait-laced magazine editor to whom the manuscript was to be sent; while he also clearly implies that 'at the printing of the whole in volume form' all the omitted and modified passages were restored to their original form. The last-mentioned claim is virtually repeated, even more explicitly, in a later passage of the *Early Life*, when Hardy is discussing his activities during August and the autumn of 1891: 'Hardy spent a good deal of time in August and the autumn correcting *Tess of the d'Urbervilles* for its volume form, which process consisted in restoring to their places the passages and chapters of the original MS. that had been omitted from the serial publication.'[14]

What these various statements in the *Early Life* fail to mention are the many, and substantial, *permanent* alterations that entered the manuscript of the novel during the period between 25 November 1889 and the autumn of 1890, when he seems to have completed the serial version. The latter date is supplied by the following passage of the *Early Life*, wherein Hardy once again refrains

[13] Purdy, p. 304.   [14] *Life*, pp. 238-9.

they had deserved better at the hands of fate. She had deserved worse;
~~but she was the chosen one.~~ It was wicked of her to take all without
paying. She would pay to the uttermost farthing: she would tell,
there & then. This final determination she came to while she looked
into the fire, he holding her hand.

A steady crimson glare from the now flameless embers painted
the sides & back of the fireplace with its colour, & the well-polished
andirons, & the old brass tongs that would not meet. The underside
of the mantel-shelf was flushed with the ~~same~~ unwavering blood-col-
oured light, & the legs of the table nearest the fire. ~~Her ~~ Tess's face & neck
~~were reflected~~ which each ~~brilliant~~ diamond turned into an
~~with~~ the same warmth ~~a ~~
Aldebaran or a Sirius — a constellation of ~~stars~~ white, red, & green flashes, that
~~Do you remember what we ~~lightly~~ said to each other this morn-~~ interchanged
~~about telling our faults?~~ their hues
ing?" he asked abruptly, finding that she still remained immovable. with her
"We spoke lightly perhaps, & you may & well have done so. But for me — every
it was no light promise. I want to make a confession to you, love." pulsation

This, from him, so unexpectedly apposite, had the effect upon her
of a Providential interposition. "You have to confess something?" she
said quickly, and even with gladness & relief.

"You did not expect it? Ah — you thought too highly of me. Now
listen: put your head there; because I want you to forgive me,
& not to be indignant with me for not telling you before, as perhaps
I ought to have done."

How strange it was! He seemed to be her double. She did not speak,
& Clare went on:

from mentioning the introduction of permanent changes: 'In the latter part of this year [1890], having finished adapting *Tess of the d'Urbervilles* for the serial issue, he seems to have dipped into a good many books—mostly the satirists . . .'[15] The phrase 'adapting . . . for the serial issue' continues the pretence that the only changes made during the preceding period of approximately a year were temporary expurgations. It would have been far more accurate to have employed a phrase denoting a duality of changes involving both adaptation and revision.

At the time when he undertook this dual process of adaptation and revision he had written over 300 manuscript leaves, and had reached at least that point in the plot concerned with Angel Clare's wedding-night confession to his bride, as represented in this extract:

'You did not expect it? Ah—you thought too highly of me. Now listen: put your head there; because I want you to forgive me, & not to be indignant with me for not telling you before, as perhaps I ought to have done.'
How strange it was! He seemed to be her double. She did not speak, & Clare went on . . . (f. 319)

The foliation number, 319, on the leaf from which the above extract is taken is the final number given to it by Hardy. The original number, 305, formed part of the foliation series that Hardy was employing for his manuscript at the time when he submitted it to Mowbray Morris (as will be shown, in detail, in the next chapter); the leaf was thus written before the process of adaptation and revision previously referred to was begun. There is, of course, a strong possibility that Hardy had progressed even beyond this point in the plot and that he later destroyed all leaves containing such subsequent plot material when he began his reconstruction of the novel; but on this matter there is no evidence, with the result that any discussion concerning the number of leaves written as at 25 November 1889 must remain essentially conjectural. All that can be added, with certainty, is that Morris did not actually see all the material that Hardy had written by this date, for he was clearly unsure of the outcome of the courtship at Talbothays when he

[15] *Life*, p. 230.

commented in his letter that Angel Clare '*seems* inclined to "make an honest woman" of Tess'.

Hardy's reconstruction of his manuscript novel began with the omission of the two episodes that he knew would prove to be the most troublesome when he came to approach the next editor on his list, Arthur Locker of the *Graphic*. These, as we have seen, were subsequently published in the *National Observer* and the *Fortnightly Review* under the titles 'Saturday Night in Arcady' and 'The Midnight Baptism' respectively, and were not restored to their original positions in the novel until the First Edition. That these two 'adaptations' for the serial publication were made *before* any of the permanent revisions occurred may be established from evidence concerning changes in the villain's name, as contained in the B.M. MS. The original form of the villain's name in the manuscript was 'Hawnferne', and it was only after 25 November 1889 that it became 'Turberville', and then 'D'Urberville'. In the two sections of the manuscript under discussion, however, the intermediate form 'Turberville' does not appear: instead, 'Hawnferne' has been altered directly to 'D'Urberville' and the absence of 'Turberville' from these sections, although not from surrounding folios, indicates that Hardy laid them aside as soon as he began the reconstruction. Indeed, they were not restored to the manuscript of the novel until after it had been returned to Hardy by the *Graphic* printers, as the absence of serial foliation on these leaves clearly shows.

It is also probable that during his reconstruction of the 300-odd leaves already completed, as well as during the composition of the 240 or so leaves that were subsequently written, Hardy was influenced, at times, by serial requirements in a manner that has previously not been suspected. If, as has been indicated, the manuscript version being written after November 1889 was, in effect, the *serial* version, and remained so until after the *Graphic* text had been set from it, there is every likelihood that some of the artistic flaws in the definitive text of the novel are attributable to this unusual method of composition. Certainly, the more melodramatic later incidents, such as Angel's dangerous crossing of the flooded Frome River during his sleep-walking, the appearance of Alec as an evangelical preacher in the barn at Evershead, and the blood-stain on the ceiling at Sandbourne, may well have been included as a result of the author's awareness that he was now composing a text that would be sent directly to the editor of a nineteenth-century family magazine, whose taste would exclude 'immoral situations' but not sensationalism and surprises. Correspondingly, the strict reticence and avoidance of detail in Hardy's treatment of the heroine's wedding-night confession to Angel Clare (on f. 323 of the manuscript) may be due to the same cause.

When Hardy came to prepare the text of the First Edition he worked only occasionally from the manuscript; indeed, most of the First Edition was set up directly from the *Graphic* text. In a broad sense, therefore, he was justified in claiming in his Preface to the First Edition, dated November 1891, that the *Graphic* version represented 'the trunk' of his novel. But in claiming that the episodic sketches in the *Fortnightly Review* and the *National Observer* represented its 'limbs' Hardy was being less frank. The relevant sentence from his Preface, here termed an 'Explanatory Note', runs as follows: 'My thanks are tendered to the editors and proprietors of those periodicals for enabling me now to piece the trunk and limbs of the novel together, and print it complete, as originally written two years ago.' As I have earlier pointed out, the *Fortnightly Review* text of 'The Midnight Baptism', admittedly, supplied the main textual source for the second part of chapter 14 of the novel. However, the first part of that chapter was based, predominantly, not on the printed source but on the manuscript; while the influence exerted by the *National Observer* text of 'Saturday Night in Arcady' on the published novel was even less important.

But it is the words 'and print it complete, as originally written two years ago' that represent the most serious distortion of the publishing history of *Tess*. The manuscript that existed 'two years ago' was the manuscript of November 1889: for Hardy to imply to his readers that the text of the First Edition was identical with this manuscript version, whose rejection by Mowbray Morris had led to a major reconstruction, was an act that showed scant regard for the truth. In addition, the claim ignored the fact that while most of the text of the First Edition represents a conflation of readings from earlier texts—the *Graphic*, the manuscript, and the two printed sketches—a number of readings are entirely new, and illustrate Hardy's continuing interest in the novel, an interest that was to show itself again in the revisions of the 1892, 1895, 1902, and 1912 editions.

Hardy originally explained that his proposed amendments for the 1902 Macmillan edition of *Tess* consisted of some changes in the wording in chapter 46, as the following extract from his letter to his publishers, dated 9 July 1902, clearly shows:

> There is no other reason why you should not begin printing. I suppose you would not mind my making a few corrections in three of the vols. They are confined to particular pages, and are not scattered over the books. Neither do they overrun. They are mainly these:
> To rewrite the preface to *F. M. Crowd*, and change a few words in Chaps. 2 and 51.
> Change some words in Chap. 46 of *Tess*.
> Change a few words in one Chap. of *Jude*.
> I can send up these few pages with the corrections marked. It does not strike me that they are unreasonable for 17 vols. But if they are I would pay for the labour.[16]

The 'corrections' were speedily sent by Hardy, and when *Tess* appeared in print later in the year, as one of the volumes in Macmillan's new Popular Uniform Edition of Hardy's works, they were duly incorporated, even though no indication was given in the volume itself that any amendments had been made. Moreover, as it turned out, the changes affected not only chapter 46, but also chapter 45 and, to a lesser extent, three later chapters of the novel.

Finally, we may examine a curious claim made by Hardy in the Preface of the Wessex Edition of 1912, a claim which is virtually repeated in the *Catalogue of Additions to the Manuscripts in the British Museum*. The relevant passage from the 1912 Preface reads as follows: 'The present edition of this novel contains a few pages that have never appeared in any previous edition. When the detached episodes were collected as stated in the preface of 1891, these pages were overlooked, though they were in the original

16 *M138*, p. 64.

manuscript. They occur in Chapter X.' The entry in the *Catalogue*, for its part, records the acceptance by the Museum authorities of the manuscript of Hardy's novel (as Additional MS. 38182), and after noting that two of the portions of the manuscript omitted from the *Graphic* serial issue had been published separately, it goes on to comment that one of these separately published sketches included 'a preliminary description of a country-people's dance accidentally omitted in the three-volume and subsequent editions until 1912: see ff. 59 sqq. in the MS.'[17] It will thus be seen that in both of the above passages the assertion is being made that the Chaseborough dance episode, which appears in chapter 10 of the 1912 edition of *Tess*, was omitted from all preceding editions by chance, and not by design.

Since this matter is dealt with at length in Part Four of the present book, the only observation required here is that when the First Edition is compared with both the manuscript and the printed sketch ('Saturday Night in Arcady'), the only tenable conclusion is that the omission of the dance episode from the First Edition was a deliberate act on Hardy's part, effected by the telescoping into a single scene of incidents separated in the manuscript by the description of events at the dance. Hardy's motives for omitting the dance episode from the First Edition cannot now be determined with any certitude; all that is certain is that the statements in the 1912 Preface and the British Museum *Catalogue* are not in accordance with the facts.

Some of the circumstances and motives which led Hardy to resurrect the dance episode in the 1912 edition are made clear in a letter he wrote to Macmillan on 27 September 1907:

Did I ever tell you that I found some time ago that about ⅓ of a chapter in the original MS. of Tess of the d'Urbervilles had been accidentally omitted from all the volume forms of the story? It appeared as part of an episode from the story that was printed in the 'National Observer', but somehow was dropped out of the complete form. I don't know if it would be a good commercial stroke to keep this private till we bring out a new edition of the book, and then announce it in literary paragraphs, etc. Nobody, of course, would remember reading it in the National Observer.[18]

---

[17] *Catalogue of Additions to the Manuscripts in the British Museum in the Years MDCCCCXI-MDCCCCXV*, London, 1925, pp. 89–90.   [18] *M138*, p. 121.

The matter was, in fact, kept 'private' for the next few years and the eventual announcement in 1912 no doubt constituted what Hardy termed 'a good commercial stroke'. But the decision to publish this omitted section may have owed something also to Sydney Cockerell's visit to Hardy at the end of July 1911, 'mainly to enquire about Hardy's old manuscripts', as the *Life* tells us.[19] As a result of this inquiry Hardy handed over several manuscripts, and in October of that year the manuscripts of *Tess* and *The Dynasts* were presented by Cockerell to the British Museum. Such public interest in the manuscript of *Tess* at a time when its author was preparing the novel for a definitive edition may well have provided an additional stimulus for disinterring this important episode.

[19] *Life*, p. 356.

II

THE MANUSCRIPT

I

THE manuscript of *Tess* differs from most other Hardy manuscripts
—notably those of *Under the Greenwood Tree*, *The Mayor of Casterbridge*, *The Dynasts*, and all the poetry volumes—in being a working manuscript, instead of a fair copy. Like the manuscripts of *The
Return of the Native* and *Jude the Obscure* it is full of intriguing
textual amendments, which pose many problems in interpretation.
Indeed, of all the extant Hardy manuscripts, it presents, without
any doubt, the greatest challenge, by virtue of its confused foliation, changes in characters' names, alterations in chapter numbers,
missing folios (40 out of a total of 565), and manifold amendments
to plot, images, thematic concepts, and character portrayals. In
this chapter most of the attention will be directed towards an
examination of the foliation systems and the naming of characters,
which together provide the keys to two important questions—the
nature of the various layers discernible in the manuscript, and the
relationship between an earlier and a later group of layers in terms
of authorial intentions. As a result, it will be seen that there are
five main layers in the manuscript of *Tess* and that these can be
identified in detail; moreover, with the assistance of two passages in
the letter written by Mowbray Morris, it will also be possible to
see that there exists an Ur-text, which corresponds to the two
earliest of the five main manuscript layers.

II

A close study of the foliation difficulties eventually confirms that
Hardy employed, in all, three main systems of foliation during the
period when he was working on his manuscript. These may be
signified by their chronological order, as System 1 (S1), System 2

(S2), and System 3 (S3). Vestiges of yet other systems linger in some of the older leaves, but need not concern us here; neither should the foliation added by the British Museum in 1911, which merely gave a number to each of the 525 extant leaves. Throughout this study of *Tess* I have made use of Hardy's final foliation system (S3) whenever I have wished to identify leaves in the manuscript: thus, if I have cited a leaf as f. 319 it should be understood that I am referring to the leaf which carries 319 as Hardy's final number. (The correspondences between Hardy's three systems and the B.M. system are tabulated in the Appendix.)

The earliest system (S1) may be discerned on many leaves, although not after f. 319 (B.M. no. 280), on which leaf the S1 number is 305.[1] S1 is most easily found by examining the substantial section that begins with f. 117 and finishes with f. 319. In this section, the S1 numbers run from 110 to 305 on 189 extant leaves, and on only 14 of these leaves are S1 numbers lacking: as a result, 175 leaves bearing S1 numbers are identifiable in this section of the manuscript alone. A further large group of such leaves is soon discovered when ff. 76–113 are examined. Here, the corresponding S1 numbers run from 61 to 98, each of the 34 extant leaves bearing its appropriate S1 number.

S1 may be dated with the assistance of one of the previously mentioned passages from Mowbray Morris's letter, which yields the information that this was the system in use during November 1889, and, hence, was the foliation system of the Ur-version. Demonstration is best offered by quoting the reference in Morris's letter to the number of the manuscript page on which a certain word appeared. The reference is to Hardy's employment of the word 'venust' on 'p. 214': 'But you also sometimes use words which do not seem to me English at all. *Venust*, for example, on p. 214. The meaning is clear enough, of course; but surely the word is no English one. Surely one might as well say of a brave man that he was *fort*, or of a learned man that he was *doct*, as of a pretty woman that she was *venust*.'[2] If one examines the B.M. MS. of *Tess*, one discovers that the word 'venust' has been cancelled on f. 222. This

---

[1] See sample page from MS. (f. 319), facing p. 15.
[2] See p. 11 above. Morris's italics.

leaf also bears the numbers 214 (the number cited by Morris) and 176. The citing of 214 makes it clear that the foliation system to which it belongs (S1) was the system in use during November 1889.

Further investigation shows that the other early number on the leaf (176) belongs to the system I have termed S2, which is present on most leaves of the B.M. MS. S2 is not present, however, on those leaves put aside after November 1889 and kept apart from the remainder of the manuscript until after the text of the serial version had been printed for the *Graphic*. In other words, S2 is missing from ff. 77/8–99, ff. 107–11, and ff. 117–35. Thus, it eventually becomes clear that S2 constitutes the serial foliation, that is, the numbers added to the manuscript during the time when Hardy was putting together the serial version which was eventually accepted by the *Graphic*. S2 runs from 1 to 518.

S3 numbers run from 1 to 565 and are found on all leaves of the manuscript. (An initial cause of confusion to anyone examining the manuscript for the first time is that on ff. 1–77/8, the S2 numbers also serve as the S3 numbers.) S3 was not employed until after the *Graphic* printers had returned the serial version of the manuscript to the author, although it was added to the final arrangement of manuscript material prior to the publication of the First Edition. The last point is made clear by the fact that the B.M. MS. contains brief authorial notes employing S3 numbers on f. 141 and f. 520.[3] These notes are, virtually, reminders written by Hardy to himself that a certain episode (the heroine's visit to the d'Urberville church at Kingsbere) was to be transferred, in the 'volumes', to a later position in the story. This was, in due course, done, as a comparison of the First Edition version of the story with that of the manuscript and the *Graphic* shows. As a result, S3, although Hardy's final foliation system, must clearly antedate the publication of the First Edition by some little time.

Whereas the presence of an S1 number signifies that the folio once formed part of the Ur-version, and S2 that it was included in the

---

[3] Hardy's note in the margin of f. 141 reads: 'For volumes transfer this to p. 520.' The note on f. 520 reads: 'For Vols. transfer visit to D'Urberville Aisle, etc. from p. 141 to this chap.'

serial version of the manuscript (as finally dispatched to the *Graphic* printers), a finer differentiation among the various strata of manuscript material is attainable through a close study of nomenclature. We can profitably begin with a study of the sequence of Christian names bestowed upon the heroine.

In the earliest extant parts of the B.M. MS. the heroine is known variously as Love, Cis, and Sue. Later, she is given the name Rose-Mary, and eventually Tess. Thus, on ff. 22, 24, and 25 we find the sequence of changes running Love/Rose-Mary/Tess. On ff. 34, 35, 36, and 37 the sequence is Cis/Rose-Mary/Tess; while on most folios from 59 to 113 the sequence has become Sue/Rose-Mary/Tess.

From foliation evidence it is possible to arrive at tentative conclusions as to the periods of time when the earlier Christian names— Love, Cis, Sue, and Rose-Mary—were in use. But Mowbray Morris's letter, once again, supplies the invaluable link in the chain of evidence, in that the letter permits a positive dating of the introduction of the final name, Tess, into the novel. The following passage is one of several which establish the fact that the heroine's name was Tess at the time when Morris read the manuscript: 'Even Angel Clare, who seems inclined to "make an honest woman" of Tess, has not as yet got beyond a purely sensuous admiration for her person. Tess herself does not appear to have any feelings of this sort about her; but her capacity for stirring & by implication for gratifying these feelings for others is pressed rather more frequently and elaborately than strikes me as altogether convenient, at any rate for my magazine.'[4] Morris's letter does not reveal, of course, the important qualification that at this time Hardy was using the name Tess only in amended readings. But the presence of the name in the letter is significant because it proves, conclusively, that all folios bearing among their cancellations any of the earlier variants—Love, Cis, Sue, or Rose-Mary—must have belonged to the Ur-version of the novel.

Thus, it may be stated that the Ur-text of the B.M. MS. may be divided into two clearly distinguishable chronological layers. The first is marked by the presence of S1 numbers and the names

4 See p. 11 above.

Love, Cis, or Sue, and the second by S1 numbers and the names Rose-Mary or Tess (the latter as an amendment). Nomenclature may also be employed to distinguish three later layers in the manuscript, as the following section of this chapter will show. We may therefore conclude the chapter with an analysis of all five layers in the manuscript, in terms of the variants in characters' names enabling identification of layers to be made and the S3 numbers associated with each layer.

III

We shall begin with an analysis of the first layer (L1). Herein, the heroine is always called Love, Cis, or Sue, the full combinations that occur being Love Woodrow, Cis Woodrow, Sue Woodrow, and occasionally Sue Troublewell[5] and Sue Troublefield.[6] The villain's name is Hawnferne; but there is as yet no occurrence of any name for the ancient family. L1 occurs as the original text, and in occasional amendments, on the following folios (the numbers in parentheses indicating missing folios): 22, (23), 24, 25; 34, 35, 36, 37; 59, 60, 61, 62, (63), 64, 65, (66), 67, 68, 70, (71), 72, 73, 74, 75, 76, 77/8, 79, 80, 81, 82, 83, 84, 85, 86, 87, 88, 89, 90, 91, 92, 93, 94, 95, 96, 97, 98, 99, (100), (101), 102, 103, 104, 105, 106, 107, 108, (109), 110, 111, 112, 113, (114), (115), (116), 117, 118, 119, (120), (121), (122), 123, (124), (125), (126), 127, 128, 129, 130, 131, 132, 133, (134), (138), (139), 140, 142, 143, (144), (145), (146), 147, 148, 149, 150, 151, 152, 153 (?), 154, 155 (?).

In the second layer (L2), the heroine is called Rose-Mary, in both original and amended readings, or else Tess, in amended readings only. The full combination with Rose-Mary is Rose-Mary Troublefield, while that with Tess is Tess Woodrow. (The full name Tess Woodrow does not appear as an *original* reading anywhere in the manuscript, but the single name Tess appears as an original reading from L3 onwards.) The villain's name, which is recorded infrequently in this layer, remains Hawnferne, while the old family name of Turberville now makes its first appearance in the manuscript, although only among folios written almost at

---

[5] Namely, on f. 110. [6] Namely, on f. 150.

the end of the period of time during which L2 was being composed. L2 is often found among amendments on the previous group of leaves. It also occurs as the original text, and in some of the amendments, on the following large group of folios: 135, 136, 141, 142 verso; 156–319 {*excluding* 170, 180, 269, 270, 271, 295, 312, 313, 314, 315}. (f. 179 is missing.)

In the third layer (L3), as well as in succeeding layers, the heroine is called Tess in both original and amended readings. Her full name in L3 is now Tess Troublefield, while the villain and the ancient family have as their common name Turberville. L3 is found among amendments on many of the folios of the two groups listed above, although, as I have earlier noted, it does not appear on any folios from 77/8 to 99, 107 to 111, or 117 to 135, all of which folios Hardy temporarily excluded from the manuscript, when he began to revise his novel, with serial requirements in mind, after November 1889. Nor does L3 occur among amendments on any folios after 150, for at approximately this point in his revision Hardy began to embark on the next layer (a fact which is indicated on ff. 150, 194, 212, and elsewhere, by the direct substitution of Durbeyfield for Woodrow, instead of via the intermediate stage of Troublefield). L3 is found also as the original text, and in some of the amendments, on the following folios: 1, 2, 3, 4, 5, 6, 6a, 6b, 7, (8), (9), 10, 11, 12, 13, 14, (15), (16), (17), 18, 19, 20, (21); 26, 27, 28, 29, 30, (31), (32), (33); 38, 39, (40), (41), 42, 43, 44, 45, 46, 47, (48), 49, 50, 51, 52, 53, 54, (55), (56), (57), (58), 60 verso; 69.

In the fourth layer (L4), the heroine's full name is Tess Durbeyfield, while the name of both the villain and the ancient family is D'Urberville. (Note the capital D.) The heroine's name of Durbeyfield occurs in this layer only as a substitution (for Troublefield, Woodrow, or sometimes for [Tess] Hawnferne). Similarly, D'Urberville, as the ancient family's name, is always an insertion or a substitution (for Turberville) in this layer, except on five substitute folios (180, 269, 270, 271, and 314) where it occurs as the original reading. L4 is found among the amendments on folios of the three groups listed above (except on ff. 77/8–99, 107–11, and 117–35). It also occurs as the original text, and in some of the amendments, on the following folios: 137, 150 verso, 155 verso (?),

170, 180, 236 verso, 269, 270, 271, 293 verso, 295, 301 verso, 312, 313, 314, 315.

In the fifth and final layer (L5), the heroine's name is Tess Durbeyfield in the original, as well as amended, readings; similarly, the name of both the villain and the ancient family is D'Urberville in all readings. L5 is almost synonymous with ff. 322–565, although, to be more precise, it begins on a pasted-in section on the bottom half of f. 320/1. L5 comprises both the original and amended readings of ff. 322–565, together with a few amendments on the four groups listed above, especially on ff. 77/8–99, 107–11, and 117–35, which had remained excluded from the manuscript from shortly after November 1889 until after the printing of the *Graphic* serial version of the novel. As it exists in ff. 322–565, L5 is a homogeneous and relatively stable section of the manuscript, comprising over 240 leaves, or approximately 46 per cent of the total extant manuscript.

PART TWO

THE UR-NOVEL

III

PLOT AND THEMES

FROM the 232 leaves of L1 and L2, which embody the Ur-text material, it is possible to make a partial reconstruction of the Ur-novel. Accordingly, the present chapter will deal with the elements of plot and theme that characterized the novel at the time when Hardy was attempting to interest Tillotson's, *Murray's Magazine*, and *Macmillan's Magazine* in its serial publication. Imagery will be dealt with in the next chapter.

I

In broad terms, the different direction taken by the early plot, when compared with that of the completed manuscript, is suggested by the following passage in Mowbray Morris's letter to Hardy: 'It is obvious from the first page what is to be Tess's fate at Trantridge; it is apparently obvious also to the mother, who does not seem to mind, consoling herself with the somewhat cynical reflection that she may be made a lady *after* if not *before*. All the first part therefore is a sort of prologue to the girl's seduction, which is hardly ever, & can hardly ever be out of the reader's mind.'[1] Morris's opening sentence clearly does not apply to the novel as it exists in its final manuscript form, where the first six and a half leaves ('Chapter 1') are devoted, as they are in all subsequent versions, to incidents associated with the homeward journey of the inebriated John Durbeyfield, father of the heroine, and, more specifically, to his conversations with 'the antiquary, of Stagfoot Lane' (Parson Tringham) and 'the lath-like stripling' (Fred). Moreover, the events of the next twenty-eight extant leaves of the completed manuscript continue to be almost identical with the events of the definitive text, and, as such, afford, once again, no evidence for Morris's remark that during 'all the first part', the

---

[1] See p. 11 above. Morris's italics.

heroine's seduction 'is hardly ever, and can hardly ever be out of the reader's mind'. These twenty-eight leaves (ff. 6b–45) describe the setting (the Vale of Blakemore), the 'club-walking' and dance at Marlott, Angel Clare's glimpse of Tess before he leaves the dance, the visit of John and Joan Durbeyfield to Rolliver's Inn, Tess's drive to market, the death of Prince, and Tess's reluctant acquiescence in her mother's plan that she should go to Trant-ridge to 'claim kin' of the supposed relatives; and it is only after the heroine has undertaken this journey that she has her first en-counter with the man who is to be her seducer, the meeting being described on f. 45, which is almost half-way through what would now be called 'Phase the First' (the seduction scene itself being described from f. 99 onwards). In view of the wide discrepancy between the tenor of Morris's comments and the events recorded in the completed manuscript it is scarcely surprising to discover that among the first forty-three extant leaves of the completed manuscript (ff. 1–54) thirty-six leaves belong to L3.

It is only after scrutiny of the variant Ur-text readings that it becomes possible to establish, more specifically, some of the dif-ferences between Ur-plot and final manuscript plot. Thus, it is a cancelled reading on f. 141 that reveals the fact that it would not have been possible for the Ur-plot to have begun with a scene such as now constitutes chapter 1 of the novel, since in the Ur-text the heroine is shown to have been aware of her noble ancestry 'ever since her infancy'. Folio 141 is an L2 leaf forming part of the account of the heroine's journey to Talbothays dairy-farm in quest of work, during which she veers briefly from her course (as she does *not* do in the editions) in order to enter the church of her ancestors at Kingsbere (called Greenhill-Regis in L2). The rele-vant cancelled reading will be seen at the end of the following passage, the substitution of 'Parson Tringham's announcement' for 'her infancy' being made later, at the L3 stage:

> Tess's ~~whim to do~~ entered   two in
> . . . ~~Rose-Mary did, entering~~ the church about ~~the middle of~~ the afternoon,
> *and beheld*
> ~~She stood~~ for the first time in her life ~~upon~~ the spot whereof her father
>   *Parson Tringham's announcement.*
> had spoken or sung to painfulness ever since ~~her infancy~~ ‸   (f. 141)

The Ur-novel lacked not only the opening incident of the sudden revelation of ancient lineage, but also the account of the heroine's first visit to the home of her supposed rich relatives, undertaken for the purpose of 'claiming kin'. This visit, which takes up most of the fifth chapter in all the editions, first entered the manuscript at the L3 stage in a number of interpolated leaves (38–54). Indeed, the whole concept of 'claiming kin' was extraneous to the Ur-plot: the villain's name being Hawnferne, no question of kinship based on a similarity of names between heroine and villain could possibly have arisen.

In the Ur-plot it would also seem that the first sighting of the heroine by the villain had, in fact, occurred among the first few leaves of the novel, probably at the 'club-meeting' and 'dance', which had been attended, not by Angel Clare, but by 'Hawnferne'. The evidence for these deductions is available in a number of brief sections of Ur-text material, for example on f. 36 (L1), where the heroine, distressed by the accident in which Prince has been killed, recalls the dance when she exclaims (in an uncancelled section): 'Why, I *danced* and laughed only yesterday.' Later in the story, on f. 61 (L1), the heroine's mother observes with surprise the arrival of a dog-cart to take her daughter to Trantridge, and in the original, as in the final, reading recognizes the driver. However, whereas in the final reading we are told that she recognizes him as the visitor of 'a week or two before', in the original reading she recalls him as 'a handsome horsey dandy who had visited her on the day of the club-meeting':

> *with a cigar between his teeth ; ~~&~~ wearing*
> The driver was a young man of one-or two-&-twenty, ~~in~~ ∧ a low hat,
> *tightly buttoned, trousers of the same hue*
> drab frock-coat ~~& trousers~~, white neckcloth, stick-up collar, & brown
> *he was the*   *young buck*
> driving gloves—in short ~~a~~ ∧ handsome horsey ~~dandy~~ who had visited
> *a week or two before to get her answer about Tess.*
> her ~~on the day of the club-meeting~~.
>   (f. 61)

A passage in the heroine's reverie on f. 34 (L1), during her drive through the early-morning darkness towards the Casterbridge markets, illuminates the opening situation even more, by its Ur-text reference to her awareness of the favourable impression created on the mother by this 'handsome horsey dandy' and his smart 'gig':

Then examining the mesh of events in her own life, it [?] she seemed
　　vanity of her father's news:　the gentlemanly match of
to see the ˄ ~~young man who had so greatly taken~~ her mother's fancy;
but as yet unbeheld by herself;　　　　　　*laughing at her poverty, &*
˄ to see him as a grimacing personage, ~~whose gig was a part~~
her shrouded knightly ancestry.
~~of his body~~
　　　　　　　　　　　　　　　　　　　　　　　　　　　(f. 34)

Indeed, so much had this young man 'taken her mother's fancy' that the mother had consulted a fortune-telling book, or 'dream-book', which a 'fetishistic fear' prevented her from ever allowing to remain in the house all night. The heroine had therefore been compelled to take the book to an outhouse, where she had stuffed it into the thatch. During her return through the garden, on f. 22 (**L1**), the heroine originally guesses (and guesses correctly, we are told) that the consulting of the 'dream-book' was related to 'that gentleman who saw me', presumably at the club-meeting earlier that day. (The text was later altered to include a reference to Parson Tringham's revelation, instead.) The relevant passage runs as follows:

Returning　　　　　　　　~~Rose-Mary~~ *Tess*
~~Walking~~ along the garden-path ~~Love~~ ˄ mused on what her mother could have
　　　　　from the dream-book　　　　　　　　　*our*
wished to ascertain ˄ on this particular day, '~~Ah something about that~~
　being　　　　*laughed at*　　　　　　　　*Tess*
~~gentleman who saw me, perhaps!' she said. ¶ Rose-Mary conjectured rightly~~
⟨*& readily guessed it to bear upon the recent discovery.*⟩　　(f. 22)

In the Ur-text, as in the final manuscript text, the heroine goes to work at Trantridge and is seduced in The Chase. After she has lost her child, Sorrow, she sets out for Talbothays. It is on her arrival at Talbothays that we notice the next important difference in plot between the Ur-text and the final manuscript text. This is the absence of a 'recognition scene' on the occasion when the heroine and Angel Clare see each other in the barton, caused by the fact that in the Ur-novel Angel Clare had not attended the Marlott dance and hence had not seen the heroine before. The manuscript, which is heavily amended at this point, reads as follows:

　Tess　　　　　　　　　　　　　　　　　　　*white*
~~Rose-Mary~~ could then see him at full length. He wore the ordinary ˄

   & leather leggings
pinner ˄ of a dairy-farmer when milking, & his boots were clogged
~~with the mulch of the yard; but this was all of his local livery.~~
     it
~~Beneath ˄ was something educated, reserved, subtle, sad, differing.~~
            could
  ~~The details of his corporeal aspect she did not readily observe, so~~
~~much was her mind arrested by his presence & air, and at the best~~
         took   *was apt to neglect particulars in*
~~of times latterly she was but little conscious of ˄ outward things/~~
~~She saw for the general impression. But she saw by degrees that he~~
   shapely
~~had a —— & thoughtful face,~~ —— —— a young man's incipient
~~beard &~~ moustache & beard—the latter of the palest straw colour where
it began upon his cheeks, & deepening to a warm brown further from its root.
            & leggings   *woollen trousers,*
 Under his milking-pinner ˄ he wore a dark velveteen jacket, ˄ & a
   white
starched ˄ shirt.   (ff. 156–157/8)

The final lines of the next paragraph go on to mention explicitly
that the young man was 'a stranger' to her:

   she
. . . & ˄ was unable to indulge in more than transitory observation of
a stranger, interesting in a general sense as he might be.   (f. 157/8)

It is not until we reach the *Graphic* that we find the first extant
passage containing the information that the heroine has seen Angel
Clare before and that she recognizes him as 'the pedestrian who
had joined in the club-dance at Marlott':

Tess could then see him at full length. He wore the ordinary white
pinner and leather leggings of a dairy-farmer when milking, and his
boots were clogged with the mulch of the yard; but this was all his local
livery. Beneath it was something educated, reserved, subtle, sad, differing.

But the details of his corporeal aspect she could not readily observe,
so much was her mind arrested by the discovery that he was one whom
she had seen before. Such vicissitudes had Tess passed through since
that time that for a moment she could not remember where she had
seen him; and then it flashed upon her that he was the pedestrian who
had joined in the club-dance at Marlott—the passing stranger who had
come she knew not whither, had danced with others but not with her,
had slightingly left her and gone on his way with his friends.

A momentary dismay lest he should recognise her also, and by some
means discover her story, passed away when she found no sign of re-
membrance in his face. But the flood of memories brought back by this

revival of an incident dating from a time anterior to the troubles which had arisen from the disclosure of her descent, destroyed her equanimity for a while. But the recuperative instinct calmed her, and she saw by degrees that since their first and only rencounter his shapely face had grown more thoughtful, and had acquired a young man's incipient moustache and beard—the latter of the palest straw-colour where it began upon his cheeks, and deepening to a warm brown further from its root.

Under his milking-pinner and leggings he wore a dark velveteen jacket, woollen trousers, and a starched white shirt.   (G. 190)

Somewhat illogically the *Graphic* retained the next paragraph of the manuscript, in which the reference to Clare as 'a stranger' occurs, this paragraph being omitted only from the First Edition onwards.

From the evidence of the numbers used in S2 (the serial foliation of the manuscript), which indicate that there was an additional leaf in this section of the copy at the time when it was sent to the printers of the *Graphic*, it would seem that the 'recognition scene' made its first appearance on an L4 folio bearing the serial numbering of 111 and the final numbering of 157. The leaf, for some unknown reason, was missing at the time when Hardy presented the manuscript to the British Museum. It was probably at the same stage of revision (L4) that Hardy introduced the amendments apparent in the following extract, which occurs further on in the story following the heroine's acceptance of Clare's proposal of marriage:

> *stay*
> 'Why didn't you ~~come~~ & love me when I—was seventeen;
>   *& you danced on the green*
> living with my little sisters & brothers, ‸ —O why didn't you,
> why didn't you!' ⟨*she cried, impetuously clasping her hands.*⟩   (f. 281)

Here, the words 'stay' and 'you danced on the green' appear not to have formed any part of the original (L2) text.

It is also clear that in the Ur-novel the heroine agreed to marry Clare without telling him of her ancient lineage. Indeed, even as late as the wedding-day, Clare remained ignorant of his bride's 'Turberville' ancestry, as the original (L2) readings in the two following passages show. In the first extract, Clare, speculating on the dejected appearance of his bride after the wedding ceremony,

ers of the family
~~oddly enough, he had never perceived in her own name a corruption of~~
see or hear this old coach whenever—But I'll tell you another day—
~~the name he had pronounced, & as it would have been awkward to~~
it is rather gloomy. Evidently some ~~dim~~ dim knowledge of it has been
  listen to
~~question him on the story now without disclosing her membership with the~~
brought back to your mind by the sight of this, venerable caravan.'
        banished
~~family, she immediately changed the subject till a more convenient~~
           fear
~~season should come, with the remark: 'It is gloomy, I know: don't let~~
~~us talk of it now.'~~

(f. 306)

D

In view of the two preceding passages, it is not surprising to discover that the scene in the B.M. MS. in which the heroine confesses to Angel her d'Urberville ancestry during a drive through the rain to the railway station occurs on three leaves (269–71) belonging to L4, which have been substituted for some L2 leaves concerned with a different and somewhat shorter explanation, the exact nature of which can no longer be reconstructed.

The only other plot difference requiring comment at this juncture is the absence of the 'jewels' episode from the honeymoon section of the Ur-novel. In the B.M. MS. the description of the delivery of the jewels and Angel's insistence that Tess bedeck herself in this new finery are to be found on four leaves (312–15) interpolated at the L4 stage into an otherwise continuous section of L2 leaves. The richly ironic jewels incident was 'an idea of Mrs Hardy's', according to the journalist Raymond Blathwayt, whose reported interview with Hardy appeared in *Black and White* on 27 August 1892. The manuscript account of the incident differs, however, from the account given in the editions in one important detail, in that in the manuscript old Mr Clare's letter states that the jewels are Tess's 'absolute property', while in all the editions the terms of the bequest allow the heroine 'the use of them for her lifetime' only, as family 'heirlooms'. This, as will be emphasized later,[2] was a change that was to have a beneficial effect on those parts of the novel dealing with her later financial situation in the period of her life following her rejection by her idealistic but priggish husband.

II

Four of the major themes of the definitive text of *Tess* were already well developed by November 1889. Of these, the theme of Nature as norm had played a significant role in many of Hardy's earlier novels, especially in the pastoral passages of *Under the Greenwood Tree* (1872), *Far From the Madding Crowd* (1874), and *The Woodlanders* (1887), where the close relationship between rural dwellers and their environment had been vividly portrayed. Two of the other three main themes of the Ur-novel had also played

[2] See pp. 164–5 below.

their parts in earlier Hardy novels, namely, the importance of the individual's will and foresight and (paradoxically) the insignificance of the individual in relation to an immense and indifferent Cosmos and the ceaseless flux of Time.

The only important new theme of the Ur-novel was the proposition that the heroine's intentions, rather than her actions, should be the criterion for judging her purity and innocence. Not surprisingly, this is a theme that has been seized on by several Hardy critics in their quest for a central unifying thread in *Tess*. As early as 1892 Clementine Black, reviewing Hardy's novel in the *Illustrated London News* (9 January), observed that its supremacy was due mainly to a profound moral earnestness which had not always been conspicuous in Hardy's writing. She continued: 'Its essence lies in the perception that a woman's moral wealth is measurable not by any one deed, but by the whole aim and tendency of her life and nature.'[3] More recently, Ian Gregor in *The Moral and the Story* (1962) restated this view in a more sophisticated form:

If *Tess* has a centre capable of formulation in abstract terms, then such a statement is found in Clare's reflections on 'the old appraisements of morality. He thought they wanted adjusting. Who was the moral man? Still more pertinently, who was the moral woman? The beauty and ugliness of a character lay not only in its achievements, but in its aims and impulses; its true history lay not among things done, but among things willed.' This is a forceful passage, making the point succinctly and without rhetorical flourish. Hardy is here feeling his way towards a criticism of 'behaviour' as an adequate moral register—'not things done, but things willed'.[4]

As the following pages will show, the theme of intention, although important, is not the 'centre' of *Tess*. Another critic, Bernard J. Paris, has argued that the theme that comes closest to becoming 'an ethical centre' for the novel is 'Hardy's vision of the dignity of the individual, of consciousness'. 'But', Paris continues, 'I am not claiming that it constitutes the real thematic core of the novel. The novel has no real thematic core.' There can be no doubt that this last statement by Paris is quite correct; and so also is Paris's

[3] Quoted by R. G. Cox in *Thomas Hardy, The Critical Heritage*, London, 1970, p. 187.
[4] Gregor, p. 146.

explanation that the lack of a thematic core is due to the fact that there existed in Hardy's mind, at the time when he was writing *Tess*, 'a confusion of many standards'.[5] As a result the themes are narrow and inconsistent. To use the words of another critic (Robert C. Schweik), they each offer only 'limited moral perspectives' and 'partial insights'.[6]

These 'limited moral perspectives' or 'partial insights' constitute quite a different effect from the discreteness Michael Millgate is suggesting by his observation that in *Tess* 'Hardy's philosophical formulations . . . serve rather as notations of the immediate context pointing up and intensifying, in a quite limited way, the effects being sought in a particular scene or chapter.' Indeed, Hardy's passages of philosophical comment—whether directly or dramatically rendered—are far more fully 'integrated' than Millgate allows, when he observes that they are not 'integrated elements in an articulated pattern of statement and implication'.[7] While it is true that they do not form part of any *single* 'pattern' of this kind, they nevertheless do constitute 'integrated elements' in a *series* of such 'articulated' patterns of 'statement and implication'. Hardy himself was well aware of both the presence of such patterns of thought running through his later novels and their often tentative and self-contradictory qualities as argument. His defence of his practice is summed up in the following well-known passage from the preface to *Jude*: 'Like former productions of this pen, *Jude the Obscure* is simply an endeavour to give shape and coherence to a series of seemings, or personal impressions, the question of their consistency or their discordance, of their permanence or their transitoriness, being regarded as not of the first moment.' Such a defence is equally appropriate to *Tess*.

The first of Hardy's themes, or 'seemings', to require examination is that of intention, which in the Ur-text is embodied in purely dramatic terms. Here, the author shows his heroine attempting to preserve her purity in her dealings with the villain and her integrity in her dealings with Angel Clare. Thus, in the following

---

5 Paris, pp. 59, 73–5.
6 'Moral Perspective in *Tess of the d'Urbervilles*', *College English*, xxiv, 1962, 18.
7 Millgate, p. 271.

typical passage we see her trying to avoid the villain's company on
the walk home from Chaseborough:

~~Rose-Mary~~
~~She~~ had never got over her original mistrust of him; &, with
                                                          folk
all their tardiness, she preferred to walk home with the work~~people.~~
                                                   frigidly.   can
'I am much obliged, ~~to 'ee sir~~ [?],' she answered ‸ 'But I ~~will~~ not
with 'ee.
go ‸ I have said that I will wait for 'em, & it will be better to
do it now.'
                                                            (f. 85)

Later in the plot, at Talbothays, she resolves on more than one
occasion to tell Angel of her past experience, although each time
her courage subsequently fails her. The following passage records
one such decision, taken after the three other love-sick milkmaids
have congratulated her on her engagement to Angel:

                                    Tess's ~~hot~~ salt stinging
     They were not aware that at these words ~~Rose-Mary's~~ ‸ tears
                 Tess's   anew
trickled down upon ~~her~~ pillow ‸ ; & how she resolved with a bursting
heart to tell all her history to Angel Clare, despite her mother's
command; to let him for whom she lived & breathed despise her if he
would, & her mother regard her as a fool, rather than preserve a
silence which might be deemed a treachery to him, & which somehow
seemed a wrong to these.
                                                         (ff. 286–7)

The commentary becomes associated with the theme of intention for the first time at the L5 stage, and takes both direct and
indirect forms. At the end of the chapter describing Clare's return
to his father's parsonage, three weeks after his wedding with Tess,
we find the author drawing attention to his theme in direct fashion:

~~n~~o prophet had told him, & he was not prophet enough to tell himself,
that essentially this young wife of his was as deserving of the praise
of King Lemuel as any other woman endowed with the same dislike of evil,
                having   not
~~that~~ her moral value ~~was not~~ to be reckoned ‸ by achievement but by tendency.
                                                            (f. 380)

Later, in Brazil, a much chastened and wiser Angel Clare expresses
the same thematic idea:

                        mysticism
Having long discredited the old systems of ~~theology~~ he now began
to discredit the old appraisements of morality. He thought they

> *pertinently,*
> wanted readjusting. Who was the moral man? Still more ∧ who
> *or ugliness*
> was the moral woman? The beauty ∧ of a character lay not in its
> *its   history*
> achievements, but in its aims & impulses; ~~the~~ true ~~record~~ lay not
> among things done, but among things conceived.[8]   (f. 488)

On the eve of her family's eviction from their Marlott home it is Tess who expresses the idea, while reluctantly admitting to herself the bitter truth that the treatment meted out to her by Angel has been unjust:

> Never in her life—she could swear it from the bottom of her soul—
> *ever*
> had she ∧ intended to do wrong; yet these hard judgments had come.
> Whatever her sins, they were not sins of intention, but of inadvertence,
> & why should she ~~had~~ have been punished so persistently?   (f. 508)

For the theme of Nature as norm, both description and commentary were employed from the start. Typical of the many passages of natural description in the Ur-text is the following:

> *Frome*
> Amid the oozing fatness & warm ferments of ~~Var~~ Vale, at a season
> *below   es*
> when the rush of juices & the hiss ∧ of fertilization could almost be
> heard ∫ it was impossible that the most fanciful love should not grow
> *ready*
> passionate. The ~~human~~ hearts existing there were impregnated by their
> *surroundings.*
> ~~environment.~~   (f. 210) (L2)

In the next extract we see the theme implied by an authorial comment, which comes at the end of a passage devoted to the heroine's life after the death of Sorrow:

> *that of*
> . . . her aspect was handsome, & arresting: ∧ a woman whom the turbulent
> experiences of the last year or two had quite failed to demoralize.
> *possible   simply*
> ~~But for the worlds~~ ∧ ~~opinion that experience would have been~~ ~~rather~~
> ~~a liberal education.~~   (f. 136) (L2)

[8] The familiar reading 'things willed' was substituted for 'things conceived' at the *Graphic* stage of composition.

Here, the final sentence was temporarily cancelled. However, as the broken underlining indicates, the passage was restored for the printing of the *Graphic* version and was retained in the editions.

Some of the commentary in the Ur-text is concerned with a special aspect of the Nature-as-norm theme—the difference between the rules and values of Nature and those of Society. This aspect is apparent in Angel's reflections, prompted by his realization of the gulf that has developed between his new ways of thinking while at Talbothays and the evangelical spirit of his parents' home at Emminster:

Latterly he had seen only Life, felt only the great passionate pulse
of ~~human~~ existence, unwarped, uncontorted, ~~by tradition~~ untrammelled
  those
by ⌄ conventional ~~cheeks~~ rules which futilely attempt to check what
wisdom would be content to regulate.   (f. 224)

A similar realization of the compulsive power of Nature over human conduct and its supremacy over the laws of man comes to the heroine on the afternoon when she finally accepts Angel's plea that she should marry him, although in this instance the comment is essentially the author's rather than the character's:

So they drove on through the gloom, forming one bundle inside the
sail-cloth, the horse going as he would, & the rain driving against them.
She had consented. She might as well have agreed at first. The 'appetite
                tremendous
for joy', which stimulates all creation: that ⌄ force which ~~lifts~~ sways
humanity to its purpose, as the tide sways the helpless weed, was not to
be controlled by a vague sense of self-abnegation on the score of
~~a moral —— precontract~~ [?]
~~social justice correctness.~~   (ff. 272-3)

Hardy's emphasis on Nature as norm is by no means confined to the Ur-text of *Tess*, and we find in L5 Hardy broadening the theme to take in the Darwinian idea of man's kinship with his 'weaker fellows in nature's teeming family'. This is the essence of Tess's reflection at the end of the passage describing her sympathy for the dying pheasants, brutally maimed by the huntsmen:

. . . like the inhabitants of the Malay peninsula, they ran amuck, & made it
their purpose to destroy life—in this case harmless feathered creatures,

                                                          the
brought into being by artificial means solely to gratify ~~this~~ propensity;
so unmannerly, so unchivalrous, towards their weaker fellows in nature's
teeming family.   (f. 400)

In the three-volume First Edition Hardy took his idea further when
he inserted a passage suggesting that 'maidenhood' might possess a
'recuperative power' similar to that displayed by 'organic nature':

> Was once lost always lost really true of chastity? she would ask herself.
> She might prove it false if she could veil bygones. The recuperative
> power which pervaded organic nature was surely not denied to maiden-
> hood alone.   (I. 195)

In the Fifth Edition (1892) and the Wessex Novels edition (1895)
new Darwinian implications come through, in the form of insertions stressing the 'animalism' and 'brute' element present in
human sexuality. Thus, in the Fifth Edition Hardy added this
italicized passage of comment on Angel Clare:

> It was the third day of the estrangement. *Some might risk the odd para-*
> *dox that with more animalism he would have been the nobler man. We do*
> *not say it. Yet* Clare's love was doubtless ethereal to a fault, imaginative
> to impracticability.   (X. 316)

Tess's opinion on the matter assumes a more morbid colouring.
She finds it difficult to dismiss the thought that physical coupling
is more binding than a marriage ceremony, as the italicized passage,
added in 1895, makes clear:

> 'Who was the gentleman?' asked her mother. 'Your husband?'
> 'No. He'll never, never come,' answered Tess in stony hopelessness.
> 'Then who was it?'
> 'Oh, you needn't ask. You've seen him before, and so have I.'
> 'Ah! What did he say?' said Joan curiously.
> 'I will tell you when we are settled in our lodgings at Kingsbere to-
> morrow—every word.'
> *It was not her husband, she had said. Yet a consciousness that in a brute*
> *sense this man alone was her husband seemed to weigh on her more and*
> *more.*   (Y. 464)

The Ur-text, itself, is not entirely free from these Darwinian
concepts, of which undertones may be detected in the following
basically L2 passage. Here, we are concerned at one level of mean-

ing with Angel's opinion that the heroine's limited education is of little importance. However, the deeper, philosophic meaning of the passage is that human nature, at its present stage of evolution, has been little influenced by 'moral and intellectual' systems of training, especially at the level of instinctive life:

He held ~~with all the ardour of his~~ that education had as yet but
       beats
little affected the ~~waves~~ of emotion & impulse on which domestic
happiness depends. It was probable that, in the lapse of ~~countless~~
ages, improved systems of moral & intellectual training would appreciably,
perhaps considerably, elevate the involuntary, & even the unconscious,
instincts of human nature; but up to the present day, culture, as far
    might   *only*
as he could see, ~~can~~ be ~~only~~ said , to have affected ˄ the mental epidermis
    had
of those lives which ~~have~~ been brought under its influence.   (f. 234)

Nevertheless, Roy Morrell was right in his book, *Thomas Hardy: The Will and the Way* (1965), to stress the importance in Hardy's novels of the individual's conscious exercise of will, intelligence, and choice. Although acknowledging the validity of the view that 'nature is no mere backcloth to human actions . . . but continuously active and changing' and that 'it affects man's life at point after point', Morrell went on to remind his readers that Hardy's world is by no means one of complete natural determinism: 'In Hardy's world, in short, man sometimes can and should strive *against* the natural flow of things; there is a margin for choice and action and intelligent intervention, a chance to "bend a digit the poise of forces, And a fair desire fulfil".[9] The chance to act effectively may or may not come often, but it comes.'[10] Unfortunately, none of the major characters in *Tess* displays these positive virtues consistently. There is no equivalent, in other words, of Gabriel Oak, who, with his solid, reliable, countryman qualities constitutes the moral and thematic centre of *Far From the Madding Crowd*. Nevertheless, what might be termed the theme of will is a major one in *Tess*.

In the Ur-text we find constant illustrations of the disasters occasioned by the lack of will, intelligence, and conscious choice

---

[9] From 'He Wonders About Himself', *C.P.*, p. 480.   [10] pp. 14–15. Morrell's italics.

in the characters. The heroine's parents, for example, seek escape
from reality in intoxication at Rolliver's Inn, where 'a sort of halo,
an occidental glow, came over life then', so that 'Troubles & other
realities took on themselves a metaphysical impalpability'. At
Rolliver's, the mother recaptures the unthinking sensations of the
courtship days, when she had refused to recognize her future
husband's faults, 'regarding him only in his ideal character of a
lover' (f. 22). The heroine herself, driving to market with the bee-
hives, falls 'more deeply into reverie' and ultimately into a deep
sleep, which contributes, in no small degree, to the death of the
family horse, Prince; and on the night of the seduction she helps to
bring about her own downfall by a similar lack of mental alertness,
in that when the villain returns to her through the fog he discovers
that she is 'sleeping soundly' (f. 99). During the weeks that precede
her marriage to Angel she drifts into a state of 'passive responsiveness to all things her lover suggested', with the result that an
opportunity to confess her earlier moral lapse is never created:

>   *Tess*   *without the sense of a will.*
> ~~Rose-Mary~~ was now carried along upon the wings of the hours, ∧
> The word had been given; the number of the day written down. Her naturally
>   *had ~~swerved to~~ begun to admit*
> bright intelligence ∧ ~~merged in~~ ∧ the fatalistic convictions common to
> field-folk & those who associate more extensively with natural ~~phe-~~
> phenomena than with their fellow-creatures; & she accordingly drifted
>   *that*
> into ∧ passive responsiveness to all things her lover suggested, ~~a~~
>   *the*
> characteristic of ~~that~~ frame of mind.   (f. 291)

In the above passage links are established by Hardy between
inaction, fatalism of outlook, and the life of nature. This idea is
reinforced by the original words of the heroine's mother in the
scene when her daughter first discloses what has befallen her at
Trantridge:

>   *fond ~~warm~~*
> Her mother was subdued. 'I thought if I spoke of his ∧ feelings, ·
>   *they mid*
> & what ~~it might~~ lead to, you would dislike him, & lose your chance,'
> she murmured, wiping her eyes with her apron. 'Well, we must make
>   *what pleases God.*
> the best of it—I suppose 'tis all ~~in the course of nature.~~   (f. 111)

In the version of this passage found in the First Edition, the mother's concluding words show her deriving a facile consolation for her passivity and fatalism not from the alternatives of nature and the divine will but from a combination of the two: "'Tis nater, after all, and what pleases God' (I. 160).

Equally disastrous as passivity and fatalism are the opposite qualities of precipitancy and recklessness, and in his study of Angel Clare, the 'modern' man, Hardy gives us a portrait of a person who is often merely wilful. The following basically L2 passage makes the point:

> Despite Angel Clare's plausible representations to himself & to
> *Tess*
> Rose-Mary of the practical need for their immediate union, there was,
> *in*
> in truth, an element of precipitancy about the step, as became apparent
> *ideally*
> at a later date. He loved her dearly, though perhaps rather intellectually
> *thoroughness*
> & imaginatively than with the impassioned warmth of her feeling for him.
> He had entertained no notion, when doomed as he had thought to an
> *singular*
> unintellectual bucolic life, that such natural charm as he beheld in
> this idyllic creature would be found behind the scenes. Unsophistication
> was a thing to talk of; but he had not known how it really struck one till
> he came here. But he was very far from seeing his future track clearly;
> & it might be a year or two before he would be able to consider himself
> fairly started in life. ⟨*The secret lay in the tinge of recklessness*
> *career & character*
> which had been *imparted to his* life ∧ *by the sense that he had been made*
> *to miss his true destiny through the prejudices of his family.*⟩   (ff. 291-2)

This analysis of Clare's lack of foresight and judgement is confirmed in an L4 insertion a little later in the narrative:

> *was* *She found him*
> He had ∧ determined to spend a short time at the Wellbridge flourmills;
> & what had determined him? Less the opportunity of an insight into
> grinding & bolting than the casual fact that lodgings were to be
> obtained in that very farm-house which, before its mutilation, had been
> the mansion of a branch of the D'Urberville family. This was always how
> Clare decided practical questions; by a sentiment which had nothing to
> do with them.   (f. 293ᵛ)

Hardy's championing of will and its concomitants, foresight, alertness, and dependability, is accompanied by a healthy respect

for stoicism, when misfortune must be endured, as we see in his
sympathetic portrayal of Tess's courage during adversity after the
birth of Sorrow (during L1) and at Flintcomb-Ash farm (in L5).
It is also associated with an intense respect for the individual and
belief in the value of the individual's consciousness as the source
of all perception and knowledge. Reflecting on the death of Sorrow,
Hardy describes the child as

                    eternal
. . . a waif to whom ˄ time had been a matter of hours merely; who had
           begin &   *& centuries*
seen only days ˄ end, & knew not that such things as years ˄ ever were;
to whom the cottage interior was the universe, the season's weather
climate, new-born babyhood human existence, & the instinct to suck human
knowledge.   (f. 133)

The same underscoring of consciousness appears in Hardy's reflection on his heroine's 'whimsical fancy' as she glides through
the 'lovely hills and dales' during the evenings before the birth
of Sorrow. Here, because ff. 114–16 are missing, the first extant
reading is that of the *Graphic*: 'At times her whimsical fancy would
intensify natural processes around her till they seemed a part of
her own story. Rather they became a part of it; for the world is
only a cerebral phenomenon, by all account, and what they seemed
they were' (G. 161). The phrase 'cerebral phenomenon' was later
amended to the more felicitous 'psychological phenomenon' in the
First Edition.

Angel Clare, like Hardy, recognizes that each individual and his
consciousness possess their own intrinsic value and dignity, and
this realization leads him to resolve that he must respect and avoid
harming others. There are several revealing Ur-text passages which
convey such sentiments, for example the following, with its observa-
tions that 'Upon her sensations the whole world depended to her
[the heroine]', that Angel should not 'look upon her as of less consequence than himself', and that the heroine's 'consciousness' was
'the single opportunity of existence ever vouchsafed . . . by an
unsympathetic first cause':

  Despite his heterodox opinions Clare was a man with a conscience,
                    Tess   *animal creature*
& from any honest point of view ~~Rose-Mary~~ was no insignificant ~~being~~ ˄

                              living her precious life—a
to toy with & dismiss; but a woman ∧ ~~who at her lowest estimate as an ordinary~~
~~mortal had a~~ life which, to herself who endured or enjoyed it, possessed
as great a ~~magnitude~~ dimension & importance as the life of the mightiest
        self   ~~*he considered*,~~   *in her and to herself,* to *Tess*:
to him ∧ . Upon her sensations, ∧ the whole world depended ~~to her~~ ∧ through
her existence all her fellow-creatures existed, to her. The very universe
                              Tess ~~*Woodrow*~~
itself only came into being for ~~Rose-Mary~~ ∧ on the particular day in the
particular year in which she was born.
        (*he went on*) *consciousness upon*
    Moreover ∧ this ~~career upon~~ which he had intruded was the single
                                        Tess   *an unsympathetic*
opportunity of existence ever vouchsafed to ~~Rose-Mary~~ by ~~a niggardly~~
first cause; her all; her every and only chance. How then should he look
                                        pretty trifle
upon her as of less consequence than himself; as a ~~thing~~ to patronizingly
caress & grow weary of; & not deal in the greatest seriousness with the
affection   *her* ~~*nature*~~—*so fervid & so*
~~attachment~~ which he knew that he had awakened in ∧ ~~so quivering~~ ∧ passionate
                              ~~*as hers it was*;~~   *too*
⟨*as she was under her reserve*₎ ——⟩ ~~a creature &~~ which she ∧ had awakened in
his him
    ~~him~~ [?]; in order that it might not agonise & wreck her?   (ff. 218-19)

Similar sentiments expressed by Angel will be found in the paragraph preceding the above extract and on f. 311. The fact that
Angel does not live up to his charitable sentiments when he cruelly
dismisses Tess after her confession is one of the strongest reasons
for his standing condemned in the reader's eyes.

    Paradoxically, Hardy's celebration of will and subjectivity in
the Ur-text of *Tess* is accompanied by the melancholy thought that
the individual, so much the centre of his own world of sensations,
is completely without significance when viewed against the im-
mensity of the Universe and the eternal flux of Time. On one
occasion Hardy's heroine falls into a reverie in which 'the occasional
heave of the wind became the sigh of some immense sad soul,
coterminous with the universe in space, & with history in time'
(f. 34, L1). This is the kind of cosmic background against which,
we are reminded from time to time, Hardy's characters are playing
out their little dramas of hopes and frustrations. The presence of
such a background is partly responsible for the sombre colouring
of Hardy's novels and, in particular, for the ironic sense of the

difference between what man deserves and what he actually receives from Life. It also helps to account for the quality of nobility that attaches to those characters who courageously carry on in the face of cosmic indifference, that lack of sympathy displayed by the Universal Will towards petty individual wills.

Placed in such a context of infinite space, it is little wonder that the individual looks as insignificant as a fly:

> Tess ~~Rose-Mary~~   *upon the hemmed*
> Not quite sure of her direction ∧ ~~Sue~~ stood still ~~in the~~ ∧ expanse
>   *billiard*
> of verdant flatness, like a fly on a ~~green~~ table of indefinite length,
>   *to the situation than that fly.*
> & of no more consequence   ∧   The sole effect of her presence upon
>   *had been*
> the placid valley so far ~~was~~ to excite the mind of a solitary heron,
> which, after ~~floatin~~ descending to the ground from some distant point,
> stood with neck erect looking at her.   (f. 147) **(L1)**

The 'fly' image recurs in the Flintcomb-Ash section of the narrative, as Tess and Marian grub up turnips from the bare field, under a blank sky:

> So these two upper & nether blanks confronted each other, all day
> long the white face looking down on the brown face, & the brown face
> looking up at the white face, without anything standing between them
> but the two girls crawling over the surface of the former like flies.
>   (ff. 409-10) **(L5)**

Within the dimension of Time, the individual is equally meaningless as an insignificant speck in history. Mutability triumphs over attempts to achieve stability, and the species alone has any significance. The latter truth is devastatingly clear when we look at Hardy's description of the worlds of birds and plants:

> The season developed & matured. Another year's instalment of flowers,
> leaves, nightingales, thrushes, finches & other creatures, took up their
> positions in their allotted division of time with no aspect of surprise
> *at being there,*   *others stood in their place,* ~~when and~~   ~~neither~~ *nothing*
>   ∧   *though only a year ago*   ∧   they were ~~not~~
> ~~of those things,~~
> ~~flowers, leaves, nightingales, thrushes, nor finches, nor anything~~ more than
> *inorganic* ~~chemical~~
> dead ∧ particles ~~of earth, water, & air~~.   (f. 182) **(L2)**

The human world offers the same melancholy lesson, as the heroine points out on the occasion when Angel asks her if she wishes to take up a course of study:

'Because what's the use of learning that I am one of a long row only —finding out that there is set down in some old book somebody just like me, and to know that I shall only act her part, making me sad, that's all. The best is not to remember that your nature and your past doings have been just like thousands and thousands, and that your coming life and doings'll be like thousands and thousands.'   (G. 218)

Here, however, the text quoted is that of the *Graphic*, the relevant folio (f. 179) being missing from the manuscript. Indeed, mutability in human affairs is a concept that was not to become important until after the Ur-novel stage. The emphasis occurs in the later layers of the manuscript (L3–L5), where it is closely associated with two newly emerging patterns of meaning—both themes of decline, one involving the English agricultural community in general, the other ancient landowning families, like the d'Urbervilles, which have passed into obscurity.

IV

IMAGERY
(SYMBOLISM AND MYTH)

THE elements of symbolism and myth in Hardy's novels have received a good deal of attention from modern critics, especially since Albert J. Guerard's 'revaluation' of Hardy's achievements in 1949, which pointed out that while the older generation of critics 'saw Hardy's deliberate anti-realism (his juxtaposition of implausible incident and plausible human character) as a perverse continuation of the Victorian sensation novel', modern critics 'now accept Hardy's extreme conjunctions, in the best novels at least, as highly convincing foreshortenings of the actual and absurd world'.[1] Guerard continued:

> We are in fact attracted by much that made the post-Victorian realist uneasy: the inventiveness and improbability, the symbolic use of re-appearance and coincidence, the wanderings of a macabre imagination, the suggestions of supernatural agency; the frank acknowledgement that love is basically sexual and marriage usually unhappy; the demons of plot, irony, and myth. And we are repelled or left indifferent by what charmed that earlier generation . . .[2]

In a perceptive essay called 'The Mirror and the Sword', Richard C. Carpenter demonstrated that Hardy's imagery in *Far From the Madding Crowd* 'constitutes a secondary dimension to his ostensible narrative and theme'.[3] Observing that the novel is universally acknowledged to be 'the first of the major novels' of Hardy, Carpenter pointed out that one of the reasons for its superiority over the earlier works is to be found in its 'structure of images', which, in turn, is a characteristic of all Hardy's major novels, such as *Tess, The Mayor of Casterbridge,* and *The*

---

[1] Guerard, p. 3.
[2] Ibid., p. 6.
[3] 'The Mirror and the Sword: Imagery in *Far From the Madding Crowd*', *Nineteenth-Century Fiction*, xviii, 1964, 345.

Return of the Native. Indeed, Carpenter went on: 'One of the reasons why these novels are "major" is precisely that in them Hardy managed to create a fabric of images, repeated and "concatenated" to deepen and make complex the emotional and conceptual significance.'[4]

It is certainly true that in *Tess*, as in the other major novels, Hardy succeeded in creating a web of symbolic imagery with both emotional and conceptual significance. One of the more important aspects of emotional significance is the atmosphere of eroticism built up through such means, at a time when prudery prohibited direct literary treatment of the sexual side of human relationships. Thus, through images of landscape, for example, Hardy could, and did, suggest in *Tess* the power of sexual attraction and the violence which might result therefrom. The deepening of conceptual significance is a different matter, resulting from the employment of images to reinforce and expand concepts already explicit in the novel's plot situations and thematic commentary. Both kinds of symbolism involved the use of a certain amount of imagery drawn from myth, both in the modern anthropological sense and in the traditional sense of mythologies rooted in older literature, especially the classics of Greece and Rome, the Bible, and Milton's *Paradise Lost.* Indeed, as Michael Millgate has pointed out: 'Less obtrusively but more powerfully than in earlier novels, *Tess* resonates with allusions to larger, more universal patterns which lie beyond its own world.'[5] One reason, no doubt, for the increased reliance on the allusive world of myth was that same need to suggest what could not be openly stated, which has been remarked on above, although there was also the gain in sheer imaginative force.

The Ur-text shows that several of the final imagery patterns in *Tess* were already well developed before November 1889. Thus, as has been indicated earlier in this section and in the sections on mutability and Nature as norm,[6] one such pattern involves the use of landscape and the seasons as symbolic commentary on human and cosmic affairs. An additional illustration of such imagery may

---

[4] Ibid., p. 331.   [5] Millgate, p. 269.
[6] See above, pp. 42, 50.

E

be seen in the following L1 passage, which forms part of the description of the seduction in the fog-bound Chase:

> Darkness & silence ruled everywhere around. Above them rose
>   *in which were poised*
> the primeval yews & oaks of the Chase, & the gentle roosting birds
>   *all about*
> in their last nap; & around them were the hopping rabbits & hares.   (f. 99)

Here 'the primeval yews and oaks', especially the latter, carry with them overtones of mystical sacrificial rites deriving from classical and Druidical sources, while the helpless vulnerability of the victim and the relentless drive of Nature to reproduce the species are suggested through the images of 'the gentle roosting birds' and 'the hopping rabbits and hares'. Similar examples of symbolic landscape may be multiplied from other sections of the novel, such as the August 'harvesting' scenes, when we first learn of the birth of the heroine's child (f. 123) and the long Talbothays idyll, during which the atmosphere hangs 'heavy as an opiate' over the lush valley where Angel and the four love-sick dairymaids have their being (f. 200).

Associated with such landscape passages there are several recurring motifs, which gather symbolic significance in their own right. An important group of such motifs in the Ur-text is that which includes the images of birds and animals and those of fog and pollen. In the seduction scene, as we have noted, the images of fog, birds, rabbits, and hares are all present, while in the description of the dance held at the hay-trusser's the heroine observes that the 'fusty' mist raised by the feet kicking the 'powdery residue of peat, hay, and other products' on the floor combines with the 'perspirations and warmth' of the dancers' bodies to form what Hardy describes as 'a sort of vegeto-human pollen'. Here the mist imagery accompanies, as it does so often in *Tess*, the states of drunkenness, decline in mental alertness, and loss of a character's sense of reality, while the pollen image is but one of the many reminders of Nature's mindless, prodigal fecundity:

>   *floating*   ~~sediment~~ *debris of peat & hay*   *the*
> Through this ⌄ fusty ~~emanation of the fuel shed~~, mixed with —— &
>   *& warmth of the dancers, &   together   vegeto-*
> perspirations ~~from themselves,~~   forming ⌄ a sort of ⌄ human pollen, the

muted fiddles feebly pushed their notes, in marked contrast to the spirit

measure was trodden out.

with which the ~~dance was kept up~~ ⟨*They coughed as they danced, & laughed*

there   be discerned

as they coughed.⟩ Of the rushing couples ~~she~~ could barely ^ ~~see~~ more than

high lights—the indistinctness shaping them to

the ~~outlines—~~ ^ satyrs ~~like figures~~ clasping nymphs—a multiplicity

of Pans whirling a multiplicity of Syrinxes; Lotis attempting to elude

Priapus ^ & always failing.   (ff. 81-2)

In the scene at Talbothays when the heroine is drawn through the uncultivated garden towards Angel by the music of his harp (ff. 173-4) we read that the notes wandered in the still air 'with a stark quality like that of nudity'. 'She listened', we are told, 'like a fascinated bird' and 'could not leave the spot'. The garden is described as 'damp and rank with juicy grass which sent up mists of pollen, and tall blooming weeds emitting offensive smells'. In this blighted Eden, 'she went stealthily as a cat through this profusion of growth, gathering cuckoo-spittle on her skirts . . . and rubbing off upon her naked arms sticky blights . . . thus she drew quite near to Clare, though still unobserved. . . . conscious of neither time nor space . . . she undulated upon the thin notes as upon billows'. In this state of 'exaltation' the heroine experiences the following illusion:

The floating pollen seemed to be his notes made visible, & the dampness

weeping

of the garden the ~~tears~~ of the garden's sensibility.   (f. 174)

Even more illusioned, however, is Angel's response to the physical attractiveness of the heroine during their early-morning meetings in the meadows, when the idyllic beauty of the landscape in the summer fogs and grey half-tones of light symbolizes Angel's innocent idealizing of Tess, as Adam might have idealized Eve in Paradise before the Fall. Angel is unable to see the real Tess on these occasions, which are narrated largely through his point of view; instead, he sees her as a generalized figure, as 'a visionary essence of woman', and also as a goddess, more perfect than any mortal woman, chaste (like 'Artemis') and at the same time potentially fruitful (like 'Demeter'):

It was then, as has been said, that she impressed him most deeply. She was no longer the milkmaid, but a visionary essence of woman—a whole sex condensed into one typical form. He called her Artemis, Demeter,

half-teasingly—

& other fanciful names, ∧ which she did not like because she did not

them

understand ~~their import~~.

Tess   ~~simply~~ *askance*

'Call me ~~Rose-Mary~~,' she would say ~~softly~~; & he did.   (f. 185)

Compared with Angel's romantic idealism towards her, the heroine's illusions about Angel are moderate. Although she comes to exaggerate his moral goodness she never loses sight of the man in the idea. For this reason she is more vulnerable when Angel unjustly turns against her, and the 'wounded animal' image is therefore an appropriate one to suggest both her devotion and her helplessness, in scenes such as the following, when Angel unthinkingly casts doubt on the depth of her love during the earlier part of their wedding night:

> '~~Rose-Mary~~, you are not a bit cheerful this evening—not at
> all as you used to be. I wonder if you really love me after all?'
> He knew that she did, & the words had ~~so~~ no serious intent;
> but she was so surcharged with emotions that she winced like a
> wounded animal; & though she tried not to shed tears she could not
> help beginning.   (f. 316)

The passage occurs originally on an **L2** leaf (f. 316), although later transferred to an **L4** leaf (f. 312).

The preceding allusions to 'satyrs' and 'nymphs' (f. 82), 'Pans' and 'Syrinxes' (f. 82), 'Lotis attempting to elude Priapus' (f. 82), and 'Artemis, Demeter' (f. 185) are but some of the classical references that occur in the Ur-text. Others of interest include the description of the drunken onlookers at the dance as 'some Sileni of the throng' (f. 82) and the description of the sun, on that hazy August morning when the harvesting takes place, as 'a golden-haired, ardent-eyed, godlike creature, gazing down in the vigour and intentness of youth upon an earth that was brimming with interest for him' (f. 117). In yet another section of the dance scene, Hardy describes the couples capering through the haze of the peat dust as 'demigods' who later 'resolved themselves into the homely personalities of her own next door neighbours'. The heroine thereupon asks herself incredulously: 'Could Trantridge in two or three short hours have metamorphosed itself thus madly!' (f. 82).

The verb 'metamorphosed' testifies to an indebtedness to Ovid, rather than to other ancient authors, for most of the above classical allusions. Indeed, Hardy's debt to Ovid, and especially to the *Metamorphoses*, would seem to be somewhat more wide-ranging and deeper in *Tess* than has hitherto been recognized. For not only does Ovid seem to have provided the specific allusions: he also may well have been one of the main models for Hardy's employment of pastoral landscape as symbol and for some of the individual themes, as well as for aspects of characterization.

As Charles Paul Segal pointed out in *Landscape in Ovid's 'Metamorphoses'* (1969), nearly every major ancient poet from Homer onwards made use of the natural world to order the realities of the human world, Virgil, in particular, providing the great example in the *Aeneid* of 'the possibilities of using physical setting to evoke an atmosphere which might itself symbolically reflect major themes of the work'.[7] Ovid, although quick to learn this lesson from Virgil and the earlier writers, transformed this literary symbol in certain important ways, as Segal succinctly explains: 'Ovid achieves a special and characteristic effect, however, by using peaceful sylvan scenes as the setting for violence, often sexual violence . . . One effect of this is to intensify the sense of the victim's helplessness. Where even the place of refuge and peace is invaded, there is no safety, no escape from arbitrary force. In such a world innocence is never preservable.[8] In this transformed use of literary landscape to bring out the violence, cruelty, instability, and 'moral chaos' of existence, Ovid may well have provided Hardy with an exemplar which accorded perfectly with Hardy's own temperamental predilections. Similarly, Hardy may have taken over from Ovid the 'hunting' metaphor, which plays such an important role in *Tess* from the later stages of manuscript composition onwards.[9] In earlier pastoral, hunting had possessed mainly erotic overtones, but in Ovid, as in Hardy, it became a further symbol of violence. Like

---

[7] *Landscape in Ovid's 'Metamorphoses': a Study in the Transformations of a Literary Symbol*, Wiesbaden, 1969, p. 4.
[8] Ibid., p. 8.
[9] See pp. 91–5 below.

Ovid, Hardy also shows a deep and sympathetic understanding of feminine psychology and a frank appreciation of the sexual basis of passion, his novel constituting a defence both of his heroine and of the life force in its many manifestations and changes.

Many of the above-mentioned classical allusions occur in the Chaseborough dance episode (ff. 81–5), which was omitted from the *Graphic* version and from all editions prior to the Wessex edition of 1912. Just why Hardy omitted this richly Ovidian section is not adequately explained by his note in the 1912 edition that 'these pages were overlooked, though they were in the original manuscript'. Indeed, as I have earlier indicated, they were *not* 'overlooked', although it is not easy to understand Hardy's motive in attempting to conceal the fact.[10]

The Biblical allusions in *Tess* are numerous, but the most significant group are the Eden images, some of which have come into the novel by way of Milton. As has already been observed, the description of the uncultivated garden at Talbothays (ff. 173–4) suggests Eden blighted, although it also contains echoes of Hamlet's vision of the world as 'an unweeded garden / That grows to seed',[11] while the early-morning meetings in the meadows are reminiscent of Eden before the Fall:

> *sub-marine   which pervaded the open mead*
> The spectral, half-compounded ∧ light ∧ impressed them with a feeling
> of isolation, as if they were Adam & Eve. At this dim inceptive stage
>   *Tess*
> of the day ~~Rose-Mary~~ seemed to Clare to exhibit a dignified largeness
> *both of disposition*
> ~~of nature~~ & physique, an almost regnant power . . .   (ff. 184–5)

When Angel returns to Talbothays from his visit to Emminster, determined to marry the heroine, he embraces her 'warm as a sunned cat' after her sleep, and the Adam and Eve allusions are used once again:

>   *her eyes*
> At first she would not look straight up at him, but ~~she~~ ∧ soon lifted
> , *& his met*   *violet-black*
> ~~her eyes, & he looked into~~ their ~~violet-blue-grey~~ deepness, ~~of her~~ while
>   *regarded*   ⟨*might have*⟩ *regarded*
> she ~~looked at~~ him as Eve ∧ ~~looked at~~ Adam.   (ff. 240–1)

10 See pp. 18–20 above, and pp. 180–4 below.   11 *Hamlet*, I. ii. 135–6.

In the First Edition the above passage gains additional significance from the insertion of 'at her second waking' after the word 'Eve' (II. 81).

In the later layers of the manuscript Hardy continued to build up the Eden motif, for example in the scene at Marlott when Alec suddenly reappears as her tempter amidst the smoke of the burning couch-grass, and quotes from *Paradise Lost* the passage which almost immediately precedes Eve's Fall:

'*If I were inclined to joke I should say*
                                        How much this seems like Paradise!'
        ~~Tess~~
~~does'nt it, cozzie,~~' he said, whimsically looking at her with an inclined head.
                weakly
'What do you say?' she ₳ asked.
'*A jester might say this*   *old*
~~It~~ ₳   is just like Paradise. You are Eve, & I am the ₳ other one, come to tempt you in the disguise of an inferior animal. I
                        ~~old~~
used to be quite up in that scene of ₳ Milton's when I was theological. Some of it goes,

> "Empress, the way is ready, & not long;
> Beyond a row of myrtles, on a flat
> Fast by a fountain, one small thicket past
> Of blowing myrrh & balm: if thou accept
> My conduct I can bring thee thither soon."
> "Lead then" said Eve.

And so on. My dear dear Tess, I am only putting this to you as a thing that you might have supposed or said quite untruly, because you think so badly of me.'
'I never said you were Satan or thought it. I don't think of you in that way at all.
                                        (ff. 501–2) (L5)

It is shortly after this scene that John Durbeyfield dies and Tess is compelled to accept Alec's offer to go away with him once again, in order to save her mother and family from penury. Similarly, the closing incident of the novel, with Angel and 'Liza-Lu arising from their knees and moving on with 'joined hands' (f. 565), carries with it the overtones of the two closing lines of *Paradise Lost*, with their mixture of sadness and hope:

> They hand in hand, with wand'ring steps and slow,
> Through Eden took their solitary way.

Milton

Two of the most effective patterns of imagery in the Ur-text of *Tess* involve colour and light—the first a group of vivid, sometimes macabre, blood-red images connoting violence, passion, guilt, or fear of damnation, the second a group of white-pale images suggesting innocence, unjust suffering, illusion, or pure spirituality. Both kinds of imagery may be found elsewhere in Hardy's fiction, although not with such elaborateness or such powerful cumulative effect as in *Tess*. Thus, in *Far From the Madding Crowd* Hardy describes in the opening scene how 'the sun lighted up to a scarlet glow the crimson jacket' worn by the capricious heroine as she sits on the wagon with its load of furniture and practises her smile in the mirror; and, later, after the heroine's dress has been caught one night by Sergeant Troy's spur, we read how the heroine's lantern, opened suddenly, casts its light on the dashing Troy, 'brilliant in brass and scarlet'.[12] In *The Mayor of Casterbridge* we read a description of the buildings of the town seen from the distance, with 'the highest glazings shining bleared and bloodshot with the coppery fire they caught from the belt of sunlit cloud in the west'; and earlier in this novel we are told that the road down which Michael Henchard trudges with his wife and child has its grassy margin and the nearest hedgerow branches 'powdered by the dust that had been stirred over them by hasty vehicles'. The 'coppery fire' image evokes an atmosphere of guilt and foreboding, as the mother and Elizabeth-Jane approach the town where Michael Henchard is later discovered to be mayor, while the image of the pale dusty road leading to Weydon-Priors reinforces 'the atmosphere of stale familiarity which the trio carried along with them like a nimbus as they moved down the road' and 'the voice of a weak bird singing a trite old evening song' near by.[13]

The earliest extant occurrence in *Tess* of the first of these two motifs is to be found in the section of the manuscript which contains the account of the heroine's horrified realization that the family horse, Prince, has been killed while she has been asleep:

> *Tess* ~~Rose-Mary~~
> In consternation ₍ ~~Cis~~ jumped down, & discovered the dreadful truth. The groan had proceeded from her father's poor horse Prince. The

---

[12] Chs. 1, 24.   [13] Chs. 4, 1.

morning

ᴧ   mail-cart, with its two noiseless wheels, speeding along these lanes

slow &

like an arrow, as it always did, had driven into her ᴧ unlighted equipage.

The pointed shaft of the cart had entered the breast of the unhappy Prince

spouting

like a sword; & from the wound his life's blood was ~~pouring~~ in a stream,

with a hiss

& falling ~~hissing~~ into the road.

Tess ~~Rose-Mary~~

In her despair ᴧ ~~Cis~~ sprang forward & put her hand upon the hole,
with the only result that she became splashed from face to skirt with
the crimson drops. Then she stood helplessly looking on. Prince also
stood ~~By this time~~ firm & motionless as long as he could; ~~then~~

till he suddenly

ᴧ   sank down ~~& died~~ in a heap.   (ff. 34–5)

For the heroine's family the loss of Prince will mean further im-
poverishment. However, equally significant as the economic aftermath of the incident is the impact made on the reader's mind by
some of the images themselves—'the pointed shaft' of the mail-
cart piercing the breast of Prince 'like a sword' and the heroine
becoming 'splashed from face to skirt with the crimson drops' as
she vainly attempts to stop Prince's life blood ebbing away. In this
scene Hardy is giving us, as we later realize, a subtle but vivid fore-
warning of two later violent events—the seduction of the heroine
and her stabbing of the villain. The scene is then followed by
another, equally powerful, showing the heroine waiting by the
roadside in the pale light of early morning, staring at the huge pool
of blood and the stark, dead horse, as the mail-man drives away:

while Tess ~~Rose-Mary~~

He mounted & sped on his way;   ᴧ   ~~& Cis~~ stood & waited. The atmosphere

twittered

turned pale, the birds shook themselves in the hedges, arose, & ~~sang~~:

pale white   ~~Rose-Mary~~ *Tess*   *whiter.*

the lane showed all its ᴧ features, & ~~Cis~~   showed hers, still ~~paler.~~
The huge pool of blood in front of her was already assuming the iridescence
of coagulation; & when the sun rose a million prismatic hues were reflected
from it. Prince lay alongside still & stark; his eyes half open, the hole
in his chest looking scarcely large enough to have let out all that ~~life~~
had animated him.   (f. 35)

What emerges from the two above passages is the sense of the
helplessness and anguish of the heroine in a world of violence and

sudden illogical disaster. While it is true that by falling asleep she has incurred some of the blame for Prince's death, her subsequent suffering and punishment are out of all proportion to the degree of personal responsibility. Her paleness is the paleness of physical fatigue, innocence, and undeserved suffering, while Prince's blood is symbolic not only of mortality in general and the cruelty of external forces but of the heroine's own full-bloodedness and vulnerability, not merely as a human being but as a woman.

Similar connotations relating to the colour red are apparent in the following passage from the Chaseborough dance section, where the image of the red coal of the villain's cigar, with its phallic implications, is in keeping with the general tone of peremptoriness on the villain's part and of reluctant yielding on the part of the heroine:

> loud   ~~Rose-Mary's~~ Tess's
> A ~~burst of~~ laughter from behind   ~~Sue's~~   back in the shade of the
> garden united with the titter within the room. She looked round, & saw
>   D'Urberville
> the red coal of a cigar: Alec ~~Hawnferne~~ was standing ~~behind her~~ there
>   alone   reluctantly retreated   ~~with~~ towards
> ~~by himself.~~ He beckoned to her, & she ∧ ~~went out to~~ [?] ∧ him.   (f. 84)

It is the inclusion of such passages as this that allowed Hardy to suggest by implication what he was not permitted to describe explicitly in the scene of the heroine's seduction in the Chase.

After the heroine has left Trantridge to return home the red image takes on associations of guilt, with which are later blended fears of hell fire and damnation for her illegitimate child. The earliest illustration of the guilt connotation is to be found in the description of her encounter with the painter of religious texts, whose slogan 'THE, WAGES, OF, SIN, IS, DEATH' (which Hardy amended in the First Edition to read 'THY, DAMNATION, SLUMBERETH, NOT') is painted on a stile in 'vermillion' [*sic*] paint, whence it seems to enter the heroine's heart 'with a cold accusatory horror' (f. 108). Later in the story, after the birth of the child Sorrow, the heroine is one of a group of women taking part in the harvesting of the corn crop in a field 'hard by Marlott village'. When lunchtime comes, her sister 'Liza-Lu brings the child to be fed and Hardy once again employs the red image in the description of the heroine's 'rising of

colour' as she 'unfastened her frock and began suckling the child'
(f. 123). Early the next morning, when the child falls ill, the heroine,
contemplating its 'lack of baptism and lack of legitimacy', begins
to imagine its torment in the fires of hell, in a manner considerably
less restrained in the original than in the later version:

> arch-fiend
> [She] saw the ~~devil~~ just as she had been accustomed to see him in
> ~~with which~~ used for ing
> infancy, with his three-pronged fork—like the fork ∧ they ∧ heated the oven
> ~~with~~ on baking-days, only larger—~~tossing her own dear innocent into the~~
> ~~flames, its little limbs hissing & crackling in the heat or [?] seized by~~
> curious
> ~~junior devils in turn;~~ to which picture she added many other ∧ details of
> cheerful the instructed [?]
> torment as conveyed to her mind in ~~her~~ childhood by the ∧ doctrines ∧ taught the
> young latterly recalled
> ∧ in this Christian country, & ~~revived~~ by the man with the paint-pot. (f. 129)

The power of genuine passion to stir the blood is the implication
of the red imagery in the Talbothays section, where it is applied to
the milkmaids, Marian, Izz, and Retty, as well as to the heroine
and Angel Clare. The following passage shows this aspect of meaning clearly:

> She saw them ing light dying sun
> ~~They~~ undressed in the orange ~~blaze~~ of the ~~west~~, which flushed their forms
> she
> with its colour; ~~& then~~ dozed again; but she was reawakened by their voices,
> & quietly turned her eyes towards them.
> Neither of her three chamber companions had got into bed. They were
> standing in a group, in their nightgowns, barefooted, at the window, the
> last red rays of the west still warming their faces & necks, & the walls around
> them. All ~~three~~ were watching somebody in the garden with deep interest, their
> three faces close together: a jovial & round one, a pale one with dark hair,
> & a fair one whose tresses were auburn. (f. 192)

A little later, Retty accuses Izz of having kissed Angel's shadow on
the wall and 'a rosy spot came into the middle of Izz Huett's cheek',
Izz, in her turn, then accusing both her companions of being in
love with Angel with the result that 'Marian's full face could not
blush past its chronic pinkness' (f. 193). One of the climaxes of the
book occurs one Sunday morning when Angel meets the four milk-
maids dressed in their finery on the way to church and carries them

across a flooded section of the lane. Each of the girls is emotionally disturbed by the experience of being in the arms of the man she loves—even the heroine who has begun to realize that she, too, is falling in love. Once again the imagery of blushing is employed to suggest the strength of sexual passion:

'I did not expect such an event to-day.'
'Nor I, ~~sir~~. . . . The water came up so sudden.'
That the rise in the water was what she understood him to refer to, the state of her breathing belied. Clare stood still, & turned his face towards hers.

against her.
'O Tessie!' he said pressing ~~her~~ close ~~to him.~~
The girl's cheeks burned to the breeze, & she could not speak for her emotion. (f. 205)

Later in the Talbothays section Clare leaves the dairy-farm for a short visit to his parents' home at Emminster. He rides back to Talbothays one hot afternoon and enters the house at the moment when the heroine has come downstairs, 'her face . . . flushed with sleep' and 'her eyelids . . . heavy over their pupils'. Once again the passionate implications of the blood-red imagery are quite clear in the description of 'the red interior of her mouth', no less than of her sleep-flushed face:

She had not heard him enter, & hardly realized his presence there. ~~now.~~ She was yawning, & he saw the red interior of her mouth as if it had been a
had *so* *coiled-up cable of*
snake's. She ∧ stretched one naked arm ∧ high above her ~~head-of-twisted-up~~ hair
its delicacy above the sunburn; *was* *with*
that he could see ~~almost-to-the-shoulder~~ [?] her face ~~been~~ flushed ~~from~~ sleep, & her eyelids hung heavy over their pupils. It was a moment when a woman is
incarnate *beauty inclines to the*
more ~~the-flesh~~ than at any other time; when the most spiritual ∧ ~~is~~ corporeal; & ~~when~~ sex takes the outside place in her presentation. (ff. 239–40)

It is, thus, no wonder that the skimming was done less efficiently that afternoon than normally:

Every time she held the skimmer under the pump to cool it for the work, her hand trembled, the ardour of his affection being so palpable that
flinch *burning*
she seemed to ~~droop~~ under it like a plant in too ~~strong~~ a sun. (f. 241)

The imagery of whiteness and pale light in the Ur-text needs less illustration than the blood-red imagery, although its role is

scarcely less significant. The heroine's innocence is suggested no
more strikingly in that early-morning scene of the white-faced girl
looking in dismay at the pool of Prince's coagulating blood (f. 35)
than it is in the night scene in the Chase, with the pale moonlight
gradually lessening and the heroine's 'white' muslin frock eventually becoming indiscernible in the intense blackness (ff. 98-9). It
is her capacity to attain to a state of exalted spirituality that is
suggested by the imagery in another scene, that of the midnight
baptism, when her sudden realization that her child may still be
saved leads her to exclaim 'so brightly that it seemed as though her
face might have shone in the darkness with the joy which must
have marked itself there'. Lighting a candle, she proceeds to awaken
her younger sisters and, then, majestic in her white night-gown
she baptizes the infant herself. In the pale candle-light her appearance undergoes a complete, if temporary, transfiguration, and all
her human blemishes disappear:

> Her white figure looked tall & ~~even~~ imposing as she stood, a thick
> cable of dark braided hair hanging straight down her back to her waist.
>   *the weak taper*   *the little*
> The kindly dimness of ~~night~~   removed from her form all ∧ blemishes
>   *the stubble-scratches on her wrists included,*
> which sunlight might have revealed, ∧
> & showed   *derived*
>   ~~& she~~ her in spotless beauty, with an impress of dignity, ∧ from the
> occasion, that seemed regal . . .   (f. 130)

In the baptism scene the essential purity of the heroine's spirit is
revealed and we see more deeply into her soul than in any other
scene in the novel.

In two later scenes it is not genuine spirituality but illusion that
is associated with such imagery. When the heroine steals stealthily
through the uncultivated garden at Talbothays in her 'white gown'
(f. 174), as the evening light is lessening, she is being drawn towards
an Angel whom she sees, as if through a distorting glass, as 'an
American or Australian Abraham, commanding like a monarch his
flocks & his herds, his spotted & his ring-straked, his menservants
& his maids' (f. 177). And when the two begin to meet in the
meadows in 'the spectral, half-compounded sub-marine light' of
early morning it is Angel who is illusioned (f. 184). The pale light

imparts an unearthly look to the heroine's face, 'a sort of phos-
phorescence', with the result that 'She looked ghostly, as if she were
merely a soul at large' (f. 185). In reality, her face, like his, had
merely 'caught the cold gleam of day from the north-east'. But in
such a light Angel sees her not as a mortal creature but as an ideal
woman, as a figure of spiritualized beauty, as 'a divinity' (f. 185).

However, the image of the heroine as 'a soul at large' is not
entirely without substance, for it represents not only Angel's illusioned attitude but the heroine's own yearnings when in a certain
idealizing frame of mind. Although the image is not developed very
fully in the Ur-text, it does exist in at least one other passage, where
it forms part of the heroine's own viewpoint. This is the passage
in which she is explaining her belief that in a certain state of spiritual exaltation, 'souls . . . can be made to go outside our bodies
when we are alive':

>   *—know about*
> 'I don't ~~answer for~~ ghosts,' she was saying. 'But I do know that our
> souls can —— be made to go outside our bodies when we are alive.'
> The dairyman turned to her with his mouth~~ful~~ full, his eyes charged
>   *great*
> with serious inquiry, & his ∧ knife & fork (breakfasts were breakfasts here)
>   *What*
> planted erect on the table, like the beginning of a gallows. '—— —really
> now? And is it so, maidie?' he said.
>   ·   ~~soft & fluty~~ *Tess*
> 'A very easy way to feel th'em go,' continued ~~the rich voice~~, 'is to ~~star~~
> lie on the grass at night, & look straight up at ~~the sky, & think o'~~ some
>   ~~queer~~ *big bright*
> ~~particular~~ ∧ star, ~~you see up there;~~ & by fixing your mind upon it you will
>   *you are*
> soon find that ~~your soul is~~ hundreds & hundreds o' miles away from your body,
> which you don't seem to want at all.' ~~so that if anything were to snatch~~
> ~~away your body your soul would still stay floating about up above.'~~   (f. 169)

In her utterance the heroine is describing a highly subjective,
quasi-mystical experience which reflects a deep-seated desire to
escape from the bonds and demands of the flesh. She sincerely
desires at this point in time to be 'a soul at large', but is soon to be
thwarted by the interest that Angel begins to take in her—ironically,
from the very moment that he hears these words. Hardy does not
suggest in *Tess* that pure spirituality is either desirable or practical;

indeed, the general movement of the narrative and commentary is opposed to any such denial of the life-force. What he does show is that the only instrument by which the heroine is ultimately able to escape from what Hardy elsewhere terms her 'beautiful feminine tissue' is the hand of the executioner, and to emphasize this point Hardy incorporates in the above passage the proleptic image of a gallows.

Although Hardy's general tendency was to continue amplifying and expanding the network of blood-red and white-pale images in the later layers of the manuscript, it should also be noted, in passing, that some of the blood-red images present in the Ur-text were later modified in one or other of the editions, usually in the interest of increased subtlety of expression. A single example must serve to illustrate the process, the first version being taken from the manuscript, and the second from the First Edition. In the first version, Hardy wrote:

> But of all red things that morning the reddest were two broad flat arms
>   *painted*
> of ˄ wood which rose from the margin of a yellow corn-field hard by Marlott
>   *with two others hidden by the corn, formed the large   Maltese*
> village. They ~~were~~ ˄ ~~the blades of~~   revolving ˄ cross of
> the reaping-machine, which had been brought to the field on the previous evening,
> to be ready for operations early this day. The crimson paint with which they
>   *imparted to   an*
> were coloured, intensified in hue by the toned sunlight ~~gave~~ them ~~the~~ appearance
> of having been dipped in gore.   (ff. 117–18)

The amended version shows that 'red' has become 'ruddy', 'reddest' has become 'brightest', 'crimson' has disappeared, and 'gore' has become 'liquid fire':

> But of all ruddy things that morning the brightest were two broad arms of painted wood, which rose from the margin of a yellow cornfield hard by Marlott village. They, with two others below, formed the revolving Maltese cross of the reaping-machine, which had been brought to the field on the previous evening to be ready for operations this day. The paint with which they were smeared, intensified in hue by the sunlight, imparted to them a look of having been dipped in liquid fire.
>   (I. 169)

Modifications of a similar kind occur also in the 1892 and 1912 editions.

PART THREE

DEVELOPMENTS IN THE MANUSCRIPT

V

BOWDLERIZATION AND THEMES

I

A<small>MONG</small> the many changes introduced into the manuscript after November 1889, very few could be described simply as bowdlerizations. There were, of course, a number of temporary excisions and modifications that formed part of the process of 'adaptation for the serial issue', some of these passages being marked in a special blue ink. Such temporary adjustments need not delay us here, as they will be discussed in more detail in the chapter dealing with the *Graphic* serial version.[1] But among the amendments intended to be permanent, it would be difficult to find more than three or four of which it could be confidently asserted that they show no purpose on the part of the author apart from the desire to expurgate.

One such amendment may be illustrated, however, from the following passage, which forms part of the L1 scene in which the villain is bidding farewell to the heroine on the road to Marlott, following her flight from Trantridge. The insertion at the end of the passage conveys the information that the heroine has remained at Trantridge as the villain's mistress for a month after the seduction. But this insertion is then cancelled, and being cancelled in black ink remains cancelled in all subsequent texts:

& then she

She bowed to him slightly, her eye just lingering in his; & ∧ turned to
for   ure

take the parcels & depart ∧
Smith-D'Urberville   *bent towards her,*
~~Hawnferne~~   removed his cigar, ∧ & said, 'You are not going to turn away like that, dear? Come!'

indifferently

'~~Yes~~—'If you wish,' she answered ∧   'See how you've mastered me!'
turned   & lifted her face ————   stone

She thereupon ~~faced~~ round   ∧   to him, & remained like a ~~marble~~ term

---

[1] See pp. 149–53 below.

                                    lips
while he imprinted a kiss upon her cheek—half-perfunctorily, half as if
                      out.
zest had not yet quite died ‸ ⟨ *for only a month had elapsed since she had*
ceased to defend herself against him.⟩   (f. 105)

On the next leaf the villain pleads with the heroine to return
with him to Trantridge. She originally replies that she will never
do so because people apply to her a 'horrid word' to describe her
relationship with him. Once again, however, the author tones down
the passage and his motive is moralistic:

        I made up my mind to do this as soon as I saw—what
   'Never, never! ~~They called me your—your—I won't say the horrid~~
I ought to have seen sooner
~~word~~; & I won't come.'   (f. 106)

Here, the heroine's original (L1) words have been cancelled twice,
first in blue and later in black ink. The substitution, written in
black ink, has become the permanent reading, and the original,
blunter version has been expunged for all time.

                                II

    Three themes that assume a new prominence in the later layers
of the manuscript of *Tess* are the cosmic theme, the agricultural
theme, and the heredity theme. In his presentation of the first of
these Hardy, emphasizing the suffering and injustice endured by
the individual as a consequence of cosmic indifference, frequently
resorts to bitter outbursts against the existence of such a situation.
The agricultural and heredity themes are treated with only slightly
less emotional involvement and represent separate, but related,
developments of the theme of mutability, which in the Ur-novel
was associated more closely with the worlds of birds and plants.
Both the agricultural and heredity themes deal, quite specifically,
with decline in human affairs: the former emphasizing the author's
nostalgic regret at the collapse of the old stable order of rural society
under the pressures engendered by the Industrial Revolution, and
the latter a sense of the pathos and irony inherent in the moral debility
of much of the rural population, the effete descendants of once
vigorous and prosperous aristocratic families like the d'Urbervilles.

The genesis of Hardy's cosmic theme is to be seen in the Ur-text, where sometimes through fragments of dialogue and at other times through authorial comment it is made clear that man is dogged by ill fortune, that there is no wise and loving Providence controlling Nature, and that 'the First Cause' (which Hardy else-where calls 'First Causes') is unsympathetic towards human hopes of happiness. Thus, when Abraham is awakened by his sister during the nocturnal journey to Casterbridge and told that Prince is dead, his despondency reflects his consciousness of the role played by mere chance, in that man has been 'pitched' on to a 'blighted' planet instead of on to a 'sound' one:

> ''Tis because we be on a blighted star, & not a sound one, isn't
> ~~Rose-Mary?~~ it, Tess?'   *through his tears.*
> ~~it, Cis?'~~   ∧   murmured Abraham ∧   (f. 36)

Towards the end of the seduction episode in the Chase, after a description of how 'darkness and silence ruled everywhere around', it is the author who goes on to ask with angry irony, 'But where was Sue's guardian angel; where was Providence?'; and, clearly, for Hardy no such entities existed:

> ~~Darkness~~ & silence ruled everywhere around. Above them rose the
>   *in which were poised*
> primeval yews & oaks of the Chase, ~~& the~~ gentle roosting birds in their
>   *all about*
> last nap; & ~~around~~ them were the hopping rabbits & hares. But where was
> ~~Rose-Mary's~~ Tess's
> ~~Sue's~~   guardian angel; where was Providence? Perhaps, like that other
>   *ironical*
> god of whom the ∧ Tishbite spoke, he was talking, or he was pursuing . . .   (f. 99)

Later, during the Talbothays section of the story, it is Angel who expresses the opinion that the First Cause is without generosity ('niggardly'), and, indeed, without any feeling at all towards the human actors in Life's drama, the substituted term 'unsympathetic' suggesting an attitude of neutrality and indifference (not hostility or malignity) on the part of the forces that control the universe:

> *(he went on) consciousness upon*
> Moreover ∧ this ~~career upon~~ which he had intruded was the single
>   *Tess   an unsympathetic*
> opportunity of existence ever vouchsafed to ~~Rose-Mary~~ by ~~a niggardly~~
> first cause; her all; her every & only chance.
>   (f. 218)

It is, thus, no wonder that in other Ur-text passages the heroine reflects that it is mere 'Fate' that controls the course of human life (f. 319), and the author comments on 'cruel Nature's law' (f. 208).

The first of the extended passages of bitter comment on cosmic indifference is to be found in L3, at the end of the chapter devoted to the heroine's first visit to Trantridge to 'claim kin'. Here, Hardy designates the object of his attack as 'Nature':

> Thus the thing ~~had~~ occurred. ~~And Tess Turberville Troublefield~~ Had she
> *perceived*
> ~~seen~~ its import she might have asked why she was doomed to be seen, & marked,
> & coveted that day by the wrong man, & not by a certain other man, the right
> —
> & true one in all respects ∧ as nearly as humanity can be right & true; yet to
> him at this time she was but a transient impression half-forgotten.
>   *but*
>   In the ill-judged execution of the well-judged plan of things ∧ ~~seldom~~
>   *seldom*   s   *rarely*   s
> ~~does~~ the call ∧ *produce*∧ the comer, the man to love ∧ *coincide*∧ with the
>   *a poor*
> hour for loving. Nature does not often say 'See!' to ~~her~~ creature at a
>   *body's*
> time when seeing can lead to happy doing; or reply '<u>H</u>ere' to a ~~soul's~~ cry
> of '<u>W</u>here?' till the hide-&-seek has become an irksome outworn game. We
> may wonder whether, at the acme & summit of the human progress, these
>   *corrected*   ~~mechanic~~ *intuition, a closer*
> anachronisms will ~~have~~ become ~~adjusted~~ by a finer ~~machinery of~~
>   *of the social machinery than that which   us   and* ~~round~~ *along*
> interaction ∧ ~~than~~   now jolts ∧ round ∧ ;
>   *as possible*
> but such completeness is not to be prophesied, or even conceived ∧ . (ff. 49–50)

Such a hostile view of 'Nature', as a deterministic, indifferent, and amoral force, which conflicts strikingly with the Rousseauistic and Wordsworthian overtones of the Nature-as-norm theme, is found again in the ironic reference to 'Nature's holy plan' at the end of the following passage, which comes a little earlier in the definitive text of the novel, although the earliest extant version is to be found in the *Graphic*:

All these young souls were passengers in the Durbeyfield ship— entirely dependent on the judgment of the two Durbeyfield adults for their pleasures, their necessities, their health, even their existence. If the heads of the Durbeyfield household chose to sail into difficulty, disaster,

starvation, disease, degradation, death, thither were these half-dozen
little captives under hatches compelled to sail with them—six helpless
creatures, who had never been asked if they wished for life on any terms,
much less if they wished for it on such hard conditions as were involved
in being of the shiftless house of Durbeyfield. Some people would like
to know whence the poet, whose philosophy is in these days deemed as
profound and trustworthy as his verse is tonic and breezy, gets his
authority for speaking of 'Nature's holy plan.' (G. 74)[2]

During the later layers of the manuscript, we find that the object
of the author's bitter comments on cosmic indifference is designated
by a variety of names. Thus, on one occasion, the term used is
simply 'the night', which is said to have invaded the sitting-
room of the Wellbridge farm-house after the distracted Angel has
attempted to settle down to sleep:

> He reclined on his couch in the sitting-room, & ~~put~~ extinguished the
> light. The night came in, & took up its place there, unconcerned &
> indifferent; the night which had already swallowed up his happiness, &
> was now digesting it listlessly; & was ready to swallow up the happiness
> of a thousand other people with as little disturbance or change of mien. (f. 336)

On another occasion the comment is directed against 'the circumstantial will against enjoyment', as Tess and Marian toil
on the surface of the desolate swede-field at Flintcomb-Ash in
the rain, sustained by their memories of happier sunny days
at Talbothays. Hardy contrasts the 'will to enjoy', which is
inherent in human beings, with the 'will against enjoyment', which
is external:

> And thus, as has been said, though the damp curtain of their bonnets
> flapped smartly into their faces, & their wrappers clung about them to
>   *memories of*
> wearisomeness, they lived all this afternoon in ~~the~~ green sunny romantic
> Talbothays.
>   *a gleam of a hill within a few miles of*
>   'You can see ∧   Froome valley from here when
>   *said Marian. 'An immense way off.'*
> it is fine,' ∧
>   'Ah—can you?' said Tess, awake to the new value of the locality.
>   So the two forces were at work here as everywhere, the congenital
> will to enjoy, & the circumstantial will against enjoyment. (f. 411)

---

[2] The relevant folio (f. 23) is missing.

The 'circumstantial will against enjoyment' later reappears under the title of 'the universal harshness', out of which the 'harshnesses' of men and women grow:

Clare had been harsh towards her; there is no doubt of it. Men are too often harsh with women they love or have loved; women with men. And yet these harshnesses are tenderness itself when compared with the ~~harshness~~ universal harshness out of which they grow; the harshness of the position towards the temperament, of the means towards the aims, ~~t[?]~~ of today towards yesterday, of hereafter towards to-day.   (f. 491)

The most controversial of all the terms used by Hardy to express his anger at cosmic injustice and indifference was the phrase, 'the President of the Immortals', which occurs as an insertion in the final paragraph of the manuscript:

& the President of the Immortals (in Aeschylean phrase) had ended
'Justice' was done ‸
his sport with Tess. And the D'Urberville knights & dames slept on in their
‸
tombs unknowing.

‸   The two speechless gazers bent themselves down to the earth,
as if in prayer, & remained thus a long time, absolutely motionless: the
            ed
flag continu~~ing~~ to wave silently. As soon as they had strength they arose,
joined hands again, & went on.   (f. 565)

Hardy was later forced by the notoriety gained by the opening of this paragraph to explain that 'the President of the Immortals' was a literal translation of two Greek words used by Aeschylus in line 169 of *Prometheus Bound*, and that by this phrase 'the forces opposed to the heroine were allegorized as a personality (a method not unusual in imaginative prose or poetry)', the phrase being 'a well-known trope, explained in that venerable work, Campbell's *Philosophy of Rhetoric*'. Despite such explanations, he found that the phrase continued to be misunderstood and that he was constantly being accused of postulating 'an all-powerful being endowed with the baser human passions, who turns everything to evil and rejoices in the mischief he has wrought'. Had Hardy employed in the editions the variant reading used in the *Graphic* text, which stated that 'Time, the Arch-satirist, had had his joke out with Tess', there would have been no scope for such gross misunderstanding; but with the appearance in the editions of the manuscript insertion, successive generations of careless readers unwittingly misinterpreted Hardy's meaning. Consequently, in the *Later Years* Hardy felt himself obliged to return several times to the questions of his general 'theological beliefs' and the 'philosophy' expressed in his writings (both of which he insisted were 'only a confused heap of impressions, like those of a bewildered child at a conjuring show'). On each occasion he made it clear that it was no personal god that he believed in, but something impersonal, which he labelled, variously, 'a Cause of things', 'First Causes', and 'the Unconscious Will of the Universe'.[3]

In his earlier novels, from *The Return of the Native* (1878) onwards, Hardy had occasionally commented on the cosmic situation in similar strain. Thus, in that earlier novel he had written several such passages as the following: 'That old-fashioned revelling in the general situation grows less and less possible as we uncover the defects of natural laws, and see the quandary that man is in by their operation.' But none of the earlier novels had caused such a storm of controversy as *Tess* was to do, because in none of them had Hardy commented so often, so openly, or so bitterly, on the subject.

The Ur-text contains little evidence that the agricultural theme was to be important in the definitive version of *Tess*. Indeed, one of the L2 passages indicates that 'modern life', as represented by the railway line, far from desiring to invade and destroy rural Wessex, tended to withdraw 'as if what it touched had been uncongenial'. The same passage also states that 'the feeble light' of the railway station was 'in one sense of more importance to Talbothays Dairy and mankind' than the 'celestial' light of the stars:

⟨*They crept along towards a point in the expanse* ~~~⟩ ~~expanse~~ ~~mass~~
assert its presence

of shade before them at which a feeble light was beginning to ~~show itself~~;
a spot where, by day, a fitful white streak of steam at intervals upon
the dark green background denoted intermittent moments of contact between
its steam

their secluded world & modern life. Modern life ~~had~~ stretched out a ‸
feeler to this point three or four times a day, touched the native existences,
s feeler

& quickly withdrew it ‸ again, as if what it touched had been uncongenial.

[3] *Life*, pp. 243, 244, 334, 335, 407–10.

They reached the feeble light, which came from the smoky lamp of a little
enough   *in one sense*
railway-station; a poor ——— terrestrial star, ~~enough, but~~ yet ∧ of more
Talbothays Dairy &
importance to ∧ mankind than the celestial ones to which it stood in such
new   *in the rain, Tess getting a*
humiliating contrast. The cans of ∧ milk were unladen ∧ ~~Rose-Mary standing~~
little shelter from a neighbouring holly-tree.
~~in the shelter of some.~~   (f. 266)

Another Ur-text passage (L1) describes the changed status of an
old thatched cottage on the estate belonging to the villain's mother,
which has been turned into a hen-house:

> The rooms in which dozens of infants had ~~been nursed~~ wailed at their
> nursing now resounded with the tapping of nascent chicks. Distracted
> hens in coops occupied spots where formerly stood chairs supporting sedate
> *chimney-corner & once blazing hearth was*
> agriculturalists. The ~~housewife's clean store-cupboards were~~ now filled
> with inverted beehives in which the hens laid their eggs; while out-of-
> doors the plots that each succeeding householder had carefully shaped with
> his spade, were ~~now~~ torn by the cocks in wildest fashion.   (f. 70)

Here, the decline in the fortunes of the cottage is, admittedly,
symptomatic of the destruction of the agricultural way of life; but
the point is not stressed.

It was not until the later layers that Hardy began to include
explicit comments on rural decay and on the role of farmers and
landlords in accelerating the process. What is noticeable, however,
is that even in these passages he makes no attempt to explore the
root economic causes of the decay in the way that one would have
expected from the well-known opening of Arnold Kettle's Marxian
essay on this novel: 'The subject of *Tess of the D'Urbervilles* is
stated clearly by Hardy to be the fate of a "pure woman"; in fact it
is the destruction of the English peasantry. More than any other
nineteenth-century novel we have touched on it has the quality of
a social document.'[4] There is, in fact, little of the 'social document'
element in *Tess*. Instead, there is usually only anger, puzzlement,
and regret at the passing of the old rural order, with the blame
sheeted home, indiscriminately, against a multiplicity of groups

---

[4] *An Introduction to the English Novel*, London, 1953, vol. 2, p. 49. Kettle later admitted,
in his introduction to the Harper and Row edition of *Tess* (1966), that his assessment of this
aspect of the novel had been 'somewhat one-sided'.

and influences—the selfishness of the landlords, Society's hypocritical attitudes on matters of sexual conduct, the decadence of many
old county families, the discomforts of harsh agricultural toil in the
fields, the unsettling effect of new machines, and the indifference of
the cosmic forces to the individual's hopes and fortunes.

One of the better-known **L5** passages on the agricultural theme
is the following:

> However, all the mutations so increasingly discernible in ~~the~~ village
> life did not originate entirely in the agricultural unrest. A depopulation
> was also going on. The village, ~~which~~ had formerly contained, ~~in addition~~
> ~~to the~~ side by side with the agricultural labourers, an interesting and
> better informed class, ranking distinctly above the former—the class to
> which Tess's father & mother had belonged—& including the carpenter, the
> the huckster,   farm-
> smith, the shoemaker, ‸ together with nondescript workers other than ~~Day-~~
> labourers; a set of people who ~~own~~ owed a certain stability of
> *aim*
> ~~life~~ & conduct to the fact of their being life-holders like Tess's father, or
> occasionally,   long holdings   seldom
> copyholders, or ~~even~~ small freeholders. But as the ~~houses~~ fell in they were ~~not~~
> again let to similar tenants, and were mostly pulled down, if not absolutely
> required by the farmer for his hands, ~~there being a dislike to all such petty~~
>   *cottagers*   *not*
> ~~tenants~~ ‸ who were ‸ directly employed on the land being looked upon with
>   *& the banishment of ~~the one~~ some starving the trade of the others,*
> disfavour as a rule, ‸
> *who were thus obliged to follow.*
> ‸   These families, who had formed the back-bone
> large centres
> of the village life in the past, had to seek refuge in the ~~towns~~; the process,
> humorously designated by statisticians as 'the tendency of the rural population
> towards the large towns' being really the tendency of water to flow uphill
> when forced by machinery.   (f. 506)

Here, it should be observed that Hardy's main concern is not for
the plight of the agricultural labourers, but for the disappearance
of the 'interesting and better informed class, ranking distinctly
above the former—the class to which Tess's father and mother
had belonged—and including the carpenter, the smith, the shoe-
maker, the huckster . . .'. These were the people who constituted,
as Philip Bull has pointed out, 'the group of independent workers
who sold the products of their labour and not the labour itself', and
of whom 'the most complete and sympathetic presentation . . .

given by Thomas Hardy appears in *Under the Greenwood Tree*'. Bull continues: 'Hardy sees these artisans as embodying still the "golden elements" of rural tradition—independence and a sense of belonging. He does not, however, suppose that they truly represent nineteenth century agrarian society as a whole.'[5] Indeed, Hardy usually shows in his writings that the rural labourers, or 'workfolk', are backward and over-dependent on their employers; and there is even a realization of the economic benefits that the wider horizons of urban living would offer.

The most impressive sections on the agricultural theme in *Tess* are those in which symbolism enters. Alec's role from L3 onwards, for example, is largely designed to symbolize the destructive power of the nineteenth-century industrial world as it impinges on the traditional rural world, personified by Tess. Alec's father had belonged to the newly rich class of merchants (originally, he is described in the manuscript as a 'stockbroker'): but having decided to settle as 'a county man in the south of England' he had changed his name from 'Stoke' (originally, 'Smith') to 'D'Urberville' (originally, 'Turberville'). The speed and ruthlessness with which he had usurped the family name that was rightly Tess's are well conveyed in the following L3 passage:

> *in the British Museum*
> Conning for ~~half~~ an hour ∧ the pages of works devoted to extinct, half-
> ~~clouded,~~   ing
> extinct, ∧ & obscured, & lost families ~~who which~~ appertained to the quarter
>   *D'Urberville*
> of England in which he proposed to settle he considered that ~~Turberville~~
>   *& sounded   of them D'Urberville*
> looked ∧ as well as any ∧ ; & ~~Turberville~~ accordingly was annexed to his
>   *eternally.*
> own for himself & his heirs ~~for ever~~ ∧   (f. 44)

The father's annexation of the name foreshadows the son's destruction of the daughter.

The most striking example of symbolic writing on the agricultural theme occurs during a later stage of the story, in the famous section devoted to the threshing of the last rick at Flintcomb-Ash farm (chapters 47–8 of the editions). The opening glimpse of the

---

[5] 'Thomas Hardy and Social Change', *Southern Review* (Adelaide), iii, 1969, 202–3.

red threshing machine and its sooty engineman in 'the pellucid smokelessness of this region of yellow grain and pale soil' provides an apt setting for the series of harrowing scenes that are to follow, which epitomize, in a vivid and dramatic form, the course of the agricultural theme throughout the novel:

Close under the shadow of the stack, & as yet barely visible was the red tyrant that the women had come to serve—a timber-framed construction, in shape a parallelopiped, with straps & wheels appertaining—the threshing-machine, which, whilst it was going, kept up a despotic demand upon the *endurance*
~~strength~~ of their muscles & nerves.
    A little way off there was another indistinct figure; this one black,
        sustained   that spoke
with a ~~repressed~~ hiss ∧ of strength very much in reserve. The long chimney running up beside an elm tree, & the warmth which radiated from the spot, explained without the necessity of much daylight, that here was the engine which was to ~~drive~~ act as the *primum mobile* of this little world. By the engine
            being
stood a dark motionless ~~man~~, a sooty & grimy ~~figure~~ embodiment of tallness,
        with
in a sort of trance, ~~In~~ a heap of coals by his side: it was the engine-man,
            colour
the isolation of his manner & ~~appearance~~ lending him the appearance of a creature from Tophet, who had strayed into the pellucid smokelessness of this
            with which he had nothing in common,   aborigines.
region of yellow grain & pale soil ∧ to amaze & to discompose its ~~indwellers~~
    What he looked he felt. He was in the agricultural world, but not of it. He served fire & smoke; these denizens of the fields served vegetation, weather, frost, & sun. He travelled with this engine from farm to farm, from county to county, for as yet the steam-threshing-machine was a novelty in Wessex. He
            thoughts   save on his eye on
spoke in a strange northern accent, his ~~eye~~ turned inwards upon himself, ~~&~~ ∧ his iron charge; hardly perceiving the scenes around him, & caring for them not at all; holding only strictly necessary intercourse with the natives, as if some ancient doom compelled him to wander here against his will in the service of his metallic master. The long strap which ran from the driving-wheel of his engine to the red thresher under the rick was the sole tie-line between agriculture & him.   (ff. 466–7)

Ian Gregor has pointed out that two significant threads of meaning are skilfully blended during these two chapters on the threshing of the wheat at Flintcomb-Ash—'Alec's threat to Tess, and the machine's threat to the community to which she belongs'. Consequently, 'behind Tess's resistance we feel the desperate resistance of a community', while 'on the other hand the resistance of the community to the machine is personalized in the antagonism between Tess and Alec'. And as Gregor goes on to observe: 'In Jamesian terms the whole scene is superbly "done". The whole pattern of the book is caught up and magnified, without the support of a philosophic "gloss". Every detail contributes precisely, giving just so much emphasis and no more—the stark field, the machine, the nameless engineman, the twirling cane, the shaking platform, the biblical quotations, the thrown gauntlet, the blood on the straw—to form an irresistibly powerful unity'.[6]

The agricultural theme, like the cosmic theme, is a common theme in Hardy's novels, although it is doubtful whether it has ever been handled so brilliantly in any of the other books as in the threshing scene in *Tess*. However, in the early novels, such as *Under the Greenwood Tree* (1872), *Far From the Madding Crowd* (1874), and *The Return of the Native* (1878), it appears in a different guise: the threat posed by the machine age is less strong, and the rural community has a vitality that enables it to resist the pressures of change. As a result, in these novels the theme takes the form of a conflict between two ways of life, instead of an undermining of one way of life by the other. But in *The Mayor of Casterbridge* (1886), *The Woodlanders* (1887), *Tess of the d'Urbervilles* (1891), and *Jude the Obscure* (1896) the old way of life is seen to be doomed. While the reasons for this inevitable disintegration are shown to be largely circumstantial, there is also, as John Holloway has pointed out, an 'inner defect',[7] a decline in the moral quality of the country people themselves, which in *Tess* and *Jude* is related specifically to the influence of heredity. As a result, in *Tess* the agricultural theme possesses overtones vastly different from what are found in any of the earlier Hardy novels.

More specifically, this close interweaving of the heredity and agricultural themes in *Tess* produces an especially strong sense of pathos and irony, occasioned by the spectacle of the descendants of once powerful and vigorous landowning families reduced to the

---

[6] Gregor, pp. 148-9.

[7] 'Hardy's Major Fiction', *Jane Austen to Joseph Conrad* (ed. Robert C. Rathburn and Martin Steinmann), Minneapolis, Minn., 1958, p. 235.

level of John Durbeyfield, 'haggler' and drunkard. The author's preoccupation with this aspect of heredity in relation to old Wessex families is partly autobiographical in origin, being a reflection of Hardy's romantic attitude towards the history of his father's family, which he claimed had once been of some importance in Dorset. The Dorset Hardys, Hardy tells us in the *Early Life*, had come to possess 'all the characteristics of an old family of spent social energies'. Once the proud owners of various estates in the county and numbering among their ranks such illustrious names as 'the Elizabethan Thomas Hardy who endowed the Dorchester Grammar School' and 'the Thomas Hardy captain of the *Victory* at Trafalgar', their later years had been marred by the gradual loss of most of their property and social status, according to the picture which 'the subject' (and author) of the *Early Life* gives us:

But at the birth of the subject of this biography the family had declined, so far as its Dorset representatives were concerned, from whatever importance it once might have been able to claim there; and at his father's death the latter was, it is believed, the only landowner of the name in the county, his property being, besides the acre-and-half lifehold at Bockhampton, a small freehold farm at Talbothays, with some houses there, and about a dozen freehold cottages and a brick-yard-and-kiln elsewhere.[8]

The *Early Life* also reproduces a diary entry for 30 September 1888, in which, after describing a walking-tour through the Dorset countryside around Woolcombe, Hardy comments: 'The decline and fall of the Hardys much in evidence hereabouts . . . So we go down, down, down.'[9]

In *Tess* the 'decline and fall' of old families takes the form of a deterioration not only in material prosperity but in such moral virtues as will, energy, judgement, self-respect, and dependability. The moral decline is seen most clearly in John Durbeyfield, but is also apparent in Joan Durbeyfield, Tess, and Retty Priddle. A somewhat similar spiritual malaise had affected the important rural characters in the earlier novel, *The Woodlanders*—notably Giles Winterbourne, Grace Melbury, and Marty South—whose passivity and failings in judgement had rendered them ineffective in their dealings with the more aggressive and intelligent intruders from the

outside world, Dr. Fitzpiers and Felice Charmond. The treatment of
the malaise in *The Woodlanders* had differed, however, in one important respect, from that found in *Tess*, in that the moral debility of its
rural characters had not been attributed directly to inherited traits.

The heredity theme, like the agricultural theme, would appear
to have been of little significance in the Ur-version of *Tess*, where
the heroine's ancient lineage received only passing attention. Indeed, the only substantial Ur-text reference to the ill effect of
heredity is found in a late L2 passage, in which Dairyman Crick
is telling the heroine of Angel Clare's scorn for old families in
general, and for Retty Priddle's in particular:

                                lots o'   *out by King's-Hintock*
'. . . —the old family that used to own ‸ the lands ‸ now owned by
                                & his
the Earl o' Wessex, afore even he ‸ was heard of. Well, Mr Clare
found this out, & spoke quite scornful to the poor girl for days.
Ah! he says to her! you'll never make a good dairymaid! All your
skill was used up ages ago in Palestine, & you must lie fallow
                        git
for a thousand year to ~~recover~~ strength for more deeds! . . . A boy
came here ~~the~~ t'other day asking for a job, & said his name was
                        Matt,
~~Joe, only Jock~~ ‸ & when we asked him his surname, he said he'd never
heard that 'a ever had any surname, & when we asked why, he said
he supposed his folks had'nt been 'stablished long enough. "Ah—
                        jumping up & shaking hands
you are the very boy I want!" says Mr Clare ‸
wi 'en ;   *half-a-crown*
    "I've great hopes of you"; and gave him ~~a shilling~~.
        stomach
O no—he can't ~~abear~~ old families.'   (f. 181)

It is not until we come to L3 portions of the manuscript that we
find Hardy beginning to place emphasis on the heroine's noble
ancestry, which process is examined, in detail, in my analysis of
the d'Urberville motif towards the end of the next chapter. All that
needs to be said here is that, concurrently with the expansion of
the d'Urberville motif, we find an increasing emphasis on the
decadence that may overtake ancient families, which is illustrated
most graphically in the character-study of John Durbeyfield.
A typical example of d'Urberville decadence is to be found in the
following L3 passage, in which the drunken Durbeyfield's utter

lack of dignity and self-respect are made obvious through his offer
to sell his 'title' for twenty pounds:

> 'Tell'n—I'll take a thousand pound . . . Well, I'll take less,
> when I come to think o't. He'll adorn it better than I ~~can~~ a poor
> broken down feller like myself can. Tell'n he shall hae it for a
> hundred . . . . . But I won't stand upon trifles—tell'n he shall hae
> it for fifty—for twenty pound! Yes twenty pound—that's the
> lowest. Dammy, family honour is family honour, and I won't take
> a penny less!' (f. 60ᵛ)

The heredity theme is reinforced in several **L5** sections, where
Angel Clare is bitterly blaming the heroine for her moral lapse with
Alec and her failure to confess this lapse prior to the wedding. In
the following example both the specific and the general aspects of
the theme are evoked, by references to the decline of Tess's family,
in particular, and of several other equally famous Wessex families.
The blame levelled against the heroine by Angel is excessive, but
the thematic relevance of the passage is clear:

> 'Don't, Tess; don't argue! Different societies different
> manners. You are an unappreciative peasant woman, who ~~dont~~
> *has never been initiated into*
> ~~know~~ ∧ the proportions of things. You don't know what you say.'
> 'I am only a peasant by position, not by nature.'
> *So much the worse for you.*
> '~~Who is a peasant except by position?~~ I think that parson
> who unearthed your pedigree would have done better if he had held
> his tongue. I cannot help associating your decline as a family
> *of*
> with this other fact —┼— ∧ your want of firmness. ~~Decrepit~~
> Decrepit families ~~im~~ postulate decrepit wills, decrepit conduct.
> ~~Heaven~~ *more*
> ~~God~~, why did you give me a handle for despising you ∧ by informing
> *me descent! Here was I thinking you an incipient child*
> ∧ of your ~~extraction~~ ∧
> *of nature: there were you, the seedling of an effete aristocracy!'*
> ⟨——'*Lots o'f families are as bad as mine in that. Retty's family*
> *were once large landowners, & so were Dairyman Billet's, & the*
> *Debbyhouses who now —— be carters were once the De Bayeux*
> *family. You find such as I everywhere; 'tis a feature of our*
> *county, & I can't help it.'*
> '*So much the worse for the county.*'⟩ (f. 332)

In a more restrained passage, for which the earliest extant
reading occurs in the *Graphic* (ff. 144-6 being missing from the

G

manuscript), the author himself comments on the heroine's lack
of ambition and lack of determination, and these deficiencies are
stated to be 'part of the Durbeyfield temperament':

Such high contentment with such a slight and initial performance as
that of having started towards a means of independent living was a part
of the Durbeyfield temperament. Tess really wished to walk uprightly;
to seek out whatsoever things were true, and honest, and of good report;
while her father did nothing of the kind; but she resembled him in being
content with immediate and small achievements, and in having no mind
for laborious effort towards such petty monetary and social advancement
as could alone be effected by a family so heavily handicapped as the once
knightly D'Urbervilles were now.   (G. 162)

Here, the criticism of Tess as a person is much more balanced, but
there is no doubt that Hardy takes for granted the concept of inherited moral weaknesses among members of an old family.

Finally, it must be noted that the decline of the d'Urbervilles,
like most other important concepts in the novel, is ultimately
viewed by the author against the ceaseless flow of History and
Time. As a result, even the moral weaknesses of country people
like the Durbeyfields, which have contributed so strongly to the
collapse of the old agricultural way of life, are seen to be, in the
final analysis, determined by 'the rhythm of change' and to form
part of the process of 'flux and reflux' in all things. This idea is
clearly implicit in the following authorial comment, which comes
after the announcement that by the death of John Durbeyfield the
family will be deprived of its Marlott home:

>   *once D'Urbervilles*
> Thus the Durbeyfields ∧ saw descending upon them the destiny
>   *among the*   *of*
> which, no doubt, when they were ∧ Olympians ~~in~~ the county, they
>   *severely enough,*
> had caused to descend many a time, & ∧ ~~often~~ upon the heads of
> *landless ones*
> such ∧ as they themselves were now. So ~~does~~ do flux & reflux—
>   *change*
> the rhythm of ~~motion~~—alternate & persist in everything under
> the sky.   (f. 505)

Clearly, when viewed in such a perspective, moral decline—no less
than material decline—is no longer a matter of personal, or even
human, responsibility.

VI

IMAGES AND MOTIFS

I

MOST of the imagery patterns found in the Ur-text continue to appear in the later layers of the manuscript. Thus, the use of Nature as symbolic commentary on human affairs is once again apparent in the following **L3** description of the valley setting where the nubile but innocent heroine has her home:

> This fertile & sheltered tract of country, in which the fields are never brown & the springs never dry, . . .   (f. 6a)

In an **L4** passage describing the heroine's revival of hope after a lengthy period of apathy occasioned by the death of her child, the season of Spring is seen exerting an even more active influence on her mind and desires:

> A particularly fine Spring came round, & the stir of germination was almost audible; it moved her as it moved the wild animals, & made her passionate to go. At last, one day in early May, a letter reached her from an old
>
> *long before*
> friend of her mother's to whom she had addressed inquiries ‸ —a dairyman whom she had never seen—that a skilful milkmaid was required at his
> *dairyhouse*
> place, & that he would be glad to have her for the summer months if she had found nothing to do in the interim.   (f. 137)

Similarly, one of the earlier nature motifs, that of helpless birds, reappears in the following **L5** description of the 'strange birds from behind the north pole' whose arrival at Flintcomb-Ash presages the coming of harsher winter weather:

> *After* *season*
> From this stage of congealed dampness came a spell of dry frost,
> *behind*
> when strange birds from ‸ the north pole began to arrive silently on the
> *of Flintland comb-Ash* *spectral*
> upland ‸ ; gaunt silent creatures with tragical eyes—eyes

which
~~that~~ had witnessed scenes of cataclysmal horror in ~~the~~ ₍ᵢₙₐccₑₛₛᵢᵦₗₑ₎ Polar regions, of

inaccessible

in
a magnitude such as no human being had ever conceived, ₍ₐ₎ curdling temperatures
that no man could endure; . . .   (f. 414)

In the above passage the 'gaunt' appearance and 'tragical eyes'
anticipate the increased suffering of Tess at Flintcomb-Ash, as,
for example, on the occasion when she sinks exhausted to the floor
of the barn after the exertions of 'reed-drawing' during the time
of heavy snow.

Two of the classical allusions, 'Artemis' and 'Demeter', which
occur in the L2 passage describing the lovers' early-morning meetings in the Talbothays meadows (f. 185), are reinforced in an
interesting manner in another passage, which made its first appearance at the L3 stage. The passage occurs as part of the description
of the May-time 'club-walking' on f. 7, and contains what will be
seen to be a significant alteration in phrasing, from 'traditional
rite' to 'Vestal rite':

> ~~alone survived~~ *alone lived to uphold the* ~~traditional~~ *Vestal rite.*
> The club of Marlott ₍ₐ₎
> ₍ₐ ₕᵤₙdᵣₑd₎
> It had walked for ~~fifty~~ years, & it walked still.   (f. 7)

'Vestal rite' is not the final reading, however; for in the *Graphic*
version, the expression 'Vestal rite' has become 'local Cerealia',
which remains the reading of the editions: 'The club of Marlott
alone lived to uphold the local Cerealia. It had walked for hundreds
of years, and it walked still' (G. 11).

Hardy's substitution of 'Vestal' for 'traditional' in the manuscript had the effect of drawing the reader's attention to the virginal
state of the heroine at the opening of the story and to her innocent
hope for marriage and domesticity through participation in a disguised May-Day ritual, whose deeper and more sinister significance eluded her. With the replacement of Vesta, the goddess of
the hearth, by Ceres/Demeter, goddess of the corn-bearing earth,
as the tutelary power over the ceremony, Hardy injected a harsher
note into the tale. For, by terming the ceremony a 'local Cerealia',
he introduced the notion of the subordination of the individual will
to the requirements of the general will of Nature, symbolized, at

its harshest level, within the Ceres myth by the rape of the innocent
Proserpine at the hands of the dark ruler of Hades. As a result,
a new prophetic note entered the story at this point, anticipating
some of the important plot and thematic considerations developed
later in the narrative—in particular those concerning the relationship between virginity, fecundity, and purity; love and passion;
freewill and compulsion; and life, death, and rebirth.

As has earlier been indicated, the later layers also contain examples
of the continued employment of blood-red imagery with its original
connotations. Thus, the scene in which the villain compels the
heroine to eat the ripe strawberry which he holds to her lips (f. 47)
anticipates the violence she will suffer in the Chase, as does the
scene in which she pricks her chin on the thorn of a rose at her
breast (f. 51); while it is easy to see the connotations of guilt and
fear of damnation in the hell-fire type of imagery used as the setting of Tess's wedding-night confession to Angel:

The ashes under the grate were lit by the fire vertically, like a torrid
—— waste. Her imagination suddenly beheld a Last-Day luridness in
this red-coaled glow. It still fell on his face & hand, & on hers, peering

&

into the loose hair about her brow, ₍ₐ₎ firing the delicate skin underneath. (f. 323)

The subjectivity arising from the heroine's viewpoint in the above
passage was later curtailed, when in the 1892 edition Hardy amended
the opening of the second sentence to read: 'Imagination might
have beheld a Last Day luridness . . .' (X. 292). The result was to
introduce a more speculative, and at the same time more poetic,
effect into the passage.

II

Five significant motifs that either make their first appearance
or receive a marked increase in attention during the later layers of
the manuscript are the May-Day festival, the bough of mistletoe,
the hunted animal, the altar victim, and the willing scapegoat. The
last of these, in turn, encompasses images of entombment and the
soul at large. In addition, the later layers contain several examples
of Hardy's employment of imagery based on his recollections of

various European paintings—a kind of imagery characteristic of most of his novels—together with three important new aspects of the blood-red motif.

By his use of the May-Day and mistletoe motifs Hardy deepens the thematic concept of <u>Nature as norm,</u> reminding his readers that <u>natural phenomena were once objects of veneration</u> by primitive peoples. Thus, he reminds us that the Marlott club's procession and dance (in chapter 2) was derived from the medieval May-Day dance, which, as Hardy was aware, had its origin in ancient fertility ceremonies of tree-worship, especially worship of the spirit of the mighty oak, who in classical times was Zeus himself. He also reminds us that the countryside around Marlott, like so much of England, had been 'densely wooded' until 'comparatively recent times' (f. 7), and that, although now called 'the Vale of Blackmoor', it had been 'known in former times as the Forest of White Hart' (f. 6b). Indeed, he continues:

Even now traces of its earlier condition are to be found in the old oak copses & irregular belts of timber that yet survive upon its slopes, & the hollow-trunked trees that shade so many of its pastures.   (f. 7)

Marlott thus provides a fitting location for the 'club-revel', which is described on the **L3** leaves, ff. 7–14, and is first introduced to the reader in the following mythic passage:

some   of their shades

The forests have departed, but ∧ old customs ∧ remain. Many however ~~exist~~ linger only in a metamorphosed or disguised form. The May-day dance,
was to be discerned, on the afternoon   in the guise of
for instance, ~~was figuring on the day~~ under notice, ~~as~~ ∧ the club-revel, or 'club-walking', as it was there called.   (f. 7)

It is at this 'revel' that Angel Clare later catches his first sight of Tess's white-frocked figure.

In Roman, Druidical, and Norse mythology the mistletoe was a plant believed to be endowed with supernatural powers, especially when found on oaks. The first mention of the mistletoe in *Tess* is found during the description of the Chase, that tract of ancient woodland extending behind the new, red-brick home of the villain, the relevant extract forming part of the **L3** layer of the manuscript:

. . . a truly venerable tract of forest land; one of the few remaining woodlands in England of almost primaeval date, wherein Druidical mistle-

toe was still found on aged oaks, & where enormous yew-trees, not planted
by the hand of man, grew as they had grown when they were pollarded for
bows.   (f. 42)

The plant is next mentioned in the honeymoon section of the
manuscript, in a paragraph describing the heroine's solitary
wedding-night. Entering the bedroom of the Wellbridge farm-
house, she discovers the presence of 'a bough of mistletoe' suspended from the bed-canopy:

                                          rays
In removing the light towards the bedstead its ∧ fell upon the tester of white
dimity: something was hanging beneath it, & she lifted the candle to see what
it was. A bough of mistletoe: Angel had put it there; she knew that in an
instant. This ~~had been~~ was the explanation of that mysterious parcel which
              so   *& bring*
it had been ∧ difficult to pack ∧ ; whose contents he would not explain to her,
saying that time would show her the purpose thereof. In his zest & his gaiety
                                  &
he had hung it there; & how ~~foolish~~ ∧ inopportune ~~stultified~~ that mistletoe
looked now.   (f. 334)

In the earlier passage describing the 'Druidical mistletoe' attached
to the oaks in the Chase, the motif had acquired a slightly sinister
connotation, which is here expanded by overtones of irony and
mockery. All these connotations become stronger with the recur-
rence of the image during the scene of Angel's return visit to Wellbridge farm-house, a few weeks later. When Angel goes into 'her
chamber which had never been his', he discovers that 'the mistletoe
hung under the tester just as he had placed it' and that 'it was turning colour, and the leaves and berries were wrinkled' (f. 383). These
changes in the plant parallel the decay of his hopes of happiness
with Tess. It will, thus, be apparent that the mistletoe image gains
additional meaning with each reappearance, and that one of its
functions is to act as a leitmotif associated with the heroine's original
sexual surrender.

Injustice and cruelty—on the part of both society and the cosmic
forces—are two of the main implications of the next two motifs,
those of the hunted animal and the altar victim. Both motifs may
be detected in the Ur-text, although only in rudimentary form.

The motif of the hunted animal is foreshadowed in the Ur-text
imagery of helpless animals and birds, to which attention has earlier

been drawn; it is also discernible, somewhat more clearly, in three passages where figurative language with sporting implications is applied to the actions of the villain and the heroine, although only one of these passages survived in its original position in subsequent versions of the novel. The passage to survive is the description of the villain as 'a handsome *horsey* dandy' (f. 61), which was subsequently subjected to only slight amendment in the manuscript, to read 'the handsome *horsey* young *buck*'. A second passage, which was to disappear from the novel entirely at the *Graphic* stage, contains the metaphor 'the *snaring* of his eldest daughter' (f. 127) as a description of the heroine's treatment at the hands of the villain, as viewed through the eyes of her father. There is also the passage in which the simile, 'winced *like a wounded animal*' (f. 316) is applied to the heroine, to describe her reaction to Angel's thoughtless remark: 'Rose-Mary, you are not a bit cheerful this evening . . . I wonder if you really love me after all.' Although this passage was to be cancelled on f. 316 it was subsequently to be used again, on an L4 leaf (f. 312).

With Hardy's large-scale revision of the novel after 25 November 1889 the hunted-animal motif began to assume the coherent pattern that it possesses in the definitive version, as is seen in the introduction of the L3 passage on the legend of the killing of the white hart in Blackmoor Vale:

The Vale was known in former times as the Forest of White Hart, from a curious legend of King Henry the Third's reign, in which the killing by a certain Thomas de la Lynd of a beautiful white hart which the King had run down & spared, was made the occasion of a heavy fine.   (ff. 6b–7)

This passage is followed, almost immediately, by the scenes of the May-time 'revel', in which the white-frocked Tess, who is to be hunted down in another stretch of forest land, takes part. Moreover, such cruelty as that displayed in the killing of the white hart is paralleled, later in the story, in the L5 description of the rat-hunt at Flintcomb-Ash. At this time Tess is feeling helpless and desperate: she has struck Alec on the mouth with her work-glove, drawing blood, and her 'hopeless defiance' is identified by the author with 'the sparrow's gaze before its captor twists its neck' (f. 476). Then comes the rat-hunt for which 'sporting characters of all descriptions, gents with terriers, roughs with sticks, and stones' have gathered:

> *arrived*
> The time for the rat-catching ~~came~~ at last, & the hunt began. The creatures had crept downwards with the subsidence of the rick till they were all together at the bottom, & being now uncovered from their last refuge they ran across the open ground in all directions . . .   (ff. 479–80)

The rats are mercilessly harried, as is Tess, who despite her impassioned letter to her husband in Brazil, is also unable to find any 'refuge' from the persistent attentions of those who persecute her at Flintcomb-Ash, Farmer Groby and Alec.

The metaphor of the snare, which, as we have seen, occurs once in an Ur-text passage that was subsequently suppressed (f. 127), is used again in several passages in later versions of the novel. One such passage occurs in the heroine's letter to her husband, where she expresses her fears for the future by suggesting that she may fall 'into some fearful snare' (f. 484), unless he comes, or sends for her. There is also the comparison used to describe Tess's feeling of being trapped at Flintcomb-Ash, when she recognizes her employer as 'the well-to-do boor whom Angel had knocked down at the inn for insulting her' (f. 397) and who had accosted her on her journey to the farm. On this occasion, the simile employed is 'looking like a bird caught in a springe' (f. 419), which was to be amended in the 1892 edition to 'like a bird caught in a clap-net' (X. 376). The 1912 edition contains a similar amendment, in which the word 'trap' is introduced. This occurs in the scene in which Tess, after murdering Alec, runs along the highway in pursuit of Angel, to explain her action and to beg his forgiveness for what she regards as her original sin against him. In the 1892 edition the text had read as follows: '"I have done it—I don't know how", she continued. "Still, I owed it to 'ee, and to myself, Angel. I feared long ago, when I struck him on the mouth with my glove, that I might do it some day for the wrong he did to me in my simple youth, and to you through me"' (X. 501). The 1912 edition introduces the metaphor under discussion in the manner shown below: '"I have done it— I don't know how," she continued. "Still, I owed it to you, and to myself, Angel. I feared long ago, when I struck him on the mouth with my glove, that I might do it some day for *the trap he set for* me in my simple youth, and *his wrong* to you through me" ' (Ch. 57).

During the section of the novel concerned with the heroine's first journey towards Flintcomb-Ash, Hardy employs two related metaphors, 'her hunted soul' and 'a sort of nest', together with the symbolic image, 'wounded birds', to reinforce his hunted–animal motif. As Tess makes her way along a country road she is accosted by her future employer, Farmer Groby, and the metaphor of 'her hunted soul' helps to convey the anguish she feels:

> There seemed only one escape for her hunted soul. She suddenly took to
> her heels with the speed of the wind, & without looking behind her ran
> along the road till she came to a gate which opened directly into a
> plantation.   (f. 397)

Once she has reached the protection offered by the plantation she makes for herself 'a sort of nest' from 'the dead leaves' lying on the ground:

> She scraped together the dead leaves till she had formed them into a
> large heap, making a sort of nest in the middle. Into this Tess crept.
>   (ff. 397–8)

During the night her sleep is disturbed by strange noises, which she later discovers to be caused by dying pheasants, the helpless victims of a party of hunters:

> Tess guessed at once the meaning of this. The birds had been
> driven down into this corner the day before by some shooting party;
> & while those that had fallen dead under the shot had been carried
> off, the wounded birds had escaped & hidden themselves away, or
> risen among the thick boughs, where they had maintained their
> position till their pursuers departed; when, as they grew weaker
> with loss of blood in the night-time, they had fallen one by one
> as she had heard them.
> She had occasionally caught glimpses of these men in her girl-
> hood, looking over hedges or peering through bushes & pointing their
> guns; strangely accoutred, a bloodthirsty light in their eyes.   (ff. 399–400)

Although Tess finds consolation for her own unhappy situation in the plight of these 'wounded birds'—'her recollection of the birds silently enduring their night of agony impressing upon her the relativity of sorrows, and the tolerable nature of her own' (f. 401)

—there is no doubt that the cruelty of the episode has symbolic reference to her unhappy lot in life. And, indeed, its relevance to herself is driven home by the heroine's Darwinian reflection on the callousness of those 'strangely accoutred' men, who by indulging in blood-sports are showing themselves to be

> . . . so unmannerly, so unchivalrous, towards their weaker fellows in
> nature's teeming family. (f. 400)

The 'nest' metaphor is found again in an 1892 amendment to a passage describing an incident which takes place on the night of the heroine's seduction in the Chase. The incident involves the villain's encouraging of the heroine to make herself comfortable on the ground, before he sets off in an attempt to discover their where-abouts in the fog-bound Chase. In the manuscript version, he originally hauls down 'the apron of the vehicle' (which is later altered to read simply 'the rug'), placing it upon 'the thick leaves' (f. 96). The First Edition changes the amended manuscript read-ing, 'the rug', to 'a light dust-coat' (I. 136–7). However, in the 1892 edition it is a nature image, appropriate to the hunted-animal motif, that is employed—'a sort of couch or nest', made from 'the deep mass of dead leaves':

> He turned the horse's head into the bushes, hitched him on to a bough,
> and *made a sort of couch or nest for her in the deep mass of dead* leaves.
> 'Now, you sit there,' he said. *The leaves have not got damp as yet.* Just
> give an eye to the horse—it will be quite sufficient.' (X. 87)

With such a pattern of hunting imagery running through the novel it is not surprising to find that the final authorial comment in the book, which is designed to emphasize cosmic cruelty, should take the form of a 'sporting' metaphor: '"Justice" was done and the President of the Immortals (in Aeschylean phrase) had ended his *sport* with Tess' (f. 565).

The altar-victim motif is encountered less often than the hunted-animal motif in *Tess*, but its connotations are, in many ways, similar. Virtually nothing is made of the motif in the Ur-text, where an altar image occurs only once, during the account of the heroine's first journey to Talbothays. In the relevant manuscript leaf we find that the heroine temporarily turns aside from her route (as she does *not* do in the editions) and makes her way into the church of her ancestors:

> Here   of the ~~Turbervilles~~ D'Urbervilles—formed
> ~~There~~ stood the tombs ₐ   of grey Purbeck-
> marble; canopied, altar-shaped, & plain; their carvings defaced
> & broken; & their brasses torn from ~~their~~ matrices. Of all the
>   *socially*
> reminders that she had ever received that they were ~~practically~~ an
>   *spoliation.*
> extinct family there was none so forcible as this ₐ   (f. 141)

Here, the altar image is not associated with the concept of the heroine as victim, but only with the tombs of the heroine's 'practically . . . extinct family'.

The concept of the heroine's role as 'victim' becomes clear only in the later layers of the manuscript. It is made explicit in the passage in which, after crying out to Alec to take his revenge on her for the blow she has given him with her leather gauntlet, she exclaims: 'Once victim, always victim; that's the law' (f. 476). It is also made clear, although less explicitly and more symbolically, during the Stonehenge section, when the heroine wearily murmurs that she likes 'very much' to be lying on 'the very altar on which they offered their sacrifices':

> He knelt down beside her outstretched form, & put his lips
> upon hers. 'Sleepy, are you ~~dear~~? I think you are lying on the
> very altar on which they offered their sacrifices.'
> 'I like very much to be here,' she murmured.   (f. 559)

It is shortly after this scene that the heroine is taken prisoner by the police, and she tells Angel that she is glad they have come because her happiness could not have lasted. Tess, thus, realizes that her role of victim requires that she should die to atone for the sins of the very society that condemns her to death. She also realizes that her husband, who now loves her so tenderly, would one day come to 'despise' her for the sins society had driven her to commit.

The First Edition version of the heroine's visit to the church of her ancestors strengthens the altar-victim motif even more. In this later version of the incident, the heroine enters the church after the Durbeyfield family have arrived at Kingsbere with the household furniture, following their eviction from their home at Marlott.

Inside the church, she observes the same defaced and broken tombs as are described in the Ur-text passage given above (f. 141); but the First Edition introduces a new element when her attention is suddenly attracted towards a recumbent figure on one of the altar-tombs, which appears to move. With a start she realizes that it is a living person lying there:

> She musingly turned to withdraw, passing near an altar-tomb, the oldest of them all, on which was a recumbent figure. In the dusk she had not noticed it before, and would hardly have noticed it now but for an odd fancy that the effigy moved. As soon as she drew close to it she discovered all in a moment that the figure was a living person; and the shock to her sense of not having been alone was so violent that she was quite overcome, and sank down nigh to fainting, not however till she had recognised Alec d'Urberville in the form.   (III. 206-7)

Although it is Alec d'Urberville who is lying on the altar-tomb, the real 'victim' on this occasion is Tess; for immediately after this meeting in the family church she is compelled to return to Alec— an unwilling sacrificial offering to the gods of lust and penury.

Nevertheless, there are occasions in the novel when Tess's sacrificial role is less reluctant. She is then driven by feelings of guilt to play the part of voluntary scapegoat, either punishing herself for others' sins or else allowing herself to sink into a state of despondency, in which she longs for death. Associated with the self-punishment are images of 'a soul at large'; while the mood of despondency often finds reflection in images of entombment.

An example of the self-punishment, which shows itself in a desire to be free from the demands of the flesh in future, is to be found in the scene near Cross-in-Hand, in which Tess talks with Alec for the first time since his religious conversion:

> 'Don't look at me like that!' he said abruptly.
> Tess, who had been quite unconscious of her action & mien, instantly withdrew the large dark gaze of her eyes, stammering
> *with a flush*,   *And*
> ₍ₐ₎   'I beg your pardon.' S ₍ₐ₎ There was revived in her
> *the*   *sentiment which had often come to her before*,
> ~~that~~ wretched ~~consciousness~~ ₍ₐ₎   that in——
>   *with*   *endowed*
> inhabiting the earthly tabernacle ~~with~~ which Nature had ~~given~~
> her, she was somehow doing wrong.   (f. 445)

Here, she feels a guilt which derives not only from the present situation but also from her earlier relationship with Alec, the physical
basis of which was to be underscored by the *Graphic* amendment,
'*fleshly* tabernacle' (G. 602), in place of '*earthly* tabernacle'.

Later in the story, after circumstances have compelled her to
resume that earlier relationship and she is living with Alec at Sandbourne, her acceptance of self-sacrifice for the sake of her family
takes the form of a complete indifference to the physical side of
her relationship with Alec, a complete rejection of her own body.
This is made clear in an 1892 insertion:

> 'Ah—it is my fault!' said Clare.
> But he could not get on. Speech was as inexpressive as silence. *But he
> had a vague consciousness of one thing, though it was not clear to him till
> later; that his original Tess had spiritually ceased to recognize the body
> before him as hers—allowing it to drift, like a corpse upon the current, in a
> direction dissociated from its living will.*
> A few instants passed, and he found that Tess was gone.   (X. 493–4)

Here, Tess has temporarily achieved a dichotomy between body
and spirit, and the 'original Tess' is now clearly a spiritual entity.
She has become virtually 'a soul at large', although still living on
the physical plane as Alec's mistress.

The above insertion in the 1892 edition bears a remarkable similarity to some comments made by Hardy in an interview which he
gave to a journalist, Raymond Blathwayt, earlier in the same year.
Blathwayt's article, 'A Chat with the Author of "Tess"', was published in *Black and White* on 27 August 1892, and contained the
following account of their discussion of Hardy's sub-title, 'A Pure
Woman':

> 'But now Mr. Hardy,' said I, 'I have to quarrel with you for your de-
> liberate description of "Tess" as a *pure* woman. For the moment please
> you will regard me as a representative of the British public, of the narrow-
> minded as of the liberal, of the club man in Piccadilly as of Mrs. Grundy
> in some provincial town. You must let me state the case. I can quite
> understand that you claim a purity for poor Tess after her *first* fall, the
> outcome, as she pitifully tells her mother, of sheer ignorance. But how
> on earth you can describe her as a pure woman after her absolutely un-
> necessary return to Alec D'Urberville, I cannot conceive; for you cannot
> plead with F. W. Robertson, of Brighton, that in her case "a woman's

worst fault arises from a perverted idea of self-sacrifice." And to add to her sin a cruel murder is, at first sight, absolutely unjustifiable.'

'Very well,' replied Mr Hardy, 'but I still maintain that her innate purity remained intact to the very last; though I frankly own that a certain outward purity left her on her last fall. I regarded her then as being in the hands of circumstances, not morally responsible, a mere corpse drifting with the current to her end.'[1]

The 'innate purity', to which Hardy here refers, clearly parallels the concept of the 'original Tess' in the 1892 edition, while the words that follow also have an undoubted connection with the remainder of the 1892 passage. Since the edition was published approximately a month after the interview, appearing on 30 September 1892, it seems reasonable to assume that the interview prompted the inclusion of the additional words in the edition, Hardy's motive being to refute the kind of arguments which the journalist had advanced.

The soul-at-large image takes on somewhat different implications in the Stonehenge scene, where Tess, stretched out on the altar of sacrifice, expresses the wish to Angel that he should later marry her sister, 'Liza-Lu. Once again, it was not until after the manuscript stage that the image was fully developed, for in the manuscript version of the scene there is scarcely a hint of its presence:

¶'Angel, if anything happens to me, will you watch over Liza-Lu
she asked, when they had listened a long time to the wind among the
for my sake?' ∧
pillars.

∧
'I will'
'She is so good, & simple, & pure. . . . O Angel—I wish you
, *as you will shortly.*
would marry her, if you lose me/ ∧ O if you would!'
~~'Now! You shall not be so gloomy Tessie.'~~
⟨'*If I lose you I lose all . . . . . And she is my sister-in-law.*'
'*That's nothing, dearest. People marry sister-laws continually*
about Marlott. And Liza-Lu is so gentle & sweet. . . .⟩ Well—I
have said it. I wont mention it again. (f. 560)

In the above passage there is, admittedly, a high degree of self-sacrifice present in Tess's love for Angel, which precludes jealousy

[1] Quoted by Laurence Lerner and John Holmstrom in *Thomas Hardy and his Readers*, London, 1968, p. 95. Blathwayt's italics.

towards her sister as Angel's second wife. But the suggestion that in 'Liza-Lu Angel will find a purer, and more spiritual, reincarnation of Tess did not enter the novel until the First Edition added the words indicated below:

'That's nothing, dearest. People marry sisters-in-law continually about Marlott; and 'Liza-Lu is so gentle and sweet, *and she is growing so beautiful. O I could share you with her willingly when we are spirits! If you would train her and teach her, Angel, and bring her up for your own self! . . . She has all the best of me without the bad of me; and if she were to become yours it would almost seem as if death had not divided us. . . .* Well, I have said it. I won't mention it again.'   (III. 270)

What Tess appears to be saying is that when all three of them are dead ('when we are spirits') she could willingly share Angel with 'Liza-Lu. But she makes it clear that she is also referring to the period of time when she will be dead but Angel and 'Liza-Lu will be alive and married to each other. During this period, she asserts, it would almost seem as if her original self would live on in 'Liza-Lu, because 'she has all the best of me without the bad of me'. A similar idea is conveyed in a later First Edition insertion, which occurs during the description of Angel and 'Liza-Lu walking away from the prison on the morning of Tess's execution:

One of the pair was Angel Clare, the other a tall budding creature— half girl, half woman—*a spiritualized image of Tess, slighter than she, but with the same beautiful eyes*—Clare's sister-in-law, 'Liza-Lu.   (III. 275)

The soul of Tess, freed at last from its violated 'fleshly tabernacle', would seem destined to live on in serenity in its new corporeal dwelling-place, the 'good, and simple, and pure' 'Liza-Lu.

While these two First Edition amendments have contributed to the imagery pattern of *Tess*, there can be no doubt that their presence in the definitive text has had a deleterious effect on the artistry of the closing section of the novel. For the final impact of these passages is one of artificiality. That determination to champion his heroine which led Hardy to add the sub-title, 'A Pure Woman', in the First Edition of *Tess* would seem occasionally to have undermined his powers of critical judgement, with the result that in these passages, and especially the former, Tess has become

a mere cliché, a sentimentalized angelic figure, like Dickens's Agnes
Wickfield. This artistic lapse stands out strangely when we recall
two Ur-text passages in praise of physical vitality and human imperfection. In the first, Angel accepts the idea that love depends
on an attraction that is more than 'ethereal':

> _lovable_　　　　　　_to him._
> How very ~~beautiful~~ her face was ‸　〈_There was nothing_
> _ethereal about it: all was real vitality, real warmth, real_
> _in_
> ‸ _carnation._〉　　　　　　　　　　　　　　　　　　(f. 213)

In the second, Angel, like his creator, realizes the truth that a
touch of imperfection is an essential ingredient, not only of love
('captivation') but of human nature ('humanity'):

> 　　　　　　　　　　　　　_lips & teeth_　　_actively_
> He had never before seen a woman's ~~mouth~~ ‸　　　which ‸
> 　　　　　— _mind,_　　_such_
> forced upon his —— ‸　~~with~~ ‸　~~persistent~~ iteration,
> ~~themselves without any mental seeking on his part whatever~~
> 　　　　　　　　　　　　　　　　　　　　　‸ the
> 　　　　　　　_a_
> old Elizabethan simile of　roses filled with snow. 〈_Perfect,_
> 　　　　　_might_　　　　　_offhand._　　_no:_
> _he, as a lover,_ ~~would~~ _have called them_ ‸　But ‸ _they were_
> 　_perfect._　　　　　　　　_upon_ ~~over~~ _the_
> not ~~so~~　_And it was the touch of the imperfect_ ~~on what aimed to be~~
> _intended_　　　　　　　_winsomeness_ _captivation_
> ‸　_perfect that_ ~~lent~~ _gave the_ ~~enchantment~~,　_because it was_
> 　　　　　_gave_
> _that which_ ~~lent~~ _the humanity._〉　　　　　　　(f. 213)

An early use of the entombment image occurs at the close of the
following L1 passage, which forms part of the section of the narrative concerned with the heroine's life at Marlott a few months
before the birth of Sorrow:

> 　　_despondency_
> And the ~~misery~~ of the next morning's dawn, when it was no
> 　　　　　　　　　　　　　　　　_laughing_
> longer Sunday, but Monday; & no best clothes; & the ‸ visitors
> were gone, & she awoke alone in her old bed, the innocent younger
> 　　　　　　　　　　　_In place of_
> children breathing softly around her. ‸　The excitement of her
> 　_&_
> return ‸ the interest it ~~she~~ had inspired, she saw before her a

H

>   *highway*
> long & ~~thorn~~ & stony ~~path~~ which she had to tread, without aid,
>   *sympathy*
> & with little ~~strength.~~ ⟨————————————————————————.⟩
> ~~She was disgusted with life, and~~
> ~~Her depression was then terrible, & she could have hidden herself~~
> ~~in a tomb.~~   (f. 113)

Although the final sentence has been cancelled, the broken underlining indicates that the cancellation was not permanent, as is further indicated by the appearance of the sentence in the *Graphic* and the editions.

In the L5 sleep-walking episode, after Angel has carried Tess down the staircase and across the flooded river, he eventually performs the symbolic act of burying her past in the grounds of a near-by abbey. For her part, Tess would have been happy to die in her husband's arms during the precarious journey to the abbey, and thus she passively accepts his action of depositing her on one of the graves of the monks:

>   *graves*
> Upon one of these ₍ he carefully laid her down, & having kissed her
> lips a second time breathed deeply, as if a greatly desired end were
> attained. Clare then lay | himself | down | beside her, when he immediately
> fell into the deep dead slumber of exhaustion; & remained motionless
> as a log. The spurt of mental excitement which had produced the effort
> was now over.   (f. 356)

Tess is aroused to action only by the realization that if Angel were to stay asleep in the night air he would be 'chilled to certain death' (f. 356). In the First Edition, the grave image is slightly amended, although the significance of the scene is not thereby altered: 'Against the north wall was the empty stone coffin of an abbot, without a lid. In this he carefully laid her. . . .' (II. 245).

An entombment image, with its association of despair on the part of the heroine, provides an effective conclusion to the rewritten account of her visit to the d'Urberville church, as found in the First Edition. Beneath the floor of the church lie many of Tess's knightly ancestors; but, as Alec reminds her, they are of far less use to her in her hour of need than is he, a 'sham D'Urberville'. Tess tries to persuade him to cease pursuing her, but he refuses; and her anguish is movingly conveyed in the imagery of the final lines of the extract, which are also the final lines of the scene:

'Go away!' she murmured.
'I will—I'll look for your mother,' said he blandly. But in passing her he whispered: 'Mark me; you'll be civil yet!'
When he was gone she bent down upon the entrance to the vaults, and said—
'Why am I on the wrong side of this door!'   (III. 208)

As has frequently been noted by critics, Hardy was a novelist endowed with a more highly developed visual sense than that of most other writers, which reveals itself not only in landscapes and interior settings but in significant actions and gestures of characters. For this reason it has often been remarked that he had a painter's eye, although the precision of some of his descriptions reveals the trained architect's eye as well. His vivid descriptions of cameo-like silhouettes and figures suddenly illuminated by rays of sunlight, or lamplight, are especially memorable, as is his use of colour to capture the texture of a scene. He also makes good use of perspective in his panoramic descriptions, to achieve effects of scale and movement.

Hardy's 'painter's eye' for landscape and human events undoubtedly owes a good deal to his study of European paintings, which, as F. B. Pinion reminds us, 'began in the National Gallery and was extended here and elsewhere in England and on the Continent'.[2] Hardy's allusions to paintings and painters are frequently specific, and in *Tess* they cover the works and names of Flemish and Italian artists. The fact that none of these pictorial allusions can be attributed with certainty to the Ur-version suggests that they did not play any part in the original creative process, but were introduced later to help Hardy define and refine his vision.

The earliest specific pictorial image in the manuscript of *Tess* would seem to be contained in the passage describing the heroine's 'bird's eye perspective' of the valley of the Frome, in which Hardy draws on his recollections of the works of two minor seventeenth-century Flemish painters, Van Alsloot and Sallaert, to describe the

[2] *A Hardy Companion*, London, 1968, p. 193.

effect of 'myriads of cows stretching . . . from the far east to the far west'. Both Van Alsloot and Sallaert had painted canvases crowded with tiny figures in procession, throngs of people 'whose features', as Hardy elsewhere remarks,[3] 'are indistinguishable by the very comprehensiveness of the view':

These myriads of cows stretching under her eyes from the far
                                                              one
east to the far west outnumbered any she had ever seen at a~~
                                        as thickly
glance before. The green lea was speckled ∧ with them,/ ~~like~~
~~as like~~ *as a canvas by Van Alsloot or Sallaert with burghers.*
   ∧   ~~a strawberry bed with its fruit.~~   The
       & dun   ed   evening
ripe hue of the red ∧ kine absor~~bing~~ the ∧ sunlight, which the
                      animals
white-coated ∧ returned to the eye in rays almost dazzling, even
         distant elevation on
at the ~~distance~~   ∧   ~~at~~ which she stood.   (f. 142)

As will be apparent from the above extract, the reference to the two painters did not form part of the original text (L1), and it is possible that the insertion belongs to another layer.

In a later passage Hardy employs references to two nineteenth-century Flemish painters of grotesque portraits—Anton Wiertz and Jan Van Beers—in order to suggest Angel Clare's bitter and neurotic state of mind as he approaches his father's parsonage at Emminster, three weeks after his wedding to Tess. Here, the allusions do form part of the original L5 text:

        stood before   *in*
Nevertheless, humanity ~~had for~~ him no longer ∧ the pensive sweetness of
Italian art, but in the staring & ghastly attitudes of a Wiertz museum,
& with the hideous leer of a Van Beers.   (f. 371)

But in the following L5 extract it will be seen that the pictorial reference is, once again, an insertion, as Hardy employs the first of a number of specific Italian allusions, by drawing on his memories of 'Giotto's' work (although, in fact, the fragment of fresco in the National Gallery, London, that Hardy knew as Giotto's *Two Apostles* is now known as Spinello Aretino's *Two Haloed Mourners*):

---

[3] *Return of the Native*, III. iii.

Their pale faces seemed to have shrunk to half their natural size;
                                       of their heads
                           , ~~their~~ *drooping* ‸ *being* ~~like~~
they moved on hand in hand, & never spoke a word/ ‸
that of Giotto's Two Apostles.   (f. 564)

It was not until the First Edition that Hardy inserted the highly
effective reference to Crivelli, the fifteenth-century Venetian painter,
some of whose works Hardy had seen in the National Gallery,
London. Although the manuscript contains the description of
Angel's skeleton-like appearance on his return from Brazil (ff.
523-4), it did not contain the sentence, 'He was Crivelli's dead
Christus'[4] (III. 215), later altered (in the 1912 edition) to 'He
matched Crivelli's dead *Christus*' (ch. 53). The relevant section, in
the version of the First Edition, runs as follows:

His father, too, was shocked to see him, so reduced was that figure
from its former contours by worry and the bad season that Clare had
experienced, in the climate to which he had so rashly hurried in his first
aversion to the mockery of events at home. You could see the skeleton
behind the man, and almost the ghost behind the skeleton. *He was
Crivelli's dead Christus.* His sunken eye-pits were of morbid hue, and
the light in his eyes had waned.   (III. 215)

In its context, the allusion to 'Crivelli's dead *Christus*' has a striking effect, setting up an ironic interplay between the names of
'Angel' and 'Christus', and suggesting not merely Angel's physical
emaciation but the suffering he has endured in Brazil and the
spiritual rebirth that is at present taking place. Thus, the allusion
is helping to accomplish what Hardy asserted Crivelli, himself, had
accomplished in the sister art of painting, as Hardy's note written
on 3 January 1886 makes clear: 'My art is to intensify the expression of things, as is done by Crivelli, Bellini, etc., so that the heart
and inner meaning is made vividly visible.'[5]

Finally, we may note two other pictorial allusions. The first,
which seems to have entered the text by way of the *Fortnightly
Review*, is present in the description of the moon over Marlott,
during the harvest ride, as 'resembling the outworn gold-leaf halo
of some worm-eaten Tuscan saint' (I. 180). This appears in a
section of the narrative for which the corresponding manuscript

---

[4] Hardy's italics.   [5] *Life*, p. 177.

folios are missing (ff. 124-6). The second allusion occurs during the description of Tess and Marian labouring in the swede-field at Flintcomb-Ash, for which the *Graphic* text supplies the earliest source: 'The pensive character which the curtained hood lent to their bent heads would have reminded the observer of *some early Italian conception of the two Marys*' (G. 574). Although the manuscript contains another pictorial reference, in place of this ('. . . reminded the observer of two saints by Giotto' (f. 410)), the *Graphic* reading provides a further reminder that, in *Tess*, it was Hardy's habit to define, and redefine, through pictorial allusions added at one of the revisionary stages.

The pattern of blood-red imagery is broadened in the later manuscript layers to include the new connotations of Tess as sacrificial offering and Tess as murderess; but, above all, it helps to introduce the new concept of the importance of Tess's noble ancestry. The sacrificial implications of Tess's life have an obvious connection with other motifs found in the later layers—the hunted animal, the altar victim, and the willing scapegoat; while, both as a sacrifice and a murderess, her role constitutes a natural development from the violence, passion, and guilt which the blood-red images connote in the Ur-text. The concept of Tess's noble blood, however, is first found in the novel at the L3 stage, where it accompanies and strengthens a spectacular expansion of the whole d'Urberville motif, which, in turn, continues to increase in importance during the later layers and in some of the printed versions.

During the scenes of the dying pheasants, the sufferings of the helpless birds sacrificed to human cruelty are made relevant to the heroine's sacrificial sufferings, through the frequent employment of the imagery of blood (ff. 399-401). Her mental and physical torment are conveyed, once again, by an image of blood when Hardy introduces (on ff. 429-30) the description of the 'piece of blood-stained paper, caught up from some meat-buyer's dustheap', which 'beat up and down the road' at Emminster, in front of the house of the Reverend Mr. Clare. And during the threshing of the last rick at Flintcomb-Ash, Hardy conveys much of the anguish of his cruelly oppressed heroine through sentences thickly interspersed with images of this kind:

From the west sky a wrathful shine ⟨—*all that cold March could
afford in the way of a sunset*—⟩ had burst forth after the cloudy
                         the
day ₍ₓ₎ flooding ~~them~~ tired & sticky faces of the threshers, &
dyeing them with a coppery light, as also the flapping garments
of the women, which clung to them like dull flames.
               ~~The older~~
   A panting ache ran through the rick. The man who fed
was weary, & Tess could see that the red nape of his neck was
covered with husks. She still stood at her post, her flushed
face coated with the corn-dust, & her white bonnet embrowned by
it. She was ~~incess~~ the only woman whose place was
upon   *so*   *bodily*
~~so close to~~ the machine, ₍ₐ₎ as to be shaken ₍ₐ₎ by its spinning, &
                              every fibre of her body
this incessant whirring & quivering in which   ₍ₐ₎   ~~she~~
participated had thrown her into a stupefied reverie, in which
her arms worked on independently of her consciousness.

                                                        (ff. 477–8)

It is therefore scarcely surprising that the prison in which the
heroine is finally executed should be 'a large red brick building'
(f. 565), or that in the passage which immediately follows the
threshing scene, the First Edition version should read: 'You are
as weak as a *bled calf*, you know you are; and yet you need have done
nothing since I arrived. How could you be so obstinate?' (III. 148).

   That Tess will die because she is to commit murder is prog-
nosticated at the L3 stage, during the description of the burial of
Prince:

           Durbeyfield
     Then ~~Troublefield~~ began to shovel in the earth, & the children
     cried anew. All except Tess. Her face was dry & pale as though
     she regarded herself in the light of a murderess.   (f. 38)

*Tess
- foreshadows
murderess*

Somewhat later in the story, Alec is described as 'he who was to be
the blood-red ray in the spectrum of her young life' (G. 102).
However, one of the most telling of all such passages occurs in L5,
with the description of the 'scarlet oozing' from Alec's mouth when
Tess strikes him with her leather glove, after he has attempted to
persuade her to become his mistress once again:

     One of her ~~buff~~ leather gloves, which she had taken off to
                                            , and
     eat her skimmer-cake, lay in her lap/ ₍ₐ₎ At his ~~latter~~ words,

without the slightest warning, she passionately swung the glove
~~towards~~ *directly in his face.*
by the gauntlet ~~round at [?] to [?] him at arm's [?] length~~. It
was heavy & thick as a warrior's, & it struck him flat on the
              fiercely   *his*
mouth. D'Urberville ∧ started up from ~~the~~ reclining position ~~that~~
~~he had taken~~; a scarlet oozing appeared where her blow had alighted,
in a moment the blood began dropping
&   ∧   ~~some drops from it fell~~ upon the straw. ~~In a moment~~
    But   soon
~~or two~~ ∧ he —— controlled himself, calmly drew his handkerchief
              mopped
from his pocket, & ~~applied it to~~ his bleeding lips.   (f. 475)

Alec's life's blood eventually drains away in a fashionable Sandbourne boarding-house, where the landlady, Mrs. Brooks, notices
a scarlet blot on the ceiling rapidly assuming 'the appearance of
a gigantic ace of hearts' (f. 544).

As has been observed in the previous chapter, the theme of
heredity is of little significance in the Ur-text. It is therefore
entirely consistent that the association of blood-red imagery with
the concept of noble ancestry should not be found in the first two
layers of the manuscript and that the first appearance of such
images should accompany the rapid expansion of the d'Urberville
motif in **L3**.

It is in two **L3** utterances of John Durbeyfield's that we find the
earliest examples of Hardy's employment of 'blood' to signify
lineage. Thus, after the heroine has visited Trantridge to 'claim
kin', her foolish father comes to believe that Alec wishes her to
return to Trantridge so that he may marry her to improve his
'blood':

              'He's struck wi' her—you can see that.
'But do let her go, Jacky,' coaxed his poor witless wife. ∧
He called her coz.
              He'll marry her, most likely, & make a lady of her; &
then she'll be what her forefathers was.'
              Durbeyfield
John ~~Troublefield~~ had more conceit than energy or health, & this
                                                            Mr
supposition was pleasant to him. 'Well—perhaps that's what young ∧
D'Urberville do   *he admitted:*
~~Turberville~~ ∧ means'   ∧   '& he really may have serious thoughts about

~~her~~ ⟨*improving his blood by linking on to the old line* . . . . . . *Tess,*⟩
                                            have
. . . The little rogue! And ~~has~~ she really paid 'em a visit to such an end
as this!'
                                                                    (f. 54)

And when Tess is on the point of departure, her father, in his
drunken confusion, varies the implication of the image by exclaim-
ing that his daughter is 'a comely specimen' of Alec's 'own blood':

'Goodbye, father,' said Tess, with a lumpy throat.
'Goodbye, my maid,' said Sir John, raising his head from his
~~in the chair~~ *induced by a slight excess this morning in honour of the*
breast as he suspended his nap, ˄
occasion.

˄
'Well, I hope my young friend will like such a comely specimen of his
                                                    ~~our~~ *our*
own blood. . . . And tell'n, Tess, that being reduced, quite, from ~~my~~ ˄
                            ~~*more's the pity!*~~
former grandeur, ˄   I'll sell him the title—yes, sell it—
and at no onreasonable figure.'
                                                                    (f. 60ᵛ)

Alec, himself, suffers no such delusions—either about wanting to
improve his blood or accepting Tess as a blood-relation: however,
he is fully aware of the nobility of Tess's ancestry, and the close
of the following L5 extract shows him using the blood image to
draw the distinction between her genuine d'Urberville lineage and
his own spurious claim to the distinction:

~~As she had not caught him in the~~
    ˄ 'Tess,' he added, with a sigh that verged on a groan, 'yours
was the very worst case I ever was concerned in.' Wretch that I was,
    jest with
to ~~foul~~ that innocent life. The whole blame was mine; the whole
                            You, too, the real blood of which
blackness of the sin, the awful, awful iniquity. ˄
I am but the counterfeit.

˄
                                                                    (ff. 452–3)

III

The genesis of the d'Urberville motif—perhaps the most important single motif in the novel because of its widespread influence
on title, plot, characterization, and themes—is to be found in folios

belonging to the closing stage of **L2**. But any close examination of
the history of the motif must begin with **L1**, where three brief
references to the father's descent from an old and once distinguished
family occur.

In **L1** the name of the ancient family is not specified. We are
merely told that the heroine's father (at this stage named Woodrow)
feels pride in his ancient lineage. Thus, in the earliest of such
references we read of his 'pride in the possession of a great vault
full of old family bones':

> *marble tombs &*
> Her father's pride in the ~~possession of~~ ₐ a ~~great vault~~
>   *knightly respectability of his family   forms*
> ~~full of old family bones~~ was apt to burst out in sundry ~~ways~~, the
> commonest of which was musical.   (f. 127)

This feeling on John Durbeyfield's part is reinforced by the
passage in which the heroine explains to the clergyman why she
was forced to baptize her child instead of sending for him to do so:

> He expressed his willingness to listen; & she told the
>   *how* | *had been* | *owing*
> story of ₐ the | extemporized | ordinance ₗ ~~owning~~ to her father's
>   *babe*
> family pride, & the sudden illness of the ~~child~~.   (f. 133)

However, to the heroine there seems little or no cause for such
'pride', as may be seen from her reflection on 'her useless ancestors',
in the first version of the passage describing the journey which
takes her past the church of her ancestors (on f. 143).

In **L2** the ancient family name makes its first appearance in the
novel, and is found on five folios (ff. 141, 142^v, 181, 306, 309). At
this stage the name given to the family is Turberville, but because
this was the name of one of the old historical families of Dorset
Hardy later altered it to D'Urberville (in **L4** of the manuscript)
and, finally, to d'Urberville (in the 1912 edition). One of these
five folios (f. 141) contains a rewritten version of the journey referred
to at the end of the preceding paragraph in relation to f. 143, and
in the later account the journey takes the heroine inside the ancestral
church, where she stands 'for the first time in her life upon the spot
whereof her father had spoken or sung to painfulness ever since

her infancy', and discerns on a dark stone leading to the vaults a
Latin inscription mentioning the ancient family by name: 'Ostium
sepulchri antiquae familiae Turberville.'

However, this is not the earliest of the Turberville references in
the layer: nor is the intermediate version of the passage, which
occurs on f. 142ᵛ. Indeed, the earliest of the Turberville passages
is to be found on f. 306, wherein Angel remarks to the heroine (in
the original reading): 'Oh—you have heard the story of the Turberville coach . . .', and she reflects that 'he had never perceived in
her own name a corruption of the name he had pronounced . . .'
On f. 181 (which, like f. 141 and f. 142ᵛ, is a substitute leaf) we read
that, when talking to Angel at Talbothays, the heroine 'held her
tongue about the Turberville vault'; while in a passage on f. 309
Angel and the heroine drive off to spend their honeymoon in a
farm-house that had once been the 'property and home of a
Turberville'.

The name Turberville occurs so many times in L3 that there is
no doubt that the accentuation of the motif was one of Hardy's
main preoccupations during this period of composition. The pro-
liferation of the name is immediately apparent when one reads L3
scenes such as the father's meetings with Parson Tringham and
the country lad, Fred (as recorded on ff. 1–6a), and the heroine's
exploits on her visit to Trantridge to 'claim kin' (on ff. 38–54).
Moreover, there are numerous other leaves belonging to this layer
in which the reader is constantly being reminded of the motif, for
example, through the discussions between the parents on the question of whether or not they should send their daughter to 'claim
kin' with their supposed relation 'out by Trantridge' (on ff. 20,
26, 27, 28).

At the L4 stage, the reminders of the d'Urberville motif tend to
take the form of insertions in earlier material. One of the most
revealing of such insertions is to be seen in the following extract,
wherein after the heroine has observed (in the L2 part of the leaf)
that Angel's friends may be indignant if they hear that 'you are
walking about like this with me, a milkmaid', Angel replies:

'My dear girl ⟨A D'Urberville hurt the dignity of a Clare! It
is a grand card to play—that of your belonging to such a family,

& I am reserving it for a grand effect when we are married, &
have the proofs of your descent, from Parson Tringham & the rest
of the genealogists. Apart from that⟩ my future is to be totally
my family's
foreign to ~~theirs~~ . . .' (f. 278)

An equally revealing insertion is written on the verso of an earlier **L2** leaf. Here, the **L4** insertion takes the form of the following conversation between Angel and his father:

'Not one of the ancient D'Urbervilles of King's-Bere &
asked his son
other places?' ‸ ~~'I would go forty miles any day to see~~
~~*living relic*~~ *'That curiously worn-out with its*
~~a representative of that~~ ‸ historic ‸ family, ‸
ghostly legend of the coach-&-four?'
decayed & disappeared
'O no. The original D'Urbervilles ~~died out~~ sixty or
eighty years ago—at least I believe so. This seems to be
a new family which has taken the name; & for the credit of
the former *they are spurious,*
~~that~~ knightly line I hope ‸ ~~so,~~ I'm sure. But it is odd
to hear you ~~enthusiastic~~ express interest in old families. I
thought you set less store by them even than I'. . . . (f. 236^{v})

Similar **L4** insertions of d'Urberville material occur elsewhere in the Ur-text on ff. 180, 265–6, 268–71, 293^{v}, 301^{v}, 306, and 314.

In the final layer and in some of the printed texts, notably the *Graphic* and First Edition, Hardy continued to expand the d'Urberville motif; and, indeed, even as late as the 1912 edition Hardy was still making small amendments relating to it.

The general implications of the d'Urberville motif, as it exists in the definitive version of *Tess*, are many and varied. In terms of plot, the motif supplies a useful opening incident and a plausible reason for the meeting between heroine and villain at Trantridge. The characters of Angel and Tess (to say nothing of less important personages, like John Durbeyfield) are also illuminated by it; while, thematically, its significance is extremely great, for it helps to convey not merely such major concepts as the heredity and mutability themes but a number of minor concepts as well.

The inconsistent nature of Angel Clare is well exemplified by the contrast between his democratic scorn for ancient families, as reported by Dairyman Crick in **L2** (on f. 181), and his snobbishness and romanticism, as displayed in the two d'Urberville insertions quoted almost immediately above (ff. 278 and 236ᵛ). Tess, on the other hand, stands out as more clear-sighted than either Angel or her father in her attitude towards her ancient lineage: for whereas Angel becomes fanciful at times and the father remains foolishly proud, Tess recognizes only too clearly the uselessness of her d'Urberville ancestors in her daily struggle to achieve happiness, and appreciates, also, the two-sided nature of her genetic inheritance. Both of these insights are apparent in the later L2 version of her visit to the d'Urberville church:

>   *Tess*   *church-*   *—like a Cardinal*
> ~~Rose-Mary~~ did not read ⌃ Latin ⌃   but she knew that
> this was the door of her ancestral sepulchre, & that the tall
> knights of whom her father chanted in his cups lay inside it in
>   *Pooh—what's the good of thinking about*
> their leaden shrouds. ⌃
>   *a   sigh*
> them!' she said, with ⌃ sudden ~~scorn~~. '*I have as much of mother as*
> ⌃
> *father in me* ⟨*: all my prettiness comes from her,*⟩ *& she was*
> ⌃
> *only a dairy maid.'*
> ⌃   ~~She left the church, & resumed her course.~~   (f. 141)

As early as L1 Hardy had propounded this view of the duality of genetic influences as an authorial comment, even though in the relevant passage the alteration of the main reference from 'refinement' to 'dignity' later led to cancellation of the comment:

>   *dignity*
> The natural ~~refinement~~ of the ~~young~~ girl—~~drawn rather~~
>   *strange*
> ~~from her mother than her father by the way~~—the ⌃ tenderness
> in her voice, . . .   (f. 133)

However, although the authorial 'guarantee' for the concept was withdrawn on this leaf (f. 133), it was subsequently restored, at the L3 stage, through a comment on another leaf:

> There still faintly beamed from the woman's features something
> of the freshness, & even the prettiness, of her youth; rendering
> it evident that the personal charms which Tess could boast of
>   *unknightly,*
> were in main part her mother's gift, & therefore ⌃ unhistorical.   (f. 18)

Similarly, at the L3 stage Hardy also gave his authorial stamp of approval to the opinion expressed by the heroine that from a practical viewpoint there was no advantage in the possession of knightly ancestors:

> *skeletons*   *D'Urberville*
> ⟨*Pedigree, ancestral* repute, *monumental record, the* Turberville
> *lineaments, did not help Tess in her life's battle as yet, even to*
> *the extent of attracting to her a dancing-partner over the heads of*
> *the commonest peasantry. So much for Norman blood unaided by*
> *Victorian lucre. . . .*⟩   (f. 14)

In the final sentence ('So much for Norman blood unaided by Victorian lucre') there are shades of Hardy's earlier political radicalism, which had been clearly displayed in his first attempt at novel-writing, *The Poor Man and the Lady*, although muted in most of his subsequent fiction.

The most significant of the thematic implications of the d'Urberville motif concerns the concept of the decadence of old knightly families, which bears directly on the twin themes of heredity and mutability. Once again, it is in L3 that the concept first becomes significant, especially through the dramatic presentation of John Durbeyfield's actions and speech. Most of the L5 d'Urberville passages, also, are employed to this end, a typical example being Angel's cruel comments to Tess that 'decrepit families postulate decrepit wills, decrepit conduct' and that she is 'the seedling of an effete aristocracy' (f. 332). In the same layer Hardy describes how Angel is 'embittered by the conviction that all this desolation had been brought about by the accident of her being a D'Urberville' (f. 372ᵛ).

As a consequence of such passages, it becomes apparent that Hardy sees much of the responsibility for Tess's effeteness as circumstantial, rather than personal, and believes that she should not be judged too harshly by the reader for an inherited passivity and submissiveness. On the occasion of her separation from Angel after the disastrous honeymoon period at Wellbridge Hardy points out the disadvantage under which Tess labours as a result of 'her mood of long suffering', and suggests that had she acted with more artifice Angel 'would probably not have withstood her'. Her behaviour on this occasion is attributed (in the manuscript) to 'that indifference to results too apparent in the whole D'Urberville family' (f. 363), a reading which eventually became (in the 1892 edition) 'that *reckless acquiescence in chance* too apparent in the whole D'Urberville family' (X. 328).

Similarly, we are reminded that Tess's occasionally violent behaviour is a legacy from the past, the result of some sinister taint in the d'Urberville blood. This is clearly the implication of the various references to the phantom d'Urberville coach, which stress the violence of a crime committed in a coach by one of Tess's ancestors (f. 306) and the fact that only 'one of D'Urberville blood' can now hear its approach, which inevitably presages disaster:

'. . . What is the story?'
 'If you are a genuine D'Urberville I ought not to tell you,
I suppose. As for me, I'm a spurious one, so it doesn't matter.
                              non-existent
It is rather dismal. It is that this sound of a ˄ coach can
only be heard by one of D'Urberville blood, & it is —— held
to be of ill-omen to the one who hears it. It has to do with
a murder, committed by one of the family, centuries ago.'
 'Now you have begun it, finish it.'
                                   abducted some
 'Very well. One of the family is said to have ~~murdered his~~
beautiful woman, who tried to escape from the coach in which he
was carrying her off, & in the struggle he killed her—or she
killed him—I forget which. Such is the tale . . .'   (ff. 509-10)

A concrete illustration of Tess's own tendency towards violence, in moments of extreme mental stress, is given to the reader in the manuscript description of how she strikes Alec across the mouth with her glove at Flintcomb-Ash; and in the First Edition Hardy was to add the comment that specifically relates her violent action to at least the possibility of hereditary determinism at work:

It was heavy and thick as a warrior's, and it struck him flat on the mouth.
*Fancy might have regarded the act as the recrudescence of a trick in which
her mailed progenitors were not unpractised.* Alec fiercely started up from
his reclining position. A scarlet oozing appeared where her blow had
alighted, and in a moment the blood began dropping from his mouth
upon the straw.   (III. 140-1)

Three related passages, which made their first appearance after the manuscript stage of composition, serve to place even more emphasis on this more sinister aspect of the heroine's heredity. These are the passages that allowed the introduction of the d'Urberville portraits into the story.

The earliest reference to the d'Urberville portraits is found in the following passage from the *Graphic*, none of the italicized section being present in the manuscript version of the scene:

When the carriage was gone *they ascended the stairs to wash their hands, the charwoman showing the way. On the landing Tess stopped and started.*
   '*What's the matter?*' *said he.*
   '*Those horrid women!*' *she answered, with a smile. 'How they frightened me!*'
   He looked up, and perceived two life-size portraits on panels built into the masonry. As all visitors to the mansion are aware, these paintings represent women of middle age, of a date some two hundred years ago, whose lineaments once seen can never be forgotten. The long pointed features, narrow eye, and smirk of the one, so suggestive of merciless treachery, the bill-hook nose, large teeth, and bold eye of the other, suggesting arrogance to the point of ferocity, haunt the beholder afterwards in his dreams.
   '*Whose portraits are those?*' *asked Clare of the charwoman.*
   '*I've been told by old folk that they were ladies of the D'Urberville family, the ancient lords of this manor,*' *she said. 'Owing to their being builded into the wall they can't be removed.*'
   The unpleasantness of the matter was that, in addition to their effect upon Tess, her fine features were unquestionably traceable in these exaggerated forms. He said nothing of this, however, and regretting that his romantic plan of choosing this house for their bridal time was proving to be a mistake, went on into the adjoining room. The place having been rather hastily prepared for them, they washed their hands in one basin. Clare touched hers under the water.
   'Which are my fingers and which are yours?' he said, looking up. 'They are very much mixed.'   (G. 422)

In the First Edition, two additional references to the portraits were then introduced. In the first, Angel comments on the effect of the portraits on the spirit of his bride:

   'Tess, you are not a bit cheerful this evening—not at all as you used to be. *Those harridans on the panels upstairs have unsettled you. I am sorry I brought you here.* I wonder if you really love me, after all?' (II. 180-1)

In the second, Angel's actions are influenced by their sinister influence:

He turned away to descend; then, irresolute, faced round to her door again. In the act he caught sight of one of the D'Urberville dames, whose portrait was immediately over the entrance to Tess's bedchamber. In the candlelight the painting was more than unpleasant. Sinister design lurked in the woman's features, a concentrated purpose of revenge on the other sex —so it seemed to him then. The Caroline bodice of the portrait was low— precisely as Tess's had been when he tucked it in to show the necklace; and again he experienced the distressing sensation of a resemblance between them. The check was sufficient. He resumed his retreat and descended.

(II. 214-15)

As will be clear from a reading of the above extracts the italicized insertions are by no means exempt from the charge of melodrama, if judged by purely realistic standards. As omens of disaster, however, in a novel which employs imagery symbolically, they play a valuable role during the honeymoon section of the novel. They also emphasize the thematic concept of the grim irony inherent in the whole human condition; for Angel wrongly imagines that Tess has inherited the vices depicted in the paintings and acts accordingly —to his later profound regret.

Finally, it must be observed that Tess's d'Urberville ancestry offers her one positive advantage in her battle with life's problems and hardships. Despite the many disadvantages that have been noted, Tess possesses a certain 'dignity', which as the extract from f. 133 has already indicated, differs from the quality of 'refinement', in that it has been inherited not from the mother's but from the father's line. One of the main effects that results from the building-up of the d'Urberville motif during the later layers of the manuscript is the fact that it gives to the heroine a new romantic *aura*, which sets her apart from most other young women of the district in which she was raised. During the Talbothays scenes of courtship, much of Angel's interest in her ancestry is, admittedly, snobbish and over-fanciful: however, there remains a kernel of valid historical interest in the fact that she is descended from an 'ancient and knightly line', and it is a far less illusioned Angel who, while in Brazil, recalls her face and thinks that 'he could see therein a flash of the dignity which must have graced her granddames' (f. 491).

I

VII

CHARACTERIZATION

I

IT may be an exaggeration to say, as Trevor Johnson does, that 'Tess is Hardy's most masterly portrait of a woman';[1] however, there are few readers of Hardy's fiction who would disagree with the judgement that she is one of Hardy's most successful heroines, deserving a place alongside Bathsheba Everdene, Eustacia Vye, and Sue Bridehead in the gallery of Hardy's most fascinating young women. There are, admittedly, 'genealogical' relationships between most of Hardy's heroines,[2] and Tess is no exception to the general truth that Hardy's women are classifiable in certain categories, according to temperament. Thus, in her purity and loyalty she resembles Marty South, in her beauty and resourcefulness Bathsheba Everdene, and in the sensuousness of her nature Eustacia Vye, Suke Damson, and Arabella Donn. At the same time it must be recognized, as Albert J. Guerard has pointed out,[3] that this kind of grouping is to a certain degree arbitrary and that each of these characters—Tess included—is essentially an individual, not a mere type.

One of the reasons for Hardy's success in the development of the character-study, Tess, would seem to lie buried in the mysterious region of Hardy's early life. A preliminary insight into the nature of this biographic link may be gained from the study of an insertion, which was first included in the text of the sketch, 'The Midnight Baptism' (May 1891), and was subsequently incorporated into the First Edition. In this insertion, Hardy refers to the sound of the heroine's voice in a way that suggests he was thinking of a real person, the relevant words being 'and which will never be forgotten

---

[1] *Thomas Hardy*, London, 1968, p. 151.
[2] As Guerard observes (p. 142).
[3] Guerard, pp. 142, 143.

by those who knew her'. No trace of this comment is to be found in
the manuscript version of the passage:

~~Rose-Mary~~ Next Tess
~~Then Sue~~   poured forth from the foundation of her heart the
                      uttering it
thanksgiving that followed, ∧ boldly & triumphantly, in the
~~rich stopped~~ stopt-diapason note   acquired
tender coo ∧   that her voice ~~assumed~~ when her heart was
in her speech. The ecstasy of faith almost ~~tr~~ [?] apotheosized her . . .   (f. 132)

Here, the heroine's utterance is described, first, as a 'tender coo . . .',
and, later, as 'the stopt-diapason note that her voice acquired when
her heart was in her speech'. The relevant part of the passage in
'The Midnight Baptism', which became the definitive version in
the editions, illustrates the important change: '. . . uttering it
boldly and triumphantly, in the stopt-diapason note which her
voice acquired when her heart was in her speech, *and which will
never be forgotten by those who knew her.* The ecstasy of faith almost
apotheosized her . . .' (F.R. 700).

A similar impression is conveyed by two manuscript insertions.
The first, which describes the heroine's laugh as she watches the
antics of Car Darch squirming on the grass, in an attempt to wipe
the treacle from the back of her dress during the moonlight walk
from Chaseborough, consists of the words 'in that intense low
laugh of hers which shook her shoulders':

~~Rose-Mary~~ Tess,
~~Sue . . Our heroine~~ who had hitherto held her peace, at this wild
forgot her dignity, &   ~~loudly~~   *in that intense low*
moment ∧ could not help joining ~~in~~ with the rest, ∧
laugh of hers which shook her shoulders.

∧   (f. 88)

The second insertion, which occurs on a leaf belonging to a somewhat later layer (L4), conveys the authorial explanation that, as a
consequence of the scandal occasioned by the birth of an illegitimate
child, the heroine found that 'To carry out her once fond idea of
teaching in a village school was now impossible':

She waited a long time without finding opportunity for a new departure.
⟨*To carry out her once fond idea of teaching in a village school was
now impossible.*⟩ A particularly fine Spring came round, & the stir of
germination was almost audible . . .   (f. 137)

Neither of these manuscript insertions found its way into the editions, even though the former appeared in the sketch 'Saturday Night in Arcady' (November 1891) and the latter in the *Graphic*.

The full significance of the above insertion referring to Tess's early plan of 'teaching in a village school' (f. 137) becomes clear only with the aid of biographic evidence published in relatively recent years by Lois Deacon and F. R. Southerington. In her brief monograph, *Tryphena and Thomas Hardy* (1962), Lois Deacon presented, for the first time, persuasive evidence of the existence of an engagement during Hardy's early life between himself and a cousin, Tryphena Sparks of Puddletown. At the time of this betrothal, which began in the late summer of 1867, Hardy was twenty-seven and Tryphena sixteen,[4] and, despite the fact that Tryphena went away as a student to Stockwell Teachers' Training College, London, in 1869, the engagement appears to have continued for several years. According to Lois Deacon, the monograph of 1962 presented for the first time the evidence of 'an enduring and tragic love-story', which had left its mark on a good deal of Hardy's writing: 'The truth has been told in the poems, novels, autobiography and other writings of Thomas Hardy, but told guardedly, for there were reasons for reticence during Hardy's lifetime.'[5] What these 'reasons for reticence' were she did not specify in her early monograph, and it was not until the publication of her full-length study, *Providence and Mr Hardy* (1966), written in collaboration with Terry Coleman, that they were explained. The most important revelation in the later book was her controversial assertion that Tryphena had borne Hardy's child during the betrothal period. To this claim was added a 'supposition', drawn from a tangled web of deductions and speculations, that the couple ultimately felt themselves unable to marry after discovering that their true relationship was not that of cousins, but of uncle and niece.

F. R. Southerington's book *Hardy's Vision of Man* (1971) contains the important additional piece of information that before Tryphena went away in 1869 to the Stockwell Training College

---

[4] It is noteworthy that in the *Graphic* the heroine's age is reduced to sixteen, from seventeen in the MS. (f. 281); and that in the First Edition Angel's age is increased to 'six-and-twenty', from 'three-and-twenty' in the MS. (f. 229).

[5] *Tryphena and Thomas Hardy*, Beaminster, 1962, p. 11.

she was employed in the village school at Puddletown, from 7 November 1866 until January 1868, as a pupil-teacher. It also contains the interesting suggestion that Tryphena was the pupil-teacher mentioned in the following entry in the log of the Puddletown School, dated 16 January 1868: 'Reproved pupil-teacher for neglect of duty—parents very angry in consequence—determine to withdraw her a month hence'. In the entries for 20 January, the log provides the information that Tryphena was transferred to the boys' section of the school on that day and also records that a certain Frances Dunman was 'appointed P.T. in T. Sparks's place', the implication of the latter entry being that Tryphena left the school on or about this date. No further references to her occur in the school records. Southerington also notes the curious coincidence that 'just two days after Tryphena's removal from the girls' section, the head-mistress "explained fully to 1st & 2nd classes the 7th commandment"'. As Southerington observes, '"Thou shalt not commit adultery" is unusual fare for a group of young girls in Victorian England (although there are some other recorded instances)'.[6]

Tryphena Sparks subsequently married another man, Charles Gale, in 1877 and died on 17 March 1890. The date of her death, also, has significance; for it was during the years 1890 and 1891 that Hardy was engaged in the writing of the last three layers of the manuscript of *Tess* and the preparation of the text of 'The Midnight Baptism', wherein, as we have seen, at least two of the three insertions testifying to the existence of a real-life model for Tess occur. In the poem 'Thoughts of Phena, at News of Her Death', dated March 1890, Hardy also made it clear that he still remembered her as she had been many years before, not as she was at the time when she died—'the maiden of yore', not the 'dame in her dwelling'. He also refers to her in the same poem as 'my lost prize'.[7]

The evidence presented by this poem, by at least some of the sources quoted by Deacon and Southerington, and by the three textual insertions mentioned above is sufficiently strong to validate the claim here being advanced that the news of Tryphena

[6] *Hardy's Vision of Man*, London, 1971, p. 261.
[7] *C.P.*, p. 55.

Sparks's death exerted a direct influence on the evolution of the character of Tess after March 1890. Whether or not one accepts the notion that memories of Tryphena, flooding back in Hardy's mind, were the *all*-important influence at this time is not important. What is important is that knowledge of Tryphena's life and death provides strong presumptive evidence which helps to explain an impressionistic reaction experienced by many readers of the novel. The reaction is that Hardy appeared to regard Tess as a real person, to whose welfare and good reputation he was deeply committed. One such reader was the critic Bernard J. Paris, who once observed in an article that 'Hardy was in love with Tess', and went on to note the consequences of such a close emotional involvement with a character:

> One of the consequences of Hardy's love for Tess (or, perhaps, one of the causes) is that he identifies with her strongly and presents almost everything from her point of view. Hardy is the biographer we all want, the one who sees how it is for us, who understands, accepts, and justifies. Hardy is Tess's apologist: he sees her and everything else in her terms. Where Tess is seen from the outside, from a social or cosmic perspective, it is only in order to affirm more passionately the phenomenological point of view.[8]

The tendency for Hardy to vindicate his heroine is most apparent, as will be shown, in the later manuscript layers and in changes introduced into the printed versions of the novel. Thus, for example, it was not until the First Edition was about to be published that Hardy added the famous sub-title, 'A Pure Woman | Faithfully Presented By | Thomas Hardy', and the equally sympathetic epigraph, taken from *Two Gentlemen of Verona*:

> . . . Poor wounded name! My bosom as a bed
> Shall lodge thee.

Of this kind of strong moral commitment there is little sign in the Ur-text. There, apart from a tendency to extenuate the heroine's sexual guilt by appeals to Nature as the moral norm, the author's attitude towards his heroine is, for the most part, one of moral neutrality.

[8] Paris, pp. 76–7.

It is, thus, perhaps not surprising to find that in the Ur-text, the heroine turns out to be a far less appealing character than is the heroine of the definitive text. At the same time it is necessary to acknowledge that some of the lineaments of the definitive portrait are already present in the Ur-heroine, who is known variously as Sue, Love, Cis, Rose-Mary, and Tess. In terms of physical beauty, for example, there is little to distinguish the two creations: for, although 'slender and flexible' of form (f. 205) instead of 'roundly-built' (as an amendment on f. 375 describes her), the heroine of the first two layers receives copious praise for her attractive face and figure, much of it from the author himself and most of it retained through the successive versions of the novel. A typical example of such praise is seen in the following basically L1 passage, in which the villain (Hawnferne) compliments her with genuine admiration as he spies on her attempts to perfect her whistling within the walled garden at 'The Slopes':

>   *carcase*   *was* *before*
> 'Upon my ~~soul~~ ', cried he, 'there ˄ never ~~was~~ such a beautiful
>   *"cousin" Tess.*
> thing in nature or art as you look, ˄   '   (f. 74)

In L2 it is Angel Clare who falls under her spell, and the rich mythic descriptions of their early-morning meetings in the meadows of Talbothays emphasize both her beauty of appearance and his illusioned reaction to it. In the same layer, Hardy describes some of her typical attitudes, in passages reminiscent of the style of Dutch paintings:

> All the men, & some of the women, when milking, dug their
> fore-heads into the cows & gazed into the pail. But a few—
> mainly the younger ones—rested their heads sideways. This was
> *Tess —— Durbeyfield's*
> ~~Rose-Mary's~~ ˄ habit, her temple pressing the milcher's
> flank, her eyes fixed on the far end of the meadow with the gaze
> of one lost in meditation. She was milking Old Pretty thus, &
> the sun chancing to be on the milking-side it shone flat upon
> her pink-gowned form, & her white curtain-bonnet, & upon her
> profile, rendering it dazzlingly keen, with an effect like that
> of a cameo cut from the dun background of the cow. (f. 212)

The heroine of the Ur-novel is also sexually innocent and free from any intention of becoming sexually involved with the villain

at the time of the seduction. This is made clear from the description of events which occur at the Chaseborough dance and in the
Chase, and also from her **L1** conversation with her mother on her
return home:

'You ought to have been more careful, if you did'nt mean to get
him to make you his wife!'
     O
'But ˄ mother, my mother!' cried the ~~agonised~~ girl, turning
passionately upon her parent; 'how could I be expected to know? I
was a child when I left this house four months ago. Why did'nt you
tell me there was danger? Why did'nt you warn me? Ladies know what
                                                    'em
to guard against, because they read novels that tell ~~them~~ ˄ of these
   of men;   *discovering in*
tricks ˄   but I never had the chance of ~~learning~~ ˄   that way, &
you did not help me.'   (f. 111)

This dialogue is, itself, somewhat novelettish; but, clearly, what
we are dealing with is betrayal of innocence—a common subject in
Hardy's writings.

As in the definitive version, the Ur-heroine's betrayal in the
Chase results only in part from the machinations of the villain.
Nature and Circumstance also play their part; and Nature, in particular, continues to exert a strong influence over the course of her
life during the Talbothays scenes, not only through such external
manifestations as the 'succulence and humidity' of 'that green
trough', the Frome Valley (f. 238), but also through her very pulse
'singing in her ears' (f. 252). For even though she has made up her
mind to refuse Angel's proposal of marriage, the realization later
dawns that her will is no match for the natural demands of the body,
especially its desire 'to snatch ripe pleasure':

   In reality ~~Tess~~ *she*
~~For the first time she felt that she~~ was drifting into acquiescence.
   see-saw of her breath,   *her*
Every ~~pore~~ ˄ every ~~pulse~~ wave of ˄ blood, every pulse singing in her ears,
                              in revolt
was a voice that joined with Nature ~~to rave~~ against her scrupulousness. (f. 252)

Here the concept is of Nature as norm, and such, also, is the implication of many of the mythic and symbolic touches in **L2**—the allusions to Demeter and Eve, the motifs of pollen and mist, the

blood-red motif, and the images of helpless bir~
all of which have relevance to the heroine as a d~

The Ur-text also shows the heroine's illusio
during the period of her betrothal to Angel:

> The days of declining autumn which followed her assent, beginning w~
> the month of October, formed a season through which she ~~floated~~ lived
> *altitudes*
> in ~~a~~ spiritual ~~elevation~~ more nearly approaching ecstasy than any other
> period of her life.
>   There was hardly a touch of earth in her love for Clare. To her
> sublime trustfulness he was all that goodness could be, knew all that a
> guide, philosopher, & friend should know. She thought every line in the
> contour of his person the perfection of masculine beauty; his soul
> *the soul*
> ~~that~~ of a saint; his intellect that of a seer.   (ff. 275-6)

Such a mental state does not preclude, however, the presence of
strong passion beneath the surface, and it is noteworthy that her
eventual acceptance of Angel's proposal is prompted by a deep
emotional response to his ardent and persistent love-making. Thus,
her aberration, whereby she idealizes and hero-worships to excess,
is purely temporary and arises from her ecstatic discovery of the
difference between love and lust:

> *indignation against*
> . . . & in her reaction from ~~terror of~~ the male sex she swerved to excess
> of honour for Clare.   (f. 277)

It is also noticeable that she has moments of mental clarity, in
which she perceives that Angel's tendency to idealize is far more
deeply rooted than her own. This is apparent on the occasion when
she admits to herself before the wedding that the woman he really
loves is not her, but 'one in my image; the one I might have been!'
(f. 307).

The development of the character of Tess during the later manuscript layers could be best described as a process of refining, en-
nobling, and idealizing on the part of the author. While some of
the changes may be attributed, in part, to the need to bowdlerize,
in order to forestall criticism from the editor of the *Graphic*, few
would seem to have been made solely for this purpose; and it soon

comes obvious that, as Hardy developed an increasing interest in the portrayal of Tess, artistic considerations quickly outweighed any such moralistic concerns. In a small number of examples there is insufficient evidence to date the amendments as definitely belonging to the later layers (L_3–L_5), but in the overwhelming majority of instances no difficulties of this kind arise.

A number of amendments in which the evidence for dating is incomplete and which lay increased emphasis on the heroine's moral courage, during the period before and after the seduction, may be treated first. In the first example, which forms part of the account of the drive from Marlott to Trantridge in the villain's dog-cart, we see a new determination, on her part, to conceal her fear, which replaces an earlier authorial observation that 'she was so terrified that she clutched Hawnferne's rein-arm':

>   *Rose-Mary's* Tess's   *very skin, & her*
> The wind blew through Sue's   white muslin to her ~~skin, &~~ ₍
> *washed hair flew out behind. She was determined to show no open fear, but*
> ₍ ~~she was so terrified that~~
>   ~~Turberville's~~ *D'Urberville's*
> she clutched ~~Hawnferne's~~ rein-arm.   (f. 65)

A little later, on the same leaf, when the dog-cart reaches the bottom of the hill, the heroine originally does nothing but sigh and exclaim, 'Safe thank God'; but this reading is replaced by the words '"Safe thank God in spite of your folly!" said she, her face on fire.' This new capacity for anger is then immediately stressed by an L_3 marginal comment: '"Tess—fie! That's temper!" said Turberville.' After the seduction, during the harvesting near Marlott, she is originally described as unbuttoning her frock to suckle her child, 'with a curious, stealthy movement, and rising of colour' (L_1). In the amended text we read that she performs this action 'with a curious, stealthy, *yet courageous* movement, and rising of colour' (f. 123).

In another series of amendments to which no precise date can be given the heroine's womanly warmth and education are stressed, in place of mere nervousness and intelligence:

>   *deeper-passioned Tess*
> The ~~highly strung, excited Rose-Mary~~ was very far from sleeping
> *even then*
> ~~for hours~~. This conversation was another of the bitter pills she had

been obliged to swallow that day. Scarce the least feeling of jealousy
arose in her breast. For that matter she knew herself to have the
———— *better read* *educated, more*
preference. Being more finely formed, ∧ & more intelligent ∧
woman, *perceived*
than either, she was aware that only the slightest ordinary care
was necessary for holding her own in Angel Clare's heart against these
her ————
∧ simple ∧ friends. But the grave question was, ought she to do this? (f. 195)

The most significant single development in the characterization
of the heroine during the later manuscript layers is the new emphasis given to her d'Urberville ancestry, which has already been
discussed in detail in the preceding chapter. Taken in conjunction
with the new implications of the blood-red imagery, her d'Urberville ancestry imparts to her a new personal dignity, as well as a
predetermined tendency towards violence in moments of extreme
mental stress. It is also shown to be partly responsible for her
habitual docility of temperament, which causes Angel, in his hour
of bitterness, to label her 'the seedling of an effete aristocracy'
(f. 332), even though part of the reason for her passivity and lack
of determination is to be found in the dominance exerted over her
by Nature.

During the later manuscript layers most of the developments in
the characterization of the heroine have symbolic, as well as realistic, implications. Thus, in the rewritten second chapter of the
novel (L3), the description of the May-time 'club-walking' imparts
to the heroine a youthful freshness and virginal innocence, which
contrast ironically with the cycle of seed-time, harvest, and death
symbolized by the ritual itself. In the later part of the plot, Tess
comes to be identified as 'the victim', and suffers injustice at the
hands of an indifferent Cosmos and an encroaching Industrial
System, the latter represented especially by Alec and the threshing machine. Here, additional symbols used to emphasize her role
as victim include the bough of mistletoe, the rat-hunt, snares and
nests, blood, altars, the disembodied soul, and entombment.[9]

The heroine's modesty also receives increased emphasis in the
later manuscript layers. Thus, in an L2 original reading, when Angel

[9] See pp. 89-103, 106-9 above.

clasps her unexpectedly in his arms, we read that 'she panted in her impressionability and burst into a succession of ecstatic sobs'; but this is amended in the manuscript to 'she sank upon him in her momentary joy, with something very like an ecstatic cry' (f. 214). Elsewhere in L2, Angel's memory of her, originally, is of 'so quivering, passionate a creature'; but this, also, is later amended in the manuscript to 'so fervid and so passionate as she was under her reserve' (f. 219), while in the *Graphic* and First Edition it was to be further amended to the even more modest 'so fervid and so impressionable as she was under her reserve' (G. 274). Other amendments of L2 passages motivated by a similar desire to emphasize the heroine's modesty include the substitution of 'sedate enquiry' for 'arch enquiry' to describe her expression as she speaks to Angel about his ranging of the cows for her (f. 172), the insertion of the word 'blushing' on the same leaf, and the insertion of the phrase 'her cheeks on fire' in the scene in which the heroine, after listening in the garden to Angel's playing the harp, tries to move away without being seen:

Tess, her cheeks on fire,
~~Rose-Mary~~ ∧   moved away, furtively, as if hardly moving at all.   (f. 174)

As will be seen in Part Four, modesty continues to be the subject of further amendments in the First Edition.

The Ur-heroine is not only less modest than the heroine of the later layers; she is also less scrupulous in matters of sexual morality, and this aspect of her nature is apparent in the next two passages, the former of which presents her mother's opinion on the matter and the latter her own. In the first, which constitutes an amendment belonging to the Ur-text, the mother asks her daughter, who has just returned home from her disastrous sojourn at 'The Slopes', 'And how do you get on with the gentleman? I suppose he's your open lover by this time' (f. 110). Although the reading was once again amended in the manuscript from 'suppose' to 'hear', the significant point is that Hardy at one stage is showing that the mother could 'suppose' such a thing about her daughter, a supposition which suggests a vastly different moral attitude on the part of the Ur-heroine from the one we tend to associate with the heroine of the definitive version. (Both 'suppose' and 'hear' disappear from the text in the First Edition, which makes use of the expurgated serial text of the *Graphic* at this point in the story.) The second illustration occurs in an **L2** passage in which the heroine is shown to be contemplating the possibility of entering into an illicit relationship ('another kind of union') with Angel:

>   ~~poor~~ *Tess might even*
> As a path out of her trying strait ~~she would possibly~~ have accepted
>   *purely*   *beloved*
> another kind of union with him, ∧ for his ~~own~~ ∧ sake, had he urged it
> upon her; that he might have retreated if discontented with her on
> learning her story. To be a cloud in his life was so cruel to him that
> *own standing seemed*   *and*
> her ∧ ~~career was not~~ unimportant beside it; ~~& yet~~ she could not master
> herself sufficiently to give him up altogether.   (f. 253)

Although this passage illustrates the strength of her passion and devotion, it also exhibits a strain that we recognize as alien to the scrupulous purity of her love as portrayed in the definitive text of the novel. Like the previous example, it strongly conflicts with the concept of Tess as 'a pure woman' which Hardy was to emphasize in the sub-title of the First Edition; and it is therefore not surprising to find that the whole passage was cancelled in the manuscript, probably at the **L3** stage.

To reinforce the effect of such cancellations, the later manuscript layers contain passages in which positive tributes are paid to the heroine's essential purity by other characters. In the following **L5** extract it is Alec, in his new role of evangelical preacher, who is speaking:

>   *arranged to preach*
> 'I have ∧ & I shall not be there—by reason of my burning desire
> to see a woman whom I once despised!—No, by my word & truth, I
> never despised you: if I had I should not love you now. Why I did
>   *purity*
> not despise you was on account of your intrinsic ~~chastity~~ in spite
> of all: you withdrew yourself from me so quickly & resolutely
> _____
>   ∧   —you did not remain at my pleasure; so that there was
> one victim in the world for whom I had no contempt; & you are she...'   (f. 463)

The words, 'intrinsic purity', epitomize this aspect of Tess's moral nature as it is presented in the completed manuscript version. However, Hardy was still not completely satisfied at this stage that he had emphasized her scrupulosity enough and the First Edition contains additional examples of amendments devoted to the subject.

Finally, it must be noted that the later layers place great emphasis on the heroine's resourcefulness and loyalty. Her loyalty, however, does not always receive the moral approval of the modern reader, who feels himself obliged to agree, at times, with Evelyn Hardy's assessment that there exists in Tess 'a strain likely to bring about her downfall, no matter what circumstances attend her—the tendency towards martyrdom and self-sacrifice which Hardy has touched on in his feminine characters in previous novels'.[10] This is the only conclusion that can be reasonably drawn from a number of L5 passages in which the feeling that she has betrayed Angel results in the desire for punishment or death. It is this feeling that leads her to beg Alec to 'punish' her, after she has struck him for his reminder that he, and not Angel, was her first lover:

> 'Now punish me!' she said, turning up her eyes to him with the hopeless defiance of the sparrow's gaze before its captor twists its neck. 'Whip me, crush me; you need not mind those people under the rick. I shall not cry out. Once victim, always victim; that's the law.'   (ff. 475–6)

It is this same feeling of guilt that has earlier led her to suggest, during the unhappy walk with Angel on their wedding-night, that she should take her own life:

> During the interval of the cottager's ~~coming~~ going & coming she had said to her husband, 'I don't see how I can help being the cause of much misery to you all your life. ~~& as~~ The river is down there: I can put an end to myself in it. I am not afraid.'
> 'I don't wish to add murder to my other follies,' he said.
> 'I will leave something to show that I did it myself—on account of my shame. They will not blame you then.'   (f. 333)

And at Stonehenge, just before she is arrested for having murdered Alec, she murmurs to Angel that she 'likes very much' to be lying on the altar of sacrifice (f. 559).

Whether or not Hardy ever became aware of the conflict he had introduced into the novel between his conscious role as 'Tess's apologist' and his intuitive recognition of the morbidity that underlies her self-sacrifice is not easy to determine; but without doubt Virginia Woolf was correct when she grouped Hardy with Dickens

---

[10] *Thomas Hardy: A Critical Biography*, London, 1954, p. 231.

and Scott as one of those writers who, unlike Henry James and Flaubert, was 'unconscious of many things' in his work. And she went on to observe: 'It is as if Hardy himself were not quite aware of what he did, as if his consciousness held more than he could produce, and he left it for his readers to make out his full meaning and to supplement it from their own experience.[11] Such *uncon*sciousness of what 'his consciousness held' is constantly confirmed in Hardy's writing: its operation in regard to Tess's self-martyring instinct, far from weakening the novel, adds depth and complexity to the character-study.

II

Angel Clare, although an interesting portrait of a well-intentioned but complicated young man of the times, is not a fully successful character-study, and thus cannot be ranked, artistically, on the same level as Hardy's two major male creations, Michael Henchard and Jude Fawley. Genealogically, Angel is descended from earlier ineffectual Hardy heroes such as Henry Knight of *A Pair of Blue Eyes* and Giles Winterbourne of *The Woodlanders*, whose distinctive characteristics reveal themselves in the tendency to idealize the women they love and to avoid, through timidity or scrupulosity, taking those courses of action which alone could lead to the physical consummation of their love. This is one of the reasons why Angel Clare sometimes seems unconvincing to the modern reader. But over and above such generic weaknesses, Angel's deficiencies as a character-study arise from problems which are endemic to *Tess* alone, problems which, although they may be paralleled in other Hardy novels such as *The Return of the Native*,[12] spring specifically from difficulties experienced by Hardy at the time of the original conception, and later development, of this particular character in

---

[11] 'The Novels of Thomas Hardy', *The Common Reader* (Second Series), London, 1932, pp. 247-8.

[12] Thus, John Paterson has pointed out that in *The Return of the Native*, 'The image of Diggory Venn represents a complex, then, of three clearly irreconcileable elements: the yokel, the reddleman, and the ordinary citizen', and that 'Clym's failure as a character may be said to originate, then, in Hardy's reluctance to articulate the pessimistic conclusions which the image of the character plainly justified' (Paterson, pp. 49, 66).

this particular book. A study of the Ur-text shows that uncertainties were present in Hardy's mind from the very beginning; and the later manuscript layers and the printed texts show that as the author's commitment to his heroine grew stronger his difficulties with the character of Angel Clare increased, leading to serious anomalies and inconsistencies.

It is not suggested that all the anomalies and inconsistencies present in the definitive character-study of Angel Clare fall into the category of faults, or that they are all explainable in terms of uncertainties, or other difficulties, experienced by the author during the process of composition. Indeed, some are eminently successful illustrations of the complexity of human nature, itself, and the truth of this statement is seen nowhere more clearly than in Angel's employment of a double set of standards in judging the sexual behaviour of the heroine and himself. This was observed by the journalist, Raymond Blathwayt, as early as 1892 in his published interview with Hardy as the author of *Tess*: '. . . you depict that very odious young gentleman, Angel Clare, casting off his wife for an offence of ignorance, and yet the very next week proposing to elope with her friend. I grant you that you are true to human nature.' Hardy, himself, in the same interview went on to draw attention to another fully acceptable inconsistency in Angel when he added that Angel 'always professed to despise ancient lineage, and yet as a matter of fact he was delighted that Tess was a D'Urber-ville'.[13]

The areas of temperament, motivation, and opinion in which the *un*acceptable inconsistencies reveal themselves involve a considera-tion of the two following questions. What are the true proportions, in Angel's love for the heroine, of sensual passion, chivalry, self-control, idealism, and purity of mind? And, less important, what is the true relationship between Angel's serious and logical approach to life and the whims and recklessness he displays on occasions?

An indication of Hardy's uncertainty concerning the degree of seriousness attributable to Angel is seen in one of the earliest manu-

[13] *Black and White*, 27 Aug. 1892. Quoted by Laurence Lerner and John Holmstrom in *Thomas Hardy and his Readers*, London, 1968, pp. 95–6.

script references to him, in which Angel comments on the story of William Dewy and the bull. As the following extract will show, Angel's originally serious attitude to the dairyman's tale is expressed by the word 'reflectively'. But then his attitude is temporarily seen as frivolous, as witnessed by 'Ha-ha!' and 'laughingly'. Finally, seriousness returns, with the restitution of 'reflectively' and the introduction of the comment beginning 'It's a curious story':

> ~~Ha-ha! As good as~~   *It's*
> '₍ₐ₎   ~~Quite an Orpheus!' story!'~~ ⟨¶ ₍ₐ₎ *A curious story. It carries
> us back to ~~the~~ mediæval times, when faith was a living thing.*⟩ The
>   *laughingly*
> remark was murmured ~~reflectively~~ by the voice behind the dun cow; but
>   *bearing of the words*
> as nobody understood ~~its~~ the ~~reference~~   no notice was taken, except
>   *they it*
> that the narrator seemed to think ~~it~~ ₍ₐ₎ might imply scepticism as to his
> tale.
>   (f. 156)

A few leaves later, the same uncertainty about the degree of serious-ness recurs, when Angel's mouth is at first described as 'somewhat too delicately cut for a man's, though with a sufficiently humorous turn now and then,' and later as 'somewhat too small and delicately lined for a man's, though with an unexpectedly firm close of the lower lip now and then' (f. 160).

Uncertainty about the exact nature and strength of Angel's sexual feelings pervades the following passage, as it appears in the manuscript and two of the printed versions. In the manuscript the original L2 reading attributes Angel's restraint to 'purity of mind' and 'slight coldness of nature'. The insertion of 'perhaps' before the latter phrase marks the beginning of the change which culminates in the cancellation of the phrase, and its replacement by 'chivalrous sense of duty':

>   *Tess*   *realize*
> ~~Rose-Mary~~ ₍ₐ₎ was woman enough to ~~know~~ from their avowals to herself
>   *Angel*   *Some*
> that ₍ₐ₎ Clare had the honour of all the dairymaids in his keeping. ~~Many~~
> ~~of those simple hearts might have gone weeping on her pilgrimage, as~~
> ~~she herself had done, had he chosen to abuse his position among them;~~
>   *& Tess's*
> ~~& Rose-Mary's~~ perception of his care to avoid compromising the happiness
> of either in the least degree, bred a tender respect in her for the purity

K

perhaps & *chivalrous sense of duty shown by Angel Clare, qualities*
of mind & ∧ slight coldness of nature ∧
which she had never expected to find in one of the opposite sex.   (ff. 199-200)

In the First Edition version, both 'purity of mind' and 'chivalrous sense of duty' disappear, and the words 'what she deemed the self-controlling sense of duty' take their place:

Tess was woman enough to realize from their avowals to herself that Angel Clare had the honour of all the dairymaids in his keeping, and her perception of his care to avoid compromising the happiness of either in the least degree bred a tender respect in Tess for *what she deemed the self-controlling sense of duty* shown by him, a quality which she had never expected to find in one of the opposite sex . . .   (II. 18-19)

In the 1892 edition a further insertion appears, in the form of the modifying phrase 'rightly or wrongly', with the result that the definitive reading becomes '. . . what she deemed, *rightly or wrongly*, the self-controlling sense of duty . . .' (X. 181).

In the original readings during the courtship section of the story the reader frequently finds passages in which there is strong confirmation that Angel's nature is by no means cold. One such passage is the following, in which Angel clasps the heroine in his arms and expresses his love for her. As will be seen, the original account employs the words 'He had been on the point of violently kissing that mouth of hers' and includes the hero's words 'I—am passionately devoted to you':

                            too ~~*intoxicating*~~ *tempting*
He had been on the point of ~~violently~~ kissing that ∧ mouth of
                even for tender
hers, but he checked himself, ∧ ~~for~~ conscience sake. 'Forgive me,
Tess dear   *whispered*
~~Rose-Mary,~~' he ~~stammered~~. 'I ought to have asked. I—did not know what I was doing. I do not mean it as a liberty at all—I—am
                  Tessie
~~passionately~~ devoted to you, ~~Rosie~~, dearest, with all my soul.'   (f. 214)

What emerges clearly when the manuscript amendments in the above extract are studied is the fact that Hardy has damped down the passion by the cancellation of 'violently' and 'passionately'; and similar illustrations of the same tendency are to be found on numerous other occasions, for example on f. 221, where Angel's feelings, originally described as 'a sensuous passion for her form', become 'a sensuous joy in her form', and on f. 257, where the original reading, 'pressing her chin upward to him with his hand', is deleted. After the heroine's wedding-night confession, the trend continues to be apparent, as in the passage in which the heroine inclines her mouth towards her husband as he is leaving the Wellbridge farm-house after breakfast. Here, the original reading 'Don't tempt me!' is replaced by the non-committal 'I shall be home punctually' (f. 345).

The extent of the confusion in Hardy's mind on the proportions of the non-passionate elements of chivalry, spirituality, self-control, purity of mind, solicitude, and fastidiousness present in Angel's love is clearly seen in the following passage, as it appears first in the manuscript, and later in the First Edition and the edition of 1892. In the manuscript (as in the editions) Hardy specifically mentions that Angel is 'not cold-natured'; but the remainder of the passage is devoted mainly to matters other than the passionate element. What is especially interesting is the fact that at the opening and close of the manuscript version the emphasis falls on the chivalrous and protective elements, while during the intervening section it fluctuates uneasily over a number of other qualities, as is seen in such expressions as 'rather [altered to 'more'] spiritual than animal', 'he had himself well in hand', and 'he could love intensely [altered to 'desperately']':

She had not known that men could be so disinterested, chivalrous, protective, in their love for woman as he. ~~was.~~ Angel Clare was ~~indeed~~
           in truth more
not ~~perhaps~~ all that she thought him in this respect; but he was ∧ ~~rather~~
          and he was singularly free from
spiritual than animal; he had himself well in hand, ∧
grossness.   *bright*   *less Byronic*
∧ Though not cold-natured he was rather ~~beaming~~ than hot; ∧
than Shelleyan.   *desperately*
∧   He ~~cold~~ could love ~~intensely~~; but his love ~~was~~ more
 especially inclined to
~~specifically of~~ ∧ the solicitous & cherishing mood: it was ~~with him~~
        one
an emotion which could jealously guard the loved ~~object~~ against his very self.
             (ff. 276-7)

The First Edition version goes on to substitute for 'solicitous and cherishing mood' the expression 'imaginative and ethereal' (II. 128), thereby throwing more stress on to the 'Shelleyan' concept of the manuscript insertion; while the 1892 edition introduces into the text the word 'fastidious', to describe the 'emotion which could jealously guard the loved one against his very self' (X. 252).

It is also in the 1892 edition that Hardy introduces the amendment which emphasizes the inadequacy of the sensual side of Angel's nature and passes an adverse judgement on the matter. In the manuscript version of the passage in question, which comes after Angel's rejection of his bride, the note of criticism is heard, but only in muted form:

It was the third day of the estrangement. Clare ∧ was ————
even to defectiveness, his love was ethereal to a fault, imaginative
to impracticability. With these natures corporeal presence is
sometimes
well-nigh less appealing than corporeal absence, the latter creating
an ideal presence that conveniently drops the defects of the real. She
found that her personality did not plead her cause so forcibly as she
had anticipated.   (f. 349)

Certainly in the manuscript Hardy would seem to be implying that much of the responsibility for the continuing estrangement must be attributed to Angel's deficiency in animal spirits. But it is not until the 1892 version that this criticism is driven home in a blunt and outspoken fashion:

It was the third day of the estrangement. *Some might risk the odd paradox that with more animalism he would have been the nobler man. We do not say it.* Yet Clare's love was *doubtless* ethereal to a fault, imaginative to impracticability. With these natures . . .   (X. 316)

It is true that even in the 1892 version Hardy technically limits his authorial responsibility for the judgement by including the words 'We do not say it'; but there can be little doubt in the mind of the modern reader that the sentiment bears the author's stamp of approval. As a result, he may be forgiven if he ponders over the inconsistency between this judgement and such expressions remaining in the definitive version as 'Though not cold-natured' (f. 276) or even 'what she deemed, rightly or wrongly, the self-controlling sense of duty' (X. 181). The student familiar with the manuscript may also be forgiven if he remembers that the phrase

'slight coldness of nature' had once appeared as an L2 reading on
f. 200, although later replaced by 'chivalrous sense of duty'. Thus,
this wheel has turned full circle.

Lastly, it may be noted that the comments on the whims and
impetuosity of Angel Clare belong mainly to manuscript insertions,
and would seem to have been included to explain how a serious
and philosophic young man of good family might woo and marry
a milkmaid. As has earlier been noted in this section, Hardy
rejected the temptation to humanize Angel by bestowing on him
a sense of humour; however, evidence of his impulsiveness was
required and this was provided by a series of insertions such as
occurs in the following extract:

> *Tess, at last' said he with*
> 'Well—I have betrayed my feelings, ~~Rose-Mary~~ ∧
> *curious*
> a ∧ *sigh of desperation, signifying unconsciously that his heart had*
> *outrun his judgment. 'That*
> ∧   ~~& that~~ ∧ I love you dearly & truly I need not say.
> *it distresses you—*
> But I—it shall go no further now— ∧   I am as surprised as
> you are. You will not think I have presumed upon your defencelessness—
> been too quick & unreflecting, will you?'   (f. 215)

His romantic interest in ancient families and especially in the
heroine's d'Urberville ancestry provides scope for further illustrations of this same quality:

> *~~was~~ She found him*
> ~~He had~~ ∧   determined to spend a short time at the
> Wellbridge flour mills; & what had determined him? Less the
> opportunity of an insight into grinding & bolting than the
> casual fact that lodgings were to be obtained in that very farm-
> house which, before its mutilation, had been the mansion of a
> branch of the D'Urberville family. This was always how Clare
> decided practical questions; by a sentiment which had nothing
> to do with them.   (f. 293ᵛ)

Here, the whole of the above passage appears as an L4 insertion
on the verso of the L2 leaf, f. 293.

Despite the inconsistencies of temperament which have been dwelt
on, Angel Clare is a more convincing character than the other

young man in the heroine's life, Alec d'Urberville. Alec is basically
a melodramatic figure who displays 'satanic' qualities, much in the
way that Aeneas Manston of *Desperate Remedies* and William Dare
of *A Laodicean* do. But in Alec's case, the melodramatic effect is
alleviated to some extent by the fact that his role has considerable
symbolic significance; for Alec represents the forces of moneyed
wealth and industrial progress which threaten the traditional agricultural way of life still being pursued—however precariously—by
Tess and her parents. This side of his role is seldom obscured for
long in the definitive version of the novel, and is especially strong
in certain scenes, such as the heroine's first visit to 'The Slopes' to
claim kin, the threshing of the last rick at Flintcomb-Ash, and the
meeting in the d'Urberville church at Kingsbere.

The symbolic aspects of Alec's role are not present in the Ur-text,
where the villain, who is there named Hawnferne, is a purely conventional stage-villain of Victorian melodrama. In the Ur-text
'Hawnferne' catches his first glimpse of the innocent heroine at a
country dance, calls to see her mother on the same day (presumably
to offer the girl employment at his home), and wins over the foolish
mother, who although she foresees the inevitable consequences of
his interest in her daughter deludes herself into imagining that he
will eventually offer marriage:

> ~~Troublefield~~ *Durbeyfield,' said she,*
> 'I'll tell 'ee what 'tis, ~~Woodrow~~ ⌃
> *exultingly,* '   *love* ˎ
>   he'll never have the heart not to ~~marry~~ her⌊. ~~she said~~
>   *to Tess*
> ~~exultingly.~~ 'But whatever you do, don't say too much ⌃ of his fancy for
>   *got*
> her, & this chance she has ⌃ . She is such an odd maid that it mid set her
> against him, or against going there, even now. . . .'   (f. 59)

The heroine, herself, does not foresee or desire any such outcome;
but because she feels responsible for the death of the family horse, she
reluctantly accepts the villain's offer of employment—'to get enough
money for a new horse', as her mother explains 'pacifically' (f. 60).

'Hawnferne' possesses many of the unpleasant qualities present
in the definitive portrait of Alec. During the reckless drive from
Marlott to Trantridge, he displays the same hard, aggressive streak,

while his dissolute conduct, as evidenced in the Chase, becomes so well known in the district that Angel refers to him in passing as 'a young rake-hell' (f. 245)—a reading that was later altered (in the 1912 edition) to 'a lax young cynic'. And yet, like Alec, 'Hawnferne' is not heartless: for on the occasion when the heroine insists on walking the remaining three or four miles of the journey to Trantridge, after escaping through a ruse from his speeding dog-cart, he displays a genuine, if 'fierce distress at the sense of what he had driven her to do' (f. 68); and a few weeks after the seduction when she is walking back along the road to Marlott he shows concern for her plight and expresses the wish to take care of her if she should need help (ff. 104–5). However, his generosity, like Alec's, is seldom divorced from self-interest, and he emerges throughout the Ur-text as a clever schemer, who cunningly arouses in the heroine's mind at certain critical moments a sense of gratitude and obligation.

The development of Alec's symbolic role from L3 onwards became possible only with the development of the d'Urberville motif, which permitted the introduction into the plot of the concept of a mistaken notion of kinship, based on similarity of names. It was this mistake which led Joan Durbeyfield to conceive the plan of sending her daughter to claim kin, which in turn brought about the first meeting between Tess and Alec in the L3 version of the plot:

'I've been thinking, since you brought the news, that there's a
    rich lady   *The*
great ~~gentleman~~ out by Trantridge, on the edge o' ~~Cranborne~~ Chase, of
                    D'Urberville.'
the name of ~~Turberville~~ ‸
    'Hey—what's that?' said Sir John.
                            ~~She~~ *That lady must be our relation,*'
    She repeated the information ' ‸
she said; 'and
    ‸   My project is to send Tess to claim kin.' ~~she said.~~
        a lady   a woman of the name,
    'There *is* ‸ ~~such a~~ ‸ ~~man~~ ‸   now you mention it,' said
Durbeyfield   'Pa'son Tringham didn't think of that. . . .'
~~Troublefield.~~ ‸
                                                                    (f. 27)

The d'Urberville motif also permitted Hardy to show how Alec's father had stolen from Tess's father the ancient family name; for (as has earlier been noted) it is an L3 leaf (f. 44) which describes the action whereby Alec's father, originally described as a 'stock-broker' (later amended to 'merchant') named 'Smith' (later amended to 'Stoke'), 'annexed' to 'himself and his heirs' the name 'Turberville' (later amended to 'D'Urberville'). Such an occurrence would not have been appropriate in the Ur-version of the novel, for in an L2 speech by Angel Clare the cancelled reading clearly shows that the villain's parentage was originally conceived as 'yeoman', while even the final amendment merely mentions that the villain is 'son of some landowner . . .':

'. . . a young rake-hell he met ~~with~~ somewhere about there—son of
                    business   *have*
some ~~well-to-do yeoman people who retired from~~ had retired & taken to
~~farming. I imagine that when the young man comes into the property he~~
                              landowner up that way, who has an afflicted
~~will soon make ducks & drakes of it.~~ ʌ . . .'
mother.

ʌ   (f. 245)

The First Edition insertion of the scenes at Kingsbere church (where Tess's noble ancestors lie buried) shows Hardy successfully continuing to build up the symbolic elements in the portrayal of Alec even after the manuscript stage of composition, so that there is a certain propriety in Alec's exultant words during this episode: '. . . The little finger of the sham D'Urberville can do more for you than the whole dynasty of the real underneath' (III. 207).

But many of the non-symbolic incidents relating to Alec written after the Ur-text period are not successful, for all too often melodrama and improbability intrude, as they had done in the Ur-novel. Thus, the motivation for Alec's unexpected reappearance in the story as an evangelical preacher is inadequate, while the description and dialogue during some of these later scenes are at times utterly unbelievable. No other verdict is possible on the following passage, which relates to the time when Alec is declaring his apostasy from religion and his revival of passion for Tess:

                              deliverance   till I saw you
'Tess, Tess.' I was on the way to ~~salvation,' he said~~ ʌ
again,' he ~~muttered~~ *said,*
        ʌ   shaking her as if she were a child, ~~the red of~~

temper & mood showing warm in him. 'And why then have you tempted me?
I was firm as a man could be till I saw that mouth again—surely there
never was such a maddening mouth since ~~God made~~ Eve's.' His voice sank
      purr
to a tigerish ~~fondness~~ & a hot archness shot from his black eyes. 'You
temptress, Tess; you dear witch ~~of Babylon~~— I could not resist you as soon
as I met you again!'   (ff. 463-4)

Although the First Edition version eliminates a few of the faults of
this passage, such as 'to a tigerish purr' and 'temper and mood
showing warm in him', most are retained in virtually their original
form—notably 'there never was such a maddening mouth since
Eve's', 'a hot archness shot from his own black eyes', and 'You
temptress, Tess; you dear witch of Babylon' (III. 122-3). These
unfortunate readings continue to appear, virtually unchanged, in
chapter 46 of the definitive version.

In chapters 45 and 46 of the 1902 Macmillan's Uniform Edition,
Hardy attempted to prepare his readers to accept Alec's apostasy
more readily by introducing a number of amendments designed
to reduce this character's religiosity during the later stages of his
career as a preacher. Thus, instead of the words 'the whole blackness of the sin, the awful, awful iniquity' (Y. 408) Alec employs,
in his conversation with Tess, the words 'the whole *unconventional
business of our time at Trantridge*' (Z. 408); and later, instead of
'I have broken my engagement to preach to those poor drunken
sinners at the fair' (Y. 418), he tells the heroine 'I have broken my
engagement to preach to those poor drunken *boobies* at the fair'
(Z. 418). Towards the end of chapter 46 Hardy went on to add
the comments that Alec's conversion to Christianity had been
'whimsical' and that it had been 'perhaps the mere freak of a careless man in search of a new sensation, and temporarily impressed
by his mother's death' (Z. 419). But although these amendments
of 1902 helped to prepare the reader for Alec's reappearance in
the next chapter, in his old role as Tess's admirer and tempter,
they failed to erase the general impression of unreality left by him
during the part of the story connected with his religious phase.

The only other characters whose development requires comment
are the heroine's parents, John and Joan Durbeyfield, the former

of whom tends to be denigrated by Hardy and the latter partially exonerated during the later manuscript layers.

The father's role in the Ur-version was probably of little importance, and the Ur-text references to him, under the name of Woodrow or Troublefield, are usually devoted to his drunkenness and misguided sense of family pride, as in the following L1 passage (omitted from the novel at the *Graphic* stage):

> *honour*
> It did not tarnish his ~~ancestral coat~~
>
> *line which reproduced*
> to sit at an inn from noon to night, & come home in a zigzag ⋏
> *that ~~in the map~~   voyage*
> ~~line like that~~ of St. Paul's ~~course~~ to Rome. As drunk as a lord
>   *comparison*
> was a ~~proverb~~ which he, for one, respected. But the snaring of his eldest
> daughter, though he had taken no trouble to safeguard her, and had taken
>   *the event*
> no trouble since ⋏ to lessen her strait, made him smart whenever he thought
>   *if not*
> of it—which, ~~though not~~ ⋏ always, was often, to do him justice. It was
> not the fact, however, but gossip about the fact which mortified him.   (f. 127)

As part of the revision that followed November 1889, Hardy wrote a completely new opening to his novel, which is contained on ff. 1–20 of the manuscript. Of the seventeen extant leaves belonging to this section—all of which belong to L3—seven contain scenes in which Durbeyfield is present and three contain references to him. In the next extant group of L3 leaves (ff. 26–30) Durbeyfield once again figures prominently. From this and similar evidence it becomes clear that one of the intentions of the revision was to focus attention on Durbeyfield. But from the evidence presented by the amendments (on these, and other, leaves) it also becomes clear that an equally important intention developed shortly afterwards—to present John Durbeyfield as an illustration of the more decadent aspects of the heredity and mutability themes of the novel. For while the portrayal that emerges from the *original* L3 readings on all these leaves is concerned, for the most part, with his reaction of foolish pride to Parson Tringham's revelation of his noble ancestry, the *amendments* give attention to his moral and physical, as distinct from his social, decline.

The element of denigration in these amendments is apparent in the very first paragraph of the B.M. MS.:

> *walking*
> On an evening in the latter part of May a middle-aged man was ~~riding~~
> *ward* *town*
> home ʌ from Stourcastle ~~market~~ by a lane which led into the recesses of the
> *or Blackmoor. The pair of legs*
> neighbouring Vale of Blakemore ʌ ~~He The animal~~ that carried him
> *were rickety, and there was a bias in his —— gait that inclined him*
> ~~was a feeble old white pony whose neck protruded from his shoulders like~~
> ⌐*to the left of a straight line* *somewhat*⌐. *He occasionally gave a smart*
> ~~the arm of a gallows; an empty butter-basket was strapped up under his arm,~~
> *nod, as if in confirmation of ~~the~~ some opinion; ~~yet he~~ though he was not*
> *that showed— ——*
> ~~& speckled worsted stockings~~ ʌ ~~covered~~ ʌ ~~the small of his legs~~
> *in particular.*
> *thinking ~~over~~ of anything* ʌ *An empty egg-basket was slung upon his arm,*
> ~~where exposed by the rucking ——.~~
> ~~Presently and~~ *the nap of his hat was ruffled, ⟨and a patch worn away at the*
> ʌ
> *brim where he seized it to take it off.⟩*
> ʌ
> (f. 1)

As may be observed, the original reading in the above extract describes Durbeyfield as 'riding' on 'a feeble old white pony', whose neck is compared to 'the arm of a gallows'. It then continues: 'an empty butter-basket was strapped up under his arm, and speckled worsted stockings covered the small of his legs where exposed by the rucking ——'. This version needs to be compared carefully with the amended version, in which the emphasis falls on quite different matters—Durbeyfield's inebriated state, his lack of dignity, and his customary servility towards his social superiors. The evidence that the process was one of denigration is clearly seen in the expressions, 'there was a bias in his gait', 'He occasionally gave a smart nod, as if in confirmation of some opinion; though he was not thinking of anything in particular', and 'the nap of his hat was ruffled, and a patch worn away at the brim where he seized it to take it off'.

On the next leaf, Parson Tringham asks Durbeyfield to look upwards, so that he may study his profile. In the original reading he goes on to exclaim 'Yes, that's the Turberville nose and chin';

however, in the amended manuscript version Tringham adds the comment 'a little debased':

Throw up your chin
        '. . . ~~Look up at the sky~~ a moment, so that I may catch the profile
                                    D'Urberville   —*a little debased.*
of your face better. Yes, that's the ~~Turberville~~ nose & chin ∧ . . .'   (f. 2)

Similarly, when Durbeyfield invites Tringham to go with him to 'The Pure Drop' Inn the original reading merely states 'and have a drop of beer'; but in the amended manuscript reading Durbeyfield's intemperance is accentuated by the change to 'and have a quart of beer wi' me':

                            quart   wi' me
    'But you'll turn back & have a ~~drop~~ of beer ∧ on the strength o't,
Pa'son Tringham? There's a very pretty —— brew in tap at "The Pure Drop"—though, to be sure, not so good as at Rolliver's.'
                            ~~Troublefield~~ Durbeyfield
    'No thank you—not this evening ∧ .   You've had enough already.'
Concluding thus   with doubts ~~in~~ as to his ~~own~~ discretion,
~~And~~ ∧   the parson ∧   rode on his way.   (ff. 4–5)

The parson's final 'doubts as to his discretion' is also a significant textual addition.

During the scenes at Rolliver's Inn, there may be found further illustrations of the denigration of Durbeyfield. One such illustration is the L3 passage in which his wife originally states, 'If you say she ought to go, she will go. If not she will refuse', whereas in the amended version she exclaims 'But she's tractable at bottom. Leave her to me' (f. 28). But perhaps the most memorable of all such passages is one which has already been partly quoted in relation to the blood-red motif[14] and which shows the drunken John Durbeyfield telling Tess that he will sell Alec his 'title' for 'twenty pound' (f. 60ᵛ).

In the Ur-version the heroine's mother appears to have played a more important role than did the father, and the keynotes of her character in the Ur-text are the same as in the definitive portrait. There is the same tendency to escape from reality through daydreaming and self-delusion, the same willingness to accept misfortunes fatalistically, and the same insensitivity to her daughter's

[14] See p. 109 above.

moral scrupulosity. In the later manuscript layers, she is shown, at times, in a more favourable light, as in the changed motives that impel her to persuade her daughter to accept employment at 'The Slopes'. For in the L3 version she believes Alec to be Tess's kinsman, not a mere stranger, and her nature is portrayed as 'witless' rather than unscrupulous, as the following L3 passage shows:

'*He's struck*
'But do let her go, Jacky,' coaxed his poor witless wife. ʌ
wi' her—you can see that. He called her coz.
He'll marry her, most likely,
& make a lady of her; & then she'll be what her forefathers was.'   (f. 54)

Nevertheless, her earlier amorality continues to be apparent in later parts of the story, for example in the advice she offers to her daughter in the letter written before the wedding, which remains substantially the same in the final manuscript version, and in all later versions, of the novel as it is in its original L2 form on ff. 274-5.

PART FOUR

DEVELOPMENTS IN THE PRINTED VERSIONS

VIII

EARLIER PRINTED VERSIONS
(TO THE FIRST EDITION)

I

THE study of the developments in the printed versions of *Tess*
must begin with the *Graphic* serial version, and after taking brief
account of the two independent sketches—'Saturday Night in
Arcady' and 'The Midnight Baptism'—proceed to the editions of
1891, 1892, 1895, 1902, and 1912.

Collation of the *Graphic* text with the B.M. MS. and the First
Edition reveals that two main kinds of changes entered the transmitted text of the novel at the serial stage—temporary changes,
whose effect did not extend beyond the *Graphic* text, and permanent changes, which were transmitted unaltered into the First
Edition and usually into subsequent editions. The temporary
changes that will be considered below consist of those omissions
and modifications designed to remove for the time being any
manuscript material which Hardy foresaw would be, or which
later proved to be, offensive to the delicate sensibilities of the
editor of the *Graphic*. The permanent changes most warranting
attention are those motivated by literary considerations other than
mere style and intended to remain as improvements when the novel
should appear in volume form. There are also a number of 'hybrid
changes', changes intended to be temporary but exerting an influence on the text of the First Edition as the result of oversight or
change of mind on Hardy's part. The influence of such changes is
often subtle and unexpected.

Most of the temporary alterations almost certainly made their
first appearance in the special serial manuscript, to which reference
has earlier been made and which contained only about 518 leaves
(instead of the 565 or so leaves which made up the B.M. MS.).[1]

---

[1] See pp. 6, 23 above.

The failure of the serial manuscript to survive *per se* compels us to take most of our illustrations from the printed *Graphic* text, although some of the changes are to be found in the B.M. MS., where they are usually indicated in blue ink. In the *Graphic* the two most important temporary changes to come to light consist in the omission of two substantial sections of the original story, the first of which relates to material contained on ff. 76–99 of the manuscript and the second to material on ff. 117–33.

The first of these omitted sections deals with the events preceding the seduction of the heroine, and covers her whistling lessons in the apartment of the villain's mother, her journey to Chaseborough and attendance at the dance, her quarrel with the drunken women on the way back to Trantridge, her 'rescue' by the villain, and the events in the Chase. This section was later to constitute the last thirty lines of chapter 9 and the whole of chapters 10 and 11 of the First Edition. In the *Graphic*, instead of these incidents Hardy gave a brief bridging passage of nineteen lines. Placed immediately after the villain's words, 'If you meet with any difficulties and want help here, don't go to the bailiff, come to me', it ran as follows:

It was in the economy of this *régime* that Tess Durbeyfield had under-taken to fill a place. Her first day's experiences were fairly typical of those which followed through many succeeding days. A familiarity with Alec D'Urberville's presence—which that young man carefully culti-vated in her by playful dialogue, and by jestingly calling her his cousin when they were alone—removed most of her original shyness of him, without, however, implanting any feeling which could engender shyness of a new and tenderer kind. But she was more pliable under his hands than a mere companionship would have made her, owing to her inevitable dependence upon his mother, and, through her comparative helplessness, upon him.

But where was Tess's guardian-angel now? Perhaps, like the god of whom the ironical Tishbite spoke, he was talking, or he was pursuing, or he was on a journey; or peradventure he was sleeping, and was not to be awaked. Why things should have been thus, why they should so often be thus, many thousand years of analytical philosophy have failed to explain to our sense of order. As Tess's own people down in those retreats are never tired of saying to each other, in their fatalistic way, 'It was to be.' There lay the pity of it.   (G. 134)

The second of the omitted sections describes the events of the August day on which the heroine's child, Sorrow, dies, and her subsequent visit to the vicar to inquire about the efficacy of her ex-temporized baptism. This section was later to constitute chapter 14 of the First Edition. In the *Graphic* there was not even a reference to any of these events.

As a result of these two major excisions, the *Graphic* offered its readers a nonsensical story in which no seduction took place and no child was born to the heroine. It was thus necessary for Hardy to invent a different reason for the heroine's unexpected return home from 'The Slopes' and her later suffering, and in a completely unconvincing passage the serial heroine explained to her mother that she had been tricked into a sham marriage and on discovery of the truth had left the villain, to return to Marlott:

'Well!—my dear Tess!' exclaimed her surprised mother, jumping up and kissing the girl. 'How be ye? I didn't see you till you was in upon me! Have you come home to be married?'

'No, I have not come for that, mother.'

'Then for a holiday?'

'Yes—for a holiday; for a long holiday,' said Tess.

Her mother eyed her narrowly. 'Come, you have not told me all,' she said.

Then Tess told. 'He made love to me, as you said he would do; and he asked me to marry him, also just as you declared he would. I never have liked him; but at last I agreed, knowing you'd be angry if I didn't. He said it must be private, even from you, on account of his mother; and by special licence; and foolish I agreed to that likewise, to get rid of his pestering. I drove with him to Melchester, and there in a private room I went through the form of marriage with him as before a registrar. A few weeks after, I found out that it was not the registrar's house we had gone to, as I had supposed, but the house of a friend of his, who had played the part of the registrar. I then came away from Trantridge instantly, though he wished me to stay; and here I am.'

'But he can be prosecuted for this,' said Joan. (G. 136)

Other temporary changes found in the *Graphic* text include the omission of the heroine's encounter with the painter of texts (ff. 107–8) and of Angel's request to Izz Huett that she should accompany him to Brazil (f. 386), the modification of various oaths and curses, and the masking of the fact that Tess and Alec are living together in the same apartment at Sandbourne. The mask-ing in the last-mentioned episode is apparent in the blue-ink

manuscript amendments as well as in the *Graphic* text and is
achieved through the clumsy devices of altering 'you' to 'he' and
inserting the descriptive touch, 'and Tess crossed to another apartment' (G. 726).

There is also the ludicrous change which Hardy claims was
forced on him, almost at the last minute, by the editor of the
Graphic, Arthur Locker:

> As the year [1891] drew to a close an incident that took place during
> the publication of *Tess of the d'Urbervilles* as a serial in the *Graphic*
> might have prepared him for certain events that were to follow. The
> editor objected to the description of Angel Clare carrying in his arms,
> across a flooded lane, Tess and her three dairymaid companions. He
> suggested that it would be more decorous and suitable for the pages of
> a periodical intended for family reading if the damsels were wheeled
> across the lane in a wheel-barrow. This was accordingly done.[2]

The fact that the episode was bowdlerized, in the way described,
in the *Graphic* but not in *Harper's Bazar* lends credibility to
Hardy's account of events. But the absence of serial foliation on
the extant manuscript leaves (ff. 203-4) is puzzling, since they
bear S1 numbers and give what appears to be the version to which
Locker objected. Moreover, Hardy's statement that the events
occurred 'as the year drew to a close', together with the placing of
the entry after a previous entry in the *Early Life* dated 'the first
week in November', is obviously irreconcilable with the fact that
the relevant serial episode appeared in the *Graphic* on 29 August.

Three of the *Graphic* changes given above are 'hybrid changes'.
Thus, the nineteen-line bridging passage quoted above (G. 134)
was originally inserted to replace manuscript material omitted
from the serial version: however, when the omitted material was
replaced in the First Edition much of the bridging section was
retained. The First Edition also preferred, in place of the blunt
manuscript version of the conversation between heroine and mother
on the former's return to Marlott,[3] the more discreet *Graphic*
version (G. 136), to the point at which the words 'Then Tess told'
occur—despite the fact that the *Graphic* passage had been designed
for a special set of circumstances. Again, although the First Edition

---

[2] *Life*, p. 240.   [3] See p. 160 below for the MS. version.

restored the manuscript concept of Angel's carrying the milk-maids across the flooded lane in his arms, most of the diction employed was that of the *Graphic*, readapted to the original plot situation.

The two most important permanent amendments found in the *Graphic* text—the substitution of 'local Cerealia' for 'Vestal rite' (G. 11) and the introduction of the d'Urberville portraits (G. 422) —have already been discussed in chapter VI.[4] The only other amendments which require notice are three which concern minor aspects of characterization. In the first the age of the heroine is reduced from seventeen to sixteen (G. 390). The heroine is also the subject of an amendment which reinforces the new emphasis given in 'The Midnight Baptism' to the memorable quality of her voice (as noted in chapter VII).[5] In the *Graphic* this amendment takes the form of an insertion of the word 'fluty' in the following passage:

'I waited and waited for you!' she went on, her tones suddenly resuming their old *fluty* pathos. 'But you did not come, and I wrote to you, and you did not come. . . .'   (G. 726)

In the third amendment, the villain is made slightly more prepossessing by the substitution of 'sable' for 'sooty' to describe his moustache (G. 601). A similar change was to occur in the First Edition when, at an earlier point in the story, Hardy was to substitute 'a well-groomed black moustache with curled points' (I. 70) for the earlier reading, 'a sooty fur represented for the present the dense black moustache that was to be' (G. 102).

The two most lengthy sections of manuscript material omitted from the *Graphic* were published as the independent sketches, 'Saturday Night in Arcady' and 'The Midnight Baptism', the former in the weekly magazine, the *National Observer*, on 14 November 1891 and the latter in the *Fortnightly Review* (edited by Frank Harris) on 1 May of the same year. In both sketches the name 'Tess' was suppressed and new material incorporated, the changes being somewhat more far-reaching in the former sketch than in the latter.

---

[4] See pp. 88-9, 116 above.   [5] See pp. 118-19 above.

'Saturday Night in Arcady' is a shortened and crude version of the incidents described in the manuscript on ff. 77/8–99. The sketch omits certain scenes, such as the heroine's encounter with the villain on the street corner of 'the decayed market town' (which the First Edition was to emphasize) and the seduction (which the First Edition was to retain in somewhat bowdlerized form). It also abridges the events of the dance held at the home of the hay-trusser (which the First Edition was to omit). At the end Hardy tells us indirectly that the girl, 'Big Beauty', has become the mistress of her employer's son and that he has tired of her:

They observed that to him she was deferential thence-forward, that she started when he came into the field, and when he joked jokes of the most excruciating quality she laughed with a childlike belief in them.

Two or three months afterwards she was called away from the farm to her native place, many miles off, by the sickness of a relative, which necessitated her giving up her engagement here. He made no objection to her going, and on parting she gave him her mouth to kiss, not her cheek as at one time. She implored him not to desert her. He said he would not; that the parting would not be for long; that he should soon come to see her.

But he never went.   (N.O. 675)

Only two of the changes made in this sketch had any significant influence on the transmitted text of *Tess*, one being a change in the villain's mode of transport when he has rescued the girl from the drunken women in the Chase and the other a slightly more candid description of her sexual responsiveness towards him.

As may be seen from the following manuscript passage the villain is originally described as driving a horse and gig on his way home from the dance:

The twain bowled along in the gig for some time without speech.
~~Rose-Mary~~ *Tess*
~~Sue~~   still panting in her triumph, yet in other respects indifferent.
                                                                    (ff. 91–2)

The description of this incident is altered in 'Saturday Night in Arcady', and shows that he is now riding a horse:

Meanwhile the vanished twain cantered along for some while without speech, the girl as she clung to her knight still panting in her triumph, yet in other respects dubious . . .   (N.O. 675)

In the First Edition this altered circumstance of the sketch is retained, and so are most of the textual amendments:

The twain *cantered along* for some time without speech, Tess *as she clung to him* still panting in her triumph, yet in other respects *dubious*. (I. 131)

The slightly more explicit revelation of the heroine's emotional responsiveness is found in the author's observation, 'She was silent', after she has been asked by the villain if his every attempt at love-making has angered her. The manuscript report of the conversation is as follows:

> '*Tess*
>   ʌ Why do you dislike my kissing you?'
> 'Because I don't love you.'
> 'You are quite sure?'
> 'Quite. I am angry with you sometimes.'
>   *I half feared as much.'   Nevertheless Alec*
> 'Ah, ~~no! 'Yes—I know you are.'~~ ʌ ~~Hawnferne~~ did not object to that
> confession. He knew that anything was better than frigidity. 'Why haven't
> you told me when I have made you angry?'
>   'You know very well why, sir. Because I cannot help myself here.'
>   Much more of this tentative dialogue followed, the horse keeping on
> his way; till a warm luminous fog, which had hung in the hollows all the
>   *, & enveloped them.*
> evening, became general/ ʌ   (ff. 92–3)

The version given in the sketch introduces the new evidence in the manner indicated below:

> 'Why do you always dislike my kissing you?' continued he.
> 'Because I don't love you.'
> 'You are quite sure?'
> 'Quite. I am angry with you often.'
> 'Ah! I half-feared as much.' Nevertheless, he seemed not to object to that confession: anything was better than frigidity. '*It has not been on account of my love-making?*'
> '*Sometimes—too many times.*'
> '*Every time I have tried?*'
> *She was silent*; and the horse ambled along for a considerable distance.   (N.O. 675)

By itself, the alteration, here shown in italics, would be of little importance. However, when linked with other changes introduced into the passage at the First Edition stage it assumes significance, the implications of 'She was silent' being expanded by the insertion of 'I suppose' before 'because I don't love you', the deletion of the forthright 'Quite' from the beginning of her second reply, and the substitution of 'I am angry with you sometimes!' for 'I am angry with you often':

> 'Tess, why do you always dislike my kissing you?'
> '*I suppose*—because I don't love you.'
> 'You are quite sure?'
> 'I am angry with you *sometimes*!'
> 'Ah, I half feared as much.' Nevertheless, Alec did not object to that confession. He knew that anything was better than frigidity. 'Why haven't you told me when I have made you angry?'
> 'You know very well why. Because I cannot help myself here.'
> 'I haven't offended you often by love-making.'
> 'You have sometimes.'
> 'How many times?'
> 'You know as well as I—too many times.'
> 'Every time I have tried?'
> *She was silent*, and the horse ambled along for a considerable distance, till a faint luminous fog, which had hung in the hollows all the evening, became general and enveloped them.   (I. 131–2)

The changes in the second sketch, 'The Midnight Baptism', affect mainly the beginning and the end of the episode on which it is based. Thus, its opening paragraphs offer a much abridged version of the description of early-morning activities on the day of harvesting, as given on ff. 117–19, while its closing passages, concerned with the interview between the heroine, 'Sis', and the vicar and with the burial of Sorrow, obviously represent an expansion of whatever material was contained on the missing manuscript leaf, f. 134. This expanded version of the conclusion was to find its way into the First Edition, as did a large number of minor stylistic changes.

The tone of this conclusion to 'The Midnight Baptism', and hence of the end of chapter 14 in the editions, is strongly anti-religious, and Hardy may well have been encouraged to express his hostility towards Christian orthodoxy by the relative freedom from censorship offered by the editorial policy of Frank Harris and his assistant editor, the latter of whom had commented, in a letter to Hardy dated 14 April 1891: 'I don't see why "The Bastard's

Baptism" would not do—but "The Midnight Baptism" is an effective enough title'.[6]

The only other readings in 'The Midnight Baptism' which significantly affect the transmission of the novel's text are the insertion of a descriptive clause relating to the sound of the heroine's voice and the substitution of a paragraph in which blame is transferred from the heroine's father to Chance. The inserted clause—'and which will never be forgotten by those who knew her'—has already been the subject of comment in an earlier chapter.[7] The substituted paragraph replaces a manuscript paragraph describing an early attempt by the heroine to have her child baptized, which has been thwarted by her father's misplaced family pride:

> *locked*
> As a consequence he had ~~barred~~ the door when she was going out to
> be churched, & had insisted upon a promise that there should be no christening
> *~~Rose-Mary~~ poor*
> of the child whilst it was in his house. With tears in her eyes ~~she~~ ₐ
> *Tess* *season* *~~simplicity~~*
> gave her word, though at that ~~period time of her life~~ she attached immense
> importance to rites. Since that day, therefore, she had taken no further
> *~~chance~~ opportune moment*
> step, furtively awaiting some ₐ ~~opportunity~~ for carrying out her desire.
> (ff. 127–8)

In the sketch, as in the editions, no such earlier attempt is referred to, and the key word in the substituted paragraph is 'happened'. In other words, the fault is no longer a purely personal matter; cosmic indifference and ironic 'hap' share in the responsibility for the heroine's anguish:

> It was now bedtime, but she rushed downstairs and asked if she might send for the parson. The moment *happened* to be one when her father's sense of respectability was at its highest, and his sensitiveness most pronounced, for he had just returned from his evening booze at the public-house. No parson should come inside his door, he declared, prying into his affairs just then, when, by her shame, it had become more necessary than ever to hide them. He locked the door and put the key in his pocket. (F.R. 698)

---

[6] The letter forms part of the Hardy Collection in DCM.
[7] See pp. 118–19 above.

II

The First Edition of *Tess*, published in November 1891, shows Hardy introducing a number of bowdlerizations and plot changes, emphasizing two related themes, developing certain aspects of the characterization of Tess and Angel, and dispensing with a number of authorial comments on matters not connected with the major preoccupations of the novel. The remainder of the chapter will be concerned with examining each of these aspects in turn.

One of the more surprising features of the First Edition is its occasional bowdlerization of both manuscript and *Graphic* material. It is, of course, well known that, in general terms, the First Edition offers an infinitely more honest and satisfying account of the story than does the *Graphic*: what is not widely appreciated is the fact that some of the manuscript passages, modified or omitted on moralistic grounds in the *Graphic*, were not fully restored when the First Edition appeared. This discrepancy is especially noticeable in passages relating to events of the night of the seduction. Nor is it realized by most students of the novel that the First Edition is sometimes less frank than the *Graphic* in describing the feelings and behaviour of Tess and Angel during the courtship period at Talbothays.

Although the account of the actual seduction is incomplete in the B.M. MS., owing to the fact that ff. 100-1 are no longer extant, the beginning of the scene on f. 99 is described with a certain amount of realistic detail, as the following extract shows:

obscurity

There was no answer. ~~&~~ The ~~blackness~~ was now so intense that he
The red rug, & the white muslin figure he had

could see absolutely nothing. ˄
left upon it, were now all ——— blackness alike. ~~Hawnferne~~ [?]

˄   <u>He</u> ˄   stooped, & heard a
She was sleeping soundly.

gentle regular breathing. ˄   He knelt, & bent lower, & her breath
warmed   *& with her hair,*
~~touched~~ his face, & in a moment his cheek was in contact with hers ˄

& her eyes. A ~~damp~~ wetness accompanied the touch —— of her eye

   ⌄   ~~Sue was sleeping soundly; & there was damp about her~~ lashes

upon his face,

   ⌄   as if she had wept.   (f. 99)

In the First Edition, which was the next text to contain an account of this episode, much of the realistic detail has disappeared, the paragraph now ending with the sentence 'She was sleeping soundly': 'There was no answer. The obscurity was now so great that he could see absolutely nothing but a pale nebulousness at his feet, which represented the white muslin figure he had left upon the dead leaves. Everything else was blackness alike. D'Urberville stooped; and heard a gentle regular breathing. She was sleeping soundly' (I. 140). Following this bowdlerized version, it was left to the 1892 edition to restore most of the omitted manuscript material to the transmitted text:

There was no answer. The obscurity was now so great that he could see absolutely nothing but a pale nebulousness at his feet, which represented the white muslin figure he had left upon the dead leaves. Everything else was blackness alike. D'Urberville stooped; and heard a gentle regular breathing. *He knelt and bent lower, till her breath warmed his face, and in a moment his cheek was in contact with hers.* She was sleeping soundly, *and upon her eyelashes there lingered tears.*   (X. 89–90)

Somewhat earlier in the story, the manuscript contains an account of the Chaseborough dance (ff. 81–5), which, although omitted from the *Graphic*, was to appear in an abridged form in the sketch, 'Saturday Night in Arcady'. When Hardy came to prepare the text of the First Edition, for some reason this episode was not included, although it was to be reinserted in the novel when the 'Wessex' version was published in 1912. In the preface to that edition Hardy claimed that the relevant manuscript leaves had been 'overlooked' at the First Edition stage. As has earlier been noted,[8] the omission of the Chaseborough dance could not have been accidental, and the evidence for this deduction is given in the next chapter. What is most pertinent, at this juncture, is that we should remember that the Chaseborough dance episode contains several patterns of rich erotic imagery: it is thus conceivable that one of Hardy's motives

[8] See p. 19 above.

for omitting the episode was the desire to avoid drawing upon himself criticism occasioned by its erotic tone.

On the occasion when the heroine returns home from 'The Slopes', the manuscript gives another fairly candid account of an incident later bowdlerized in the First Edition. This is the conversation between the heroine and her mother:

> *Rose-Mary my dear Tess!*   *ye*   *Have you come for a holiday?*
> 'Well, ~~Sue,~~   How be ~~you~~? ^
> I saw 'ee ~~dr~~ walk up.'
>   'Did you, mother? I thought nobody saw me . . .* Yes, I have/ for
> a ~~Yes~~ long holiday.'
>   '*~~And~~ But how do you get on with the gentleman? I ~~suppose~~ hear he's*
>
>   ^
> | *open* | *your* | *lover by this time.*'
>
>   ^
>   '*I cannot ~~say~~* speak for him.*'
>
>   ^
>   '*Have you made up a match with him?*'
>   ~~'Is he going to marry you?'~~
>   'No?'
>   *And you come back?*
>   'No? ^   Surely you might ha' got him in the mind of
> doing that!' ~~Any woman would have done it but you!~~* cried her disappointed
> mother.   (f. 110)

The above passage, as has earlier been observed,[9] was replaced in the *Graphic* by one designed to introduce an entirely different explanation of what had happened to the heroine at 'The Slopes', and the *Graphic* version became, in turn, the basis of the First Edition version of the conversation. As a result, the First Edition offers an account which is far more cautious in its handling of the question of sexual relationships than that given in the manuscript:

> 'Well!—my dear Tess!' exclaimed her surprised mother, jumping up and kissing the girl. 'How be ye? I didn't see you till you was in upon me! Have you come home to be married?'
> 'No, I have not come for that, mother.'
> 'Then for a holiday?'
> 'Yes—for a holiday; for a long holiday,' said Tess.
> '*What, isn't your cousin going to do the handsome thing?*'
> '*He's not my cousin, and he's not going to marry me.*'
> Her mother eyed her narrowly.

---

9 See p. 151 above.

'Come, you have not told me all,' she said.

Then Tess told.

'And yet th'st not got him to marry 'ee!' reiterated her mother. 'Any woman would have done it but you!' (I. 158)

In this passage the first of the italicized sections is a First Edition insertion, while the second marks the beginning of Hardy's return to the manuscript for his source material. The remainder of the extract is directly based on the expurgated *Graphic* text.

A number of other bowdlerizations are found in the First Edition in spite of the fact that they were marked in the manuscript in the blue ink intended to denote 'adaptations for serial issue only' (f. 104). Thus, in its version of the following manuscript passage, the First Edition omitted the word 'sexual', even though it was originally deleted in blue ink only:

For a moment the ~~serenity of the~~ voices cheered the heart of Tess, ~~no less~~ till she reasoned that this interview had ~~probably~~ its origin

on one side or the other, in the same

~~in the same~~ ʌ sexual attraction, ʌ which had been the prelude to her own tribulation. (ff. 449–50)

The First Edition also failed to restore the sentence 'He bought me', which was similarly amended in blue ink in a passage conveying Tess's explanation to Angel at Sandbourne of the pressures that had compelled her return to Alec:

mother,

'. . . He was very kind to me, & ʌ to all of us after father's death.
—'

He ʌ ~~bought me.~~' (f. 539)

All that the First Edition contains in place of 'He bought me' is 'He—' (III. 238).

A slightly more complicated example of the unexpected effects of blue-ink amendments is to be seen in an incident which occurs immediately before the above interview, when Angel first arrives at 'The Herons' in search of Tess. From the manuscript it becomes clear that the blue-ink amendments are designed to avoid raising in the reader's mind any questions as to the kind of relationship now existing between Tess and Alec:

The hour being early the landlady herself opened the door. Clare inquired for Teresa D'Urberville or Durbeyfield.

'*Miss D'Urberville?*'
'Mrs, or Miss?'
 '*Yes.*'
'Well—Miss.'
'There's no Miss; there's Mrs D'Urberville only.'
'Ah,' he said correctedly, 'I meant Mrs.'   (f. 537)

When the *Graphic* version appeared, the amended version was, as
usual, adhered to, with Angel merely replying 'Yes' to the landlady's question 'Miss D'Urberville?' (G. 726); but when Hardy
came to prepare the text of the First Edition, he failed to restore the
original manuscript version. Seeing before him the *Graphic* version, 'Miss D'Urberville', he contented himself with the alteration
to 'Mrs D'Urberville', leaving the remainder of the passage unchanged. As a result a scrap of conversation which had originally
been revealing and dramatic was deprived of most of its meaning
and power.

There is also present in the First Edition a group of bowdlerizations for which magazine editors cannot in any way be held
responsible. In the three examples cited immediately below, the
amendments represent a toning down of the language describing
the heroine's emotional responsiveness to Angel's advances during
the courtship scenes at Talbothays, and would seem to have been
influenced mainly by Hardy's desire to continue the trend, apparent
in the later manuscript layers, of placing increased emphasis on the
modesty of Tess. Thus, after Angel has embraced her and asked
her to be his wife, the manuscript and the *Graphic* read, 'She turned
quite pale. She had *yielded* to the inevitable result of *contact* . . .'
(G. 329); but in the First Edition this becomes, 'She turned quite
pale. She had *bowed* to the inevitable result of *proximity* . . .' (II. 82).
Later in the story, when she is standing on the staircase early one
morning, the manuscript describes how, after Angel has impul-
sively kissed her cheek, 'She *warmed as she had done when they were
at the whey-tub and* passed downstairs breathing quickly . . .' (f. 261),
which is also the reading in the *Graphic*, except for the alteration
of 'breathing quickly' to 'very quickly' (G. 358). In the First
Edition, however, all that remains of the sentence is 'She passed
downstairs very quickly . . .' (II. 107). Eventually, the heroine
accepts Angel's proposal of marriage, and when he asks her to

prove that she loves him, the manuscript and *Graphic* describe how she kisses him passionately on the lips, continuing, ' "There— now do you believe?" she asked, wiping her eyes' (G. 359). In the First Edition, however, the final sentence is amended to read: ' "There—now do you believe?" she asked, *flushed, and* wiping her eyes' (II. 123).

Two amendments, also uninfluenced by magazine editors, show a corresponding toning down of language describing Angel's embracings of the heroine, and these changes would seem to be continuing trends already noted in the later manuscript layers relating to both Angel and the heroine. One such change occurs during the flooded-lane episode, the reading in both the manuscript and *Graphic*, ' "O Tessie!" he said, pressing close against her' (G. 248), being replaced by the briefer First Edition reading, ' "O Tessy!" he exclaimed' (II. 27). Somewhat later in the story, the manuscript and the *Graphic* contain these words: 'Then he pressed her again to his side, for the unconstrained manners of Talbothays Dairy came convenient now' (G. 329). This, in turn, was to give way to a more restrained version, in which Arcadianism was to play an important part, as the italicized insertion shows: 'Then he pressed her again to his side, *and when she had done running her forefinger round the leads to cut off the cream-edge he cleaned it in nature's way*; for the unconstrained manners of Talbothays dairy came convenient now' (II. 81-2).

Two of the most important plot changes in the First Edition involve the introduction of new scenes associated with the d'Urberville motif. One of these is the episode in which the sight of the sinister d'Urberville portrait over the door of Tess's bedroom undermines Angel's resolve to enter (II. 214-15), an insertion which strengthens the plot at one of its most crucial moments. The second is the revised account of Tess's visit to Kingsbere Church, the church of her ancestors, which replaces the brief account of such a visit contained in the manuscript and the *Graphic* (f. 141; G. 162). The revised version, one of the most memorable scenes in the definitive novel, ends with the agonized words of the heroine, 'Why am I on the wrong side of this door!' (III. 208), which signify that she has reached the utmost limit of her own material, physical, and emotional resources and now has no alternative to accepting the terms offered by the sham d'Urberville, Alec.[10]

Two somewhat less important plot changes in the First Edition are concerned with letters written by the heroine to Angel. The letter written a few nights before the wedding goes under the carpet, and in the manuscript and the *Graphic* she discovers this fact only by chance, after she has 'whimsically' decided to look into Angel's room once more before leaving Talbothays for ever (G. 391). In the First Edition her motive for revisiting the room is altered: she is now 'still doubtful if he could have received it' (II. 165), and accordingly goes upstairs to investigate. The character traits of intelligence and will thus supplement the role initially dominated by chance alone. The letter written on the evening before the Durbeyfield family's expulsion from their home at Marlott is an entirely new plot element in the First Edition. Beginning with the words 'O why have you treated me so monstrously, Angel!', and ending, 'It is all injustice I have received at your hands!' (III. 187), it is waiting for Angel on his return from Brazil and exerts an important influence on his motives for delaying his journey in quest of Tess; it also reveals, in stark fashion, the state of mind which helps to drive the heroine back into Alec's arms. The manuscript (ff. 524-5) shows that there had been an earlier plot concept in which she had written a letter to Angel's father, telling him that it would not be possible for her and Angel to live together in the future; but this concept had been cancelled in the manuscript itself.

It is Tess's poverty that ultimately compels her to return to Alec, and we find in the First Edition that Hardy had made yet another plot change which makes her poverty more credible in the closing stages of the story. This arises from the amendments to the terms under which Tess receives the jewels bequeathed by Angel's godmother. In the manuscript and the *Graphic*, old Mr. Clare's note, which arrives on the wedding-night with the jewels themselves, states that they are 'your wife's absolute property' (G. 422);

---

[10] Earlier references to these scenes will be found on pp. 117, 95-7 above. It is interesting to note that the serial version in *Harper's Bazar* includes both the early and the later visits to the church.

and this absolute form of ownership is once again stressed when Tess and Angel are on the point of parting, a few days later: 'The brilliants, which were Tess's undoubted property, he had advised her to let him send to a bank for safety; and this she had agreed to. They had been deposited in her name, and he had given her the banker's receipt for the box, so that she could get them on application without hindrance from, or consultation of, anybody. "In case of need you can turn them into money," he said' (G. 482). No such right is conferred on Tess in the terms quoted in the First Edition. Here, Mr. Clare's note has been altered to read: 'They become, I believe, heirlooms, strictly speaking' (II. 183); while on the occasion of the parting of Tess and Angel the text now reads: 'The brilliants, *the interest in which seemed to be Tess's for her life only* (*if he understood the wording of the will*), he advised her to let him send to a bank for safety; and to this she readily agreed' (II. 254). As a consequence, Tess no longer possesses the 'banker's receipt' that alone would have allowed her to remain financially independent in her hour of utmost need.

Thematically, the First Edition is important for the increased emphasis it gives to the two related ideas of social intolerance and religious obscurantism, both of which have their origin in the older theme of Nature as norm. The first of these themes, which stresses the wrong-headedness of conventional nineteenth-century bourgeois attitudes towards the seduced woman occurs by implication in the manuscript in the scenes displaying Angel's incredulous horror at the news that his bride is not the virgin he had fondly believed her to be. But it was not until the printed versions—or so it would seem from the evidence still available—that Hardy employed any of the passages of explicit comment with which the reader of the definitive version is familiar.

One such passage, first found in the *Graphic* (the relevant manuscript leaf being no longer extant), stresses that the heroine ought to dismiss all feelings of guilt relating to her seduction, because her situation is 'in accord' with the natural order of things:

Walking among the sleeping birds in the hedges, watching the skipping rabbits on a moonlit warren, or standing under a pheasant-laden bough,

M

she looked upon herself as a figure of Guilt intruding into the haunts of Innocence. But all the while she was making a distinction where there was no difference. Feeling herself in antagonism she was quite in accord. She might have been a party to the tampering with a social law, but with no law known to the environment in which she fancied herself such an anomaly.   (G. 161)

The *Graphic* also includes Hardy's comment that Society is less than honest in claiming that the seduced woman has little to live for or look forward to:

Let the truth be told—women do as a rule live through such humilia-tions, and regain their spirits, and again look about them with an inter-ested eye. While there's life there's hope is a conviction not so entirely unknown to the 'deceived' as some amiable sentimentalists would have us believe.
   Tess Durbeyfield, in good heart, and full of zest for life, descended the Egdon slopes lower and lower towards the dairy of her pilgrimage.
                                                      (G. 162)

In the First Edition Hardy alters the final sentence of the first of these two *Graphic* passages, so that, instead of 'She might have been a party to the tampering with a social law . . .', it reads, 'She had been made to break a necessary social law . . .' (I. 167). Here, although it is conceded that the law is 'necessary', the emphasis is falling on compulsion, on the use of force ('*made* to break'); and later, in the 1892 edition Hardy was to alter the wording even more significantly when he wrote, 'She had been made to break an *accepted* social law . . .' (X. 108). The First Edition also inserts into that part of the text transmitted from 'The Midnight Baptism' a number of other passages of social comment, such as the following italicized sentence: '*But now that her moral sorrows were passing away a fresh one arose on the natural side of her which knew no social law*. When she reached home it was to learn to her grief that the baby had been suddenly taken ill since the afternoon' (I. 180–1).

In the following well-known comment on Angel, the statement 'when surprised back into his early teachings', represents yet another First Edition insertion: 'With all his attempted indepen-dence of judgment this advanced and well-meaning young man, a sample product of the last five-and-twenty years, was yet the slave to custom and conventionality *when surprised back into his early teachings'* (X. 343). However, the passage was not to find its definitive form, in which it is here quoted, until the edition of 1892, when the words 'and well-meaning young' and 'a sample product of the last five-and-twenty years' were inserted.

While the theme of social intolerance is at least adumbrated in *The Woodlanders*, where it takes the form of an attack on the divorce laws of England, the theme of religious obscurantism is something new in Hardy's novels. In the manuscript the references to religion are relatively innocuous, and merely note such things as the fact that Angel has become 'wonderfully free from the chronic melancholy which is taking hold of the civilized races with the decline of belief in a beneficent power' (f. 167), or that while 'The mill still worked on . . . the abbey had perished, creeds being transient' (f. 333). It is not until the First Edition that the full bitterness of the anti-religious note is heard, its reverberations being especially noticeable in the scenes involving three minor characters—the vicar of Marlott, the painter of religious texts, and the Reverend Mr Clare.

The attack on the vicar of Marlott in the First Edition represents an intensification of the anti-religious attitude already noted as a characteristic of the closing part of the sketch, 'The Midnight Baptism'.[11] The attack is levelled against both the man and the dogmas he feels compelled to uphold, and in the following quotation from the First Edition the italicized section shows a somewhat scurrilous addition to the indictment against the man:

'And now, sir,' she added earnestly, 'can you tell me this—will it be just the same for him as if you had baptized him?'
Having the natural feelings of a tradesman at finding that a job he should have been called in for had been unskilfully botched by his customers among themselves, he was disposed to say no. Yet the dignity of the girl, the strange tenderness in her voice, combined to affect his nobler impulses —or rather those that he had left in him after ten years of endeavour to graft technical belief on actual scepticism. The man and the ecclesiastic fought within him, and the victory fell to the man.
'My dear girl,' he said, 'it will be just the same.'   (I. 188-9)

A few lines further on, it is more specifically the dogmas that are the object of criticism, when that section of the churchyard wherein

---

[11] See pp. 156-7 above.

Sorrow is to be buried, described earlier in the sketch as 'that shabby corner of the enclosure where the nettles grow' (F.R. 701), is described as 'that shabby corner of *God's allotment* where *He* lets the nettles grow' (I. 191).

The First Edition version of the meeting with the painter of texts brings forth the following two additions, as italicized, to the text transmitted from the manuscript, the first being prompted by dislike of the dogmatic side of Christianity:

THY, DAMNATION, SLUMBERETH, NOT.

2 PET. ii. 3.

Against the peaceful landscape, the pale, decaying tints of the copses, the blue air of the horizon, and the lichened stile-boards, these staring vermilion words shone forth. They seemed to shout themselves out and make the atmosphere ring. *Some people might have cried 'Alas, poor Theology!' at the hideous defacement—the last grotesque phase of a creed which had served mankind well in its time. But* the words entered Tess with accusatory horror. It was as if this man had known her recent history; yet he was a total stranger.   (I. 155)[12]

In the second addition, the motivation is more personal—Hardy's dislike of the hypocritical, mechanistic approach towards religious duties adopted by certain individuals, already apparent in the earlier jibe against the 'tradesman' feelings of the vicar of Marlott:

'I think they are horrible,' said Tess. 'Crushing! killing!'

'That's what they are meant to be!' *he replied in a trade voice. 'But you should read my hottest ones—them I kips for slums and seaports. They'd make ye wriggle! Not but what this is a very good tex for the rural districts.* . . . Ah—there's a nice bit of blank wall up by that barn standing to waste. I must put one there. Will you wait, miss?'   (I. 156)

During the part of the novel concerned with Angel's early life we come across the discussion between Angel and his father, the Reverend Mr Clare, on the topic of Angel's future vocation in life. Here, too, there are a number of First Edition insertions and substitutions which were clearly designed to introduce stronger criticism of the Church and its dogmas. Thus, instead of restoring the blue-ink cancellation 'while she adheres to certain worn-out

---

[12] Cf. MS. readings quoted on p. 62 above, in which the Biblical text reads 'THE, WAGES, OF, SIN, IS, DEATH.'

portions of her teaching' (f. 163), the First Edition version of part of Angel's statement reads: '. . . but I cannot honestly be ordained her minister, as my brothers are, while she *refuses to liberate her mind from an untenable redemptive theolatry*' (I. 230). And on the following page, this passage of theological explanation by Angel makes its appearance for the first time: 'My whole instinct in matters of religion is towards reconstruction; to quote your favourite Epistle to the Hebrews, "the removing of those things that are shaken, as of things that are made, that those things which cannot be shaken may remain"' (I. 231). During most of the scenes in which the Reverend Mr Clare appears there is little personal criticism directed against him; indeed, Hardy goes out of his way to emphasize, from the manuscript stage onwards, that the author (like Angel) 'revered his practice and recognized the hero under the pietist' (f. 237). The same cannot be said, however, of Angel's two clergyman brothers, Felix and Cuthbert, who are revealed in a consistently unflattering light throughout all stages of the novel's composition.

One of the results of the bowdlerization process and the emphasis on social and religious themes in the First Edition is a stressing of certain key elements in the characterization of the two main personages—namely the modesty and purity of Tess, and the combination of idealistic ethical standards, advanced religious views, but essentially conservative social attitudes in Angel Clare. In addition, we may note two other kinds of amendments affecting Tess—one imparting to her more gracefulness and gentleness, the other accentuating her fidelity towards her absent husband—together with a series of amendments which emphasize Angel's blind idealizing of the physical fact of virginity.

The most revealing change concerned with the heroine's increased gracefulness and gentleness is to be found during the section of the novel devoted to her ride through the Chase with the villain on the night of the seduction. The manuscript describes how she is being driven in the villain's gig when she almost falls asleep from fatigue, to find herself quickly supported by his arm around her waist. The original (L1) text on f. 93 continues thus: 'This put her on the alert immediately. She started, and pushed him from her, with such unexpected force that he lost his balance, and, to her horror, rolled over the off-wheel into the road.' The manuscript shows the beginning of the process of refining, with the insertion of additional words immediately before 'pushed', which read, 'with one of those sudden impulses of reprisal to which she was liable'. But it is not until we come to the First Edition (where the two characters are now on horseback) that we find the more graceful and gentle action of the heroine that the reader of the definitive text is familiar with: 'This immediately put her on the defensive, and with one of those sudden impulses of reprisal to which she was liable she gave him a *little push* from her. *In his ticklish position he nearly lost his balance and only just avoided rolling over into the road, the horse, though a powerful one, being fortunately the quietest he rode*' (I. 133).

Tess's faithfulness to Angel, despite his unjust treatment of her, is made especially clear through the First Edition insertions which show her reacting violently to insulting remarks about him. Thus, in the manuscript and *Graphic* text, when she strikes Alec with her heavy work-glove it is in consequence of the following conversation:

'. . . Tess, my trap is waiting just under the hill, and—beauty mine—you know the rest.'
'What!' she whispered, huskily, her face rising to a dull crimson fire.
'You have been the cause of my backsliding; you should be willing to share it.'   (G. 634)

Here, it is clear that there is no insulting reference to Angel at this point in the narrative. But in the First Edition, Alec's reference to Angel as 'that mule you call husband' introduces a new dimension:

'. . . Tess, my trap is waiting just under the hill, and—*darling mine, not his!*—you know the rest.'
Her face had been rising to a dull crimson fire while he spoke; but she did not answer.
'You have been the cause of my backsliding,' he continued jauntily; 'you should be willing to share it, *and leave that mule you call husband for ever!*'   (III. 140)

Similar insertions in the passage containing Tess's distraught explanation to Angel of why she has murdered Alec illustrate the same trend: 'He heard me crying about you, and he bitterly taunted me; *and called you by a foul name*; and then I did it. *My heart could not bear it. He had taunted me about you before.* And then I dressed myself and came away to find you' (III. 252).

Angel's idealizing of virginity receives especial emphasis both in the First Edition and in the edition of 1892. Typical of such amendments is the following, in which the word 'truthful', as used in both the manuscript and the *Graphic* (G. 450), has given way to 'virginal' in the First Edition:

Nothing so pure, so sweet, so *virginal* as Tess had seemed possible all the long while that he had adored her, up to an hour ago; but

The little less, and what worlds away!   (II. 215)

Similar changes involve the replacement of 'girlishness' (G. 450) by 'maidenhood' (II. 220), and 'perfect' (G. 483) by 'spotless' (II. 276); together with the subsequent changes of the First Edition 'genuine' (I. 240) to 'fresh and virginal' (X. 155) and 'unsophistication' (II. 221) to 'innocence' (X. 308). A complementary amendment, which stresses, equally strongly, Angel's eventual realization of his earlier blindness to the true merits of Tess was also inserted towards the end of the story at the First Edition stage: 'Despite her not inviolate past, what still abode in such a woman as Tess outvalued the freshness of her fellows. Was not the gleaning of the grapes of Ephraim better than the vintage of Abi-ezer? So spoke love renascent, preparing the way for Tess's devoted outpouring, which was then just being forwarded to him by his father' (III. 163).

Hardy's tendency to intrude as commentator in *Tess* has been condemned—not always justly—by many critics over the years. Thus Lionel Johnson in 1894 observed that 'Mr. Hardy has not denied himself the luxury, or perhaps the superfluity, of comments at once inartistic and obscure', and Dorothy Van Ghent in 1953 warned the reader against 'the temptation to mistake bits of philosophic adhesive tape, rather dampened and rumpled by time, for the deeply animated vision of experience which our novel, *Tess*, holds'.[13] What has not been realized, however, is that in the First

[13] Lionel Johnson, *The Art of Thomas Hardy*, London, 1894 (new edn., 1923), p. 228. Dorothy Van Ghent, *The English Novel*, New York, 1953 (Harper Torchbook edn., 1961), p. 196.

Edition Hardy showed a tendency to eradicate some of the authorial comments earlier incorporated into the text, thus increasing, relatively speaking, the degree of objectivity present in his narrative technique.

One of the passages omitted from the First Edition (I. 22) is the following comment, found in the manuscript and *Graphic*, on the strange effect of coincidence, inspired by the arrival of Angel and his brothers at Marlott while the 'club-walking' is being held: 'Their presence here at Marlott at this hour, though it had no bearing upon the nearer events which followed, was regarded as singular in after years, when viewed by the light of subsequent incidents' (G. 14). Also omitted (I. 121) is the manuscript comment, 'an attractive phase in all her sex', which follows the description of the heroine as 'standing, moreover, on the momentary threshold of womanhood' (f. 79). A little later in the story, the First Edition substitutes the expression, 'The material distinctions of rank and wealth he *increasingly* despised' (I. 232) for '. . . he *commendably* despised' (G. 192), and '*she*' (I. 249) for '*the poor girl*' (G. 218). Then, when Angel is contemplating the possibility of marrying the heroine, we find that the First Edition (II. 51) omits another comment, this time a brief parenthesis concerning the importance of 'staunch comradeship' in marriage:

He loved her: ought he to marry her? Dared he to marry her? What would his parents and his brothers say? What would he himself say a couple of years after the event? That would depend upon whether the germs of staunch comradeship [(*without which no marriage should be made*)] underlay the temporary emotion, or whether it were a sensuous joy in her form only, with no substratum of ever-lastingness.   (G. 302)

The final illustration comes from the scene in which Tess and Angel are parting, the italicized sections in square brackets, once again, being the sections omitted from the First Edition version:

That was all she said on the matter. If Tess had been artful, had she made a scene, fainted, wept hysterically, in that lonely lane, notwithstanding the fury of fastidiousness with which he was possessed, he would probably not have withstood her. [*But she was too honest to succeed with men, who suffer artifice gladly, not as fools but as wise. Clare had, in truth, feared some such final outburst from her, with good reason.*] But her mood of long-suffering made his way easy for him, and she herself was his [*own*] best advocate. (G. 482)

Such amendments as these—albeit limited in range and number —show that Hardy was at least conscious of the technical advantage accruing from increased narrative objectivity, even though his intense moral commitment to Tess and the truths she embodied would not permit him to dilute the commentary when more fundamental issues were at stake.

IX

LATER PRINTED VERSIONS
(TO THE EDITION OF 1912)

I

ALTHOUGH *Tess* quickly established itself as Hardy's most famous novel, its reception by the reviewers was by no means uniformly favourable. While 'the majority', in Hardy's words, '. . . generously welcomed the tale', the hostile tone adopted by a small number shocked and distressed Hardy to such an extent that on one occasion, after reading a particularly vituperative attack, he recorded the following observation in his diary:

15 [April, 1892]. *Good Friday*. Read review of *Tess* in *The Quarterly*. A smart and amusing article; but it is easy to be smart and amusing if a man will forgo veracity and sincerity. . . . How strange that one may write a book without knowing what one puts into it—or rather, the reader reads into it. Well, if this sort of thing continues no more novel-writing for me. A man must be a fool to deliberately stand up to be shot at.[1]

The writer of this unsigned review, although Hardy did not know it, was Mowbray Morris, who, it will be recalled, in his capacity as editor of *Macmillan's Magazine* had rejected the manuscript of *Tess* on 25 November 1889. Morris's criticisms, which tend to restate in a particularly insulting manner views already expressed in certain other periodicals of the time—notably, the *Saturday Review* of 16 January, the *New Review* of February 1892, and the *Independent* of 25 February—are directed at the matter and the manner of Hardy's novel, both of which are labelled 'coarse and disagreeable'. Specifically, Morris notes that 'It is indisputably open to Mr Hardy to call his heroine a pure woman; but he has no less certainly offered many inducements to his readers to refuse her the name'; and he also observes that 'Poor Tess's sensual

---

[1] *Life*, p. 246.

qualifications for the part of heroine are paraded over and over
again with a persistence like that of a horse-dealer egging on some
wavering customer to a deal, or a slave-dealer appraising his wares to
some full-blooded pasha'. As the result of such a perverse attitude to
life, Morris suggests, 'the shadow of the goddess Aselgeia[2] broods
over the whole book'. It is, thus, not surprising that Morris also mocks
Hardy's 'affection of expounding a great moral law' and regrets that
'his assumption of the garb of the moral teacher' has destroyed the
charm and humour that distinguished his earlier novels.[3]

Hardy answered these and similar charges in his 'Preface to the
Fifth Edition', dated July 1892, especially in the following passage,
which is here quoted in its original form (and not in the revised
form of the 1895 edition):

Nevertheless, though the novel was intended to be neither didactic nor
aggressive, but in the scenic parts to be representative simply, and in the
contemplative to be oftener charged with impressions than with opinions,
there have been objectors both to the matter and to the rendering.

Some of these maintain a conscientious difference of sentiment concerning, among other things, subjects fit for art, and reveal an inability
to associate the idea of the title-adjective with any but the licensed and
derivative meaning which has resulted to it from the ordinances of civiliza-
tion. They thus ignore, not only all Nature's claims, all aesthetic claims
on the word, but even the spiritual interpretation afforded by the finest
side of Christianity; and drag in, as a vital point, the acts of a woman in
her last days of desperation, when all her doings lie outside her normal
character. Others dissent on grounds which are intrinsically no more
than an assertion that the novel embodies the views of life prevalent at
the end of the nineteenth century, and not those of an earlier and simpler
generation—an assertion which I can only hope may be well founded.

(X. viii)

The vigorous tone of this defence helps us to understand the
reasons for some of the changes we find in the novel itself, when it
finally appeared in its revised form on 30 September 1892, as the
'Fifth Edition'.

The relative frankness of the 1892 edition has already been noted
in relation to the description of the actions of the villain at the

---

[2] Licentiousness.
[3] 'Culture and Anarchy' [a review article devoted to three books including *Tess*], *Quarterly Review*, clxxiv, 1892. See pp. 319 ff.

beginning of the seduction scene, which was considerably bowdlerized in the First Edition. For it is the 1892 edition which publishes
for the first time the details italicized in the following extract: *'He
knelt and bent lower, till her breath warmed his face, and in a moment
his cheek was in contact with hers.* She was sleeping soundly, *and
upon her eyelashes there lingered tears'* (X. 89-90). It is also the
1892 edition which first includes the words 'I may not be able to
love you' as part of Angel's proposal to Izz Huett that she should
accompany him when he leaves for Brazil (X. 348) and Tess's
admission to Angel that the fine clothes she is wearing at Sandbourne were put on her by Alec:

> She continued—
> 'He is upstairs. I hate him now, because he told me a lie—that you
> would not come again; and you *have* come! *These clothes are what he's
> put upon me: I didn't care what he did wi' me!* But—will you go away,
> Angel, please, and never come any more?'   (X. 493)

Similarly, in the following descriptive passage the simile, 'as
if Cybele the Many-breasted were supinely extended there', was
not included in any version before that of 1892: 'Towards the
second evening she reached the irregular chalk table-land or
plateau, bosomed with semi-globular tumuli—*as if Cybele the
Many-breasted were supinely extended thore* [*sic*]—which stretched
between the valley of her birth and the valley of her love'
(X. 363).

The fact that the heroine had stayed on at 'The Slopes' as Alec's
mistress for some time after her seduction is also brought out more
specifically in the 1892 edition.[4] This is seen in the following
italicized insertion, in which the author explains that Tess had been
'temporarily blinded by his flash manners' and 'stirred to confused
surrender awhile', before suddenly despising and disliking him and
running away:

> She had never wholly cared for him, she did not at all care for him
> now. She had dreaded him, winced before him, succumbed to *a cruel
> advantage he took of her helplessness; then, temporarily blinded by his
> flash manners, had been stirred to confused surrender awhile: had suddenly*

---

[4] But see also pp. 71-2 above.

despised and disliked him, and had run away. That was all. Hate him she did not quite; but he was dust and ashes to her, and even for her name's sake she scarcely wished to marry him. (X. 102)

In the earlier part of this insertion the words 'cruel advantage he took of her helplessness' refer to the seduction itself. The words 'cruel advantage', in particular, suggest the harshness of Alec's nature and behaviour and reinforce the implications of force and compulsion conveyed by an earlier-noted amendment in the First Edition—'She had been *made to break* a . . . social law.'[5]

The implications of force are conveyed most strongly in a passage which constitutes the most significant single amendment in the 1892 edition. This is the interpolation in chapter 14, during which the field woman comments to a companion, as she watches Tess moodily kissing her baby in the cornfield near Marlott, that 'A little more than persuading had to do wi' the coming o't, I reckon':

'A little more than persuading had to do wi' the coming o't, I reckon. There were they that heard a sobbing one night last year in The Chase; and it mid ha' gone hard wi' a certain party if folks had come along.'
'Well, a little more, or a little less . . .' (X. 114)

It is this passage, more than any other in the novel, which conveys to the reader the notion that the defloration of Tess should be termed an act of rape rather than a seduction. Its introduction, without doubt, serves to win for the heroine additional sympathy and respect, and, in so doing, underlines the concept of her essential purity, which, as we have seen, is already vigorously propounded in the Preface.

The insertion of the above passage in chapter 14 necessitated the removal of a number of passages in chapter 11. One such passage was the following, whose removal was dictated primarily by the needs of consistency; for, clearly, the field woman's second sentence ('There were they that heard a sobbing one night last year in The Chase') would have conflicted with the authorial statement in the First Edition version of chapter 11 that the 'sons of the forest' did not receive 'the least inkling that their sister was in the hands of the spoiler':

[Already at that hour some sons of the forest were stirring and striking lights in not very distant cottages; good and sincere hearts among them,

[5] See p. 166 above.

patterns of honesty and devotion and chivalry. And powerful horses were stamping in their stalls, ready to be let out into the morning air. But no dart or thread of intelligence inspired these men to harness and mount, or gave them by any means the least inkling that their sister was in the hands of the spoiler; and they did not come that way.   (I. 141)]

The other passages which needed to be removed from the text were those describing how the villain forced the heroine to drink a quantity of intoxicating liquor, before leaving her temporarily in the fog-bound Chase while he ascertained their whereabouts. Once again, consistency was the main reason for the removal; for it was essential in the 1892 edition that there should not remain any suggestion that the heroine had been rendered either complaisant or unconscious by the effects of alcohol. The passages omitted in 1892 are shown by the italicized sections within square brackets:

'Nights grow chilly in September. Let me see.' [*He went to the horse, took a druggist's bottle from a parcel on the saddle, and after some trouble in opening it held it to her mouth unawares. Tess sputtered and coughed, and gasping 'It will go on my pretty frock!' swallowed as he poured, to prevent the catastrophe she feared.*]
'That's it—now you'll feel warmer,' said D'Urberville, [*as he restored the bottle to its place. 'It is only a well-known cordial that my mother ordered me to bring for household purposes, and she won't mind me using some of it medicinally.*] Now, my pretty, rest there; I shall soon be back again.'
(I. 138)

In place of this incident, Hardy included in the 1892 edition the following innocuous passage, in which all reference to a 'cordial' (or 'spirits', which is the term used in the manuscript) has disappeared:

'Nights grow chilly in September. Let me see.' *He pulled off a light overcoat that he had worn, and put it round her tenderly.* 'That's it—now you'll feel warmer,' he continued. 'Now, my pretty, rest there; I shall soon be back again.'
(X. 88)

One of the effects arising from the omission of the 'sons of the forest' paragraph from the 1892 edition was to modify slightly the attack on cosmic irony and injustice, which the paragraph had helped to illustrate in the First Edition, where it had followed the passage containing the questions, 'But where was Tess's guardian angel? where was Providence?' (I. 140). The same trend towards modification is apparent in the altered form of the questions themselves, which in the 1892 version appear as 'But where was Tess's guardian angel? where was *the* Providence *of her simple faith?*' (X. 90). And these were to be modified even more radically in the 1895 edition: 'But, *might some say*, where was Tess's guardian angel? where was the providence of her simple faith?' (Y. 90).

Concurrently with this slight decrease in emphasis on the cosmic theme, the edition of 1892 shows a slight increase in emphasis on the themes of Nature as norm and social intolerance, as is apparent from the insertion of such previously noted passages on Angel Clare as 'Some might risk the odd paradox that with more animalism he would have been the nobler man . . .' (X. 316) and 'a sample product of the last five-and-twenty years' (X. 343).[6] It should also be remembered that it was in the same edition that Hardy inserted the memorable passage on the heroine's purity, in which Angel, having located Tess at Sandbourne, senses that 'his original Tess had spiritually ceased to recognize the body before him as hers— allowing it to drift, like a corpse upon the current, in a direction dissociated from its living will' (X. 494).

II

Despite its additional prefatory material, the edition of 1895 contains relatively few significant textual changes, and of this small number most are relevant to the theme of Nature as norm. Thus, when Izz Huett agrees to go to Brazil with Angel, her words in the version of 1892 read as follows: 'It means that I shall be with you for the time you are over there—that's good enough for me' (X. 349). In the 1895 edition, however, 'be' has been amended to 'live'. Similarly, in the 1892 edition Hardy's comment on the death of Sorrow reads: 'So passed away Sorrow the Undesired—that intrusive creature, that bastard gift of shameless Nature who respects not the civil law' (X. 121). In the 1895 edition, however,

[6] See pp. 44, 136, 167 above.

Hardy has specifically emphasized the difference between the law of Nature and that of Society by substituting for 'the civil law' the reading 'the social law'. There are also insertions in the 1895 edition in which Hardy shows his two main characters temporarily oppressed by the thought that in the eyes of Nature it is Alec, not Angel, who is Tess's husband. The following italicized section illustrates this point: 'How can we live together while that man lives?—*he being your husband in Nature, and not I*' (Y. 315).[7]

Having examined the main changes in the Macmillan Uniform Edition of 1902, which are devoted to the lessening of Alec d'Urberville's religiosity in chapters 45 and 46,[8] we may pass on to the edition of 1912, where we find that the only major textual change is the one mentioned in the first paragraph of the brief prefatory statement dated March 1912: 'The present edition of this novel contains a few pages that have never appeared in any previous edition. When the detached episodes were collected as stated in the preface of 1891, these pages were overlooked, though they were in the original manuscript. They occur in Chapter X.' Here, it will be noted, Hardy is claiming that the pages had been 'overlooked' when the First Edition was being prepared for publication; and, as has earlier been noted,[9] a similar claim is made in the *Catalogue of Additions to the Manuscripts in the British Museum*, wherein there occurs, in relation to Hardy's manuscript, a statement that one of the separately published sketches included 'a preliminary description of a country-people's dance accidentally omitted in the three-volume and subsequent editions until 1912: see ff. 59 sqq. in the M.S.'[10] When all the textual evidence is examined, it becomes obvious that the claim made in both of these statements— that the section referred to was omitted by accident—is completely unfounded. And, indeed, it soon becomes apparent that only one conclusion is valid: that Hardy deliberately chose to omit from the First Edition the manuscript material in question. This material is, in essence, the account of the Chaseborough dance.

---

[7] See also p. 44 above.   [8] See pp. 7, 18, 141 above.   [9] See p. 19 above.
[10] 'ff. 59 sqq.' (B.M. numbering) is equivalent to ff. 77/8ff. in Hardy's final foliation system (S3).

The means Hardy employed for excluding the episode from the
First Edition was conflation, the telescoping into a single scene
of plot material which had originally belonged to two different
sections of the manuscript, separated from each other by the
description of the dance itself. The first of these sections of
manuscript material concludes with a meeting between the
heroine and the villain on a street corner in the main part of
Chaseborough:

This had gone on for a month or two when a Saturday came on which
a fair & a market coincided; & the pilgrims from Trantridge sought
double delights on that account. ~~They had all set out when Sue left~~
     ~~Rose-Mary's~~ *Tess's*
~~home. Sue's~~   occupations made her late in setting out, so that
her comrades reached the town long before her. It was a fine September
evening, just before sunset, when yellow lights struggled with blue
  ~~in hairy~~ *in hair-like lines,*   *forms*
shades ᴧ   & the atmosphere itself ~~is~~ a prospect,
without aid from more   *except* ~~it be~~
~~apart from~~   solid objects, ~~except than~~ the innumerable winged
             low-lit   ~~Rose-Mary~~ *Tess*
insects that dance in it. ~~Sue~~ Through this ᴧ mistiness ~~Sue~~
walked leisurely along.
          coincidence
She did not discover the ~~conjunction~~ of the market with the fair
till she had reached the place, & by which time it was close upon
  dusk
~~sunset.~~ Her limited ~~week's~~ marketing was soon completed; & then as
usual she began to look about for some of the Trantridge cottagers⸝.
~~for the sake of their company home.~~
At first she could not find them, & she was informed that most of
them had gone to what they called a private little ~~dan~~ jig at the house
        peat-   ~~& who conveniently~~
of a hay-trusser & ᴧ dealer who had transactions with their farm ᴧ.
~~kept a beer-house.~~   *townlet*
          He lived in an out-of-the-way nook of the ~~place,~~
      course   *D'Urberville*
& in trying to find her ~~way.~~ thither her eyes fell upon Mr ~~Hawnferne~~
standing at a street-corner in conversation with another young man.
     ~~Tasie?~~ *my Beauty—*
'What— ——?   you here so late?' he said.
She told him that she was simply waiting for company homeward.
        over her shoulder
'I'll see you again,' he said ᴧ   as she went on her way down
    in the twilight
the back lane. ᴧ   (ff. 79–80)

N

The second section deals mainly with a meeting between the
heroine and the villain in a garden, outside the shed in which the
dance has been in progress for some time:

     loud   ~~Rose-Mary's~~ Tess's
A ~~burst of~~ laughter from behind ~~Sue's~~   back in the shade
of the garden united with the titter within the room. She looked round,
                      D'Urberville
& saw the red coal of a cigar: Alec ~~Hawnferne~~ was standing ~~behind her~~
   alone   reluctantly retreated ~~with~~ towards
there ~~by himself~~. He beckoned to her, & she ∧ ~~went out to~~ ∧   him.
       Beauty
—'Well, my ~~pretty~~, what are you doing here?'
        at their delay   her
She was so tired ~~with waiting~~, after her long day, & ∧ walk, that she
              that she had
confided her trouble to him—'~~I have~~ been waiting ~~& waiting,~~ ever since
he   her,
~~you~~ saw —————— to have their company home, because the road at
night was   ~~at night~~ 'But   s
∧ —— strange to her ∧.   ~~But~~ ∧ it ~~do~~ seem∧ as if they will never
leave off; & I really think I will wait no longer.'
  'I am driving home. Come to The Stag & you shall ride with me.
~~Rose-Mary~~ Tess
Do, ~~Sue!~~   I will start as soon as ever you like—say in a few minutes?'
   ~~Rose-Mary~~
~~She~~ had never got over her original mistrust of him; &, with all their
                        folk
tardiness, she preferred to walk home with the work~~people~~, 'I am much
              frigidly.   can   with 'ee.
obliged ~~to 'ee sir,~~' she answered ∧ 'But I ~~will~~ not go ∧   I have said
that I will wait for 'em, & it will be better to do it now.'
       Miss Independence;
  'Very well, ~~silly~~   Please yourself. Then I shall not hurry.
   good Lord,
My ~~God~~ ∧ what an infernal kick-up they are having here!'
  He had not put himself forward, but some of them had seen him, &
                ~~& wiping of foreheads,~~
his presence ~~caused~~ led to a slight pause,   ∧   & a consideration
    the
of how ∧ time was going. As soon as he had re-lit a cigar & walked away,
    ~~workfolk~~   amid
the Trantridge people began to collect themselves from ∧ those who ~~had~~
belonged to other farms; & ~~soon~~ prepared to leave in a body. Their
bundles & baskets were gathered up, ~~from the spots whereon they had been~~
~~temporarily deposited,~~ & a quarter of an hour later, when the clock-chime
sounded half-past-eleven, they were straggling along the lane which led
up the hill towards their homes.
                               (ff. 84–5)

When we read the First Edition version, we find that only one meeting takes place between heroine and villain and this occurs on the street corner in the main part of the town; moreover, there are no references to a dance, the heroine being shown to be waiting outside a tavern, in which the Trantridge workfolk have been sitting for several hours:

This had gone on for a month or two when a Saturday came in early September, on which a fair and a market coincided; and the pilgrims from Trantridge sought double delights at the inns on that account. It was long past sunset and Tess waited for the troop till she was quite weary. While she stood at a corner by the tavern in which they sat she heard a footstep, and looking round saw the red coal of a cigar. D'Urberville was standing there also. He beckoned to her, and she reluctantly went to him.

'My Pretty, what are you doing here at this time of night?'

She was so tired after her long day and her walk that she confided her trouble to him.

'I have been waiting ever so long, sir, to have their company home, because the road is rather strange to me at night. But I really think I will wait no longer.'

'Do not. I have only a saddle-horse here to-day; but come to the "Flower-de-Luce", and I'll hire a trap, and drive you home with me.'

Tess had never quite got over her original mistrust of him, and, with all their tardiness, she preferred to walk home with the work-folk. So she answered that she was much obliged to him, but on second thoughts would not trouble him. 'I have said that I will wait for 'em, and they will expect me to now.'

'Very well, silly! Please yourself.'

As soon as he had re-lit a cigar and walked away the Trantridge villagers within began also to recollect how time was flying, and prepared to leave in a body. Their bundles and baskets were gathered up, and half an hour later, when the clock-chime sounded a quarter past eleven, they were straggling along the lane which led up the hill towards their homes. (I. 121–3)

If the two versions are closely examined, it will be seen that, although the First Edition version of these events relies on the earlier of the two manuscript passages for its setting, most of its dialogue and descriptive detail come from the later passage. A particularly revealing example of conflation may be seen in one of the villain's utterances, 'My Pretty, what are you doing here at this time of night?' Here, the first part of his question has been adapted from the later meeting—'Well, my Beauty, what are you doing here?' while the second part is an adaptation from the earlier meeting—'What—my Beauty—you here so late?'

When Hardy decided to include the Chaseborough dance episode in the edition of 1912, he prepared a special holograph manuscript consisting of eight leaves and headed 'An omitted passage from Tess of the d'Urbervilles', most of which is virtually identical, textually, with the final version in the B.M. MS. (ff. 80-5). From its opening sentence ('Tess's occupations made her late in setting out . . .') until the section beginning 'Certainly do not. I have only a saddle-horse here to-day' on the second-last leaf, the special manuscript (now held at the Dorset County Museum, Dorchester) differs from the B.M. MS. in only trifling matters; and not until we reach the brief concluding section—from 'Certainly do not' to the sentence ending '. . . straggling along the lane which led up the hill towards their homes'—do we find Hardy adopting readings from both the First Edition and the manuscript. This special manuscript was closely followed in the printed version of the episode in the 1912 edition, the differences being so few and so trivial as to be unworthy of special attention.

III

There remains for brief consideration the question of Hardy's use of dialect in the conversations of his three main Wessex-born characters—Joan, John, and Tess Durbeyfield. In the conversations of all three characters, it is noticeable that the dialectal content has received considerable emphasis in two texts—the manuscript and the edition of 1892. It is also noticeable that the dialectal content of the speech of Joan and John has received additional emphasis in the First Edition and—occasionally—in the edition of 1895, while that of the heroine has been decreased in the First Edition and the edition of 1912.

The main clue to this discrepancy as it affects the heroine is provided by amendments introduced into an authorial comment on this very matter, which occurs in the early part of the story. In the manuscript the comment tells the reader that, while Joan Durbeyfield 'still spoke portions of the dialect', Tess 'who had passed the sixth standard in the National school under a London-trained mistress, used it only when excited by joy, surprise, or grief' (f. 19). But from the 1892 edition onwards the comment was to read very differently: 'Mrs Durbeyfield habitually spoke the dialect; her daughter, who had passed the Sixth Standard in the National School under a London-trained mistress, *spoke two languages; the dialect at home, more or less; ordinary English abroad and to persons of quality*' (X. 22). When the various amendments relating to the heroine's use of dialect are examined, it is found that most of them are explainable in terms of the two forms of this comment. One important result is that most of her speech 'abroad and to persons of quality' in the edition of 1912 is free from dialect. By this means Hardy continued to impart additional dignity to his heroine, even as late as the year 1912.

PART FIVE

CONCLUSION

CONCLUSION

IT was John Paterson in his book, *The Making of 'The Return of the Native'* (1960), who first convincingly demonstrated the falsity of the notion of Thomas Hardy as 'the engineer in literature', constructing each of his novels, all too obviously, according to some kind of architectural blueprint. *The Return of the Native*, Paterson observed, was 'quite as much the product of revision as the product of vision', emerging 'out of both freedom and necessity' and shaped by both 'editorial censorship' and 'a creative force, a vision, a theme that animates and transmutes . . . form and meaning'. *Tess of the d'Urbervilles* and *Jude the Obscure*, Paterson went on to say, were less strongly influenced by editorial pressure during the period of manuscript composition than was *The Return of the Native*; however, it was 'the rule rather than the exception' for Hardy to repudiate the elaborate outline of plot which he usually prepared before undertaking the writing of a new novel.[1]

Most of the above comments by Paterson are applicable to *Tess*. The important exception is his statement that in *Tess* and *Jude* 'the artistic transaction was completed with relatively little interference of an editorial nature'. Paterson continues:

Tess was written in its entirety before it became apparent that it would have to be modified for serial publication; *Jude* was written, through a special arrangement with Harper, with publication as a book in mind and was then emasculated for its appearance as a serial. *The Return of the Native*, however, was intended for serial publication and hence was exposed to the pressures of censorship not subsequent to, but in the course of, the act of composition. Its primary text was not, therefore, like that of *Tess* and *Jude*, a faithful transcript of an imagination freely exercised, but the record of an imagination acting under straitened circumstances.[2]

As we now know from the earlier parts of the present study, Paterson's statements concerning the circumstances under which the manuscript of *Tess* was composed are completely misleading. It is

[1] Paterson, pp. 125, 126, 163, 164, 168.
[2] Ibid., pp. 163-4.

simply not true to say that '*Tess* was written in its entirety before it became apparent that it would have to be modified for serial publication'; nor is it true that the manuscript, or 'primary text', of *Tess* was 'a faithful transcript of an imagination freely exercised'.

Much of the vivid description in the Talbothays section of the novel was, admittedly, already well developed at the Ur-version stage of composition, as were many of the patterns of classical and Biblical allusions, much of the imagery of colour and light, and four of the themes—intention, Nature as norm, will, and the insignificance of the individual entity. But the characterization and plot of the Ur-novel were later to undergo fundamental changes, and it was only after the Ur-version stage that many of the important motifs and themes made their first significant appearance in the text. The evolution of *Tess* was gradual, and like *The Return of the Native* it emerged 'out of both freedom and necessity'.

The heroine's character received most of its final shaping during the last three layers of the manuscript, and the concept of Tess as 'a pure woman' continued to engage Hardy's attention during the revisions which attended the publication of the *Graphic*, the First Edition, and the edition of 1892. It was not until these printed texts, indeed, that Hardy first included the comments which emphasized Tess's innocence in the eyes of Nature, stressed that her original surrender had been a matter of compulsion rather than will, and suggested that 'with more animalism' Angel 'would have been the nobler man'. The transformation of Alec d'Urberville from a mere figure of melodrama into a character possessing considerable symbolic significance was also effected during the later layers of the manuscript, as were the expansion of John Durbeyfield's role and his transmutation into a symbol of rural decadence. Similarly, such important symbolic images as the hunted animal, the altar victim, and the willing scapegoat, date mainly from the later stage of manuscript development, as do the cosmic, agricultural, and heredity themes; while the themes of social intolerance and religious obscurantism were not to receive their main emphasis until the First Edition.

The extreme reticence which marks the treatment of some of the key scenes in the novel—such as the actual seduction, the heroine's conversation with her mother on her return home from her stay at 'The Slopes', and her confession to Angel on her wedding-night —would seem to reflect not only editorial pressures but also Hardy's growing determination after November 1889 to defend Tess as a pure and modest woman, this intention being even more clearly illustrated by the First Edition bowdlerizations of some of the courtship scenes at Talbothays. The same attitude of moral commitment to his heroine would seem to have been responsible, at least in part, for the note of sentimentality which Hardy allowed to creep into Tess's renunciation of Angel in favour of 'Liza-Lu in the First Edition, for the anomalies and inconsistencies in the character-study of Angel Clare, in both the manuscript and the printed texts, and for the artistic crudity which mars some of the First Edition passages of ironic comment relating to the painter of texts and the vicar of Marlott.

For the element of thematic confusion in *Tess*, the whole curious history of the novel's development must clearly bear much of the blame; while for the presence of melodrama in scenes involving Alec d'Urberville during the last two 'Phases' of the novel some of the responsibility must be borne by the editors of the family magazines and newspapers of the day, of whose standards of taste and morality Hardy had been made only too well aware by the time that he came to write the final layers of his manuscript.

There remains the controversial critical problem of Hardy's 'authorial intrusions' in *Tess*. These, as has earlier been noted,[3] have incurred the wrath of critics as diverse as Lionel Johnson and Dorothy Van Ghent, both of whom have condemned the intrusions as inartistic and philosophically confused. On this vexed question I shall offer three comments.

First, it should be noted that the increased bitterness of the philosophic comments from L3 onwards indicates that they represent an angry, and understandable, reaction by Hardy to the prevailing ethos of his time, as made clear to him through the hostile comments of editors such as Edward Arnold, Mowbray Morris, Arthur Locker, and, later, of reviewers such as Andrew Lang.[4]

[3] See p. 171 above.   [4] See the *New Review* of February 1892.

Secondly, it is a perfectly tenable proposition that the presence of the narrator's personality in *Tess* should be accepted as an integral part of Hardy's narrative method, which, in turn, constitutes 'the appropriate form' (to use Barbara Hardy's well-known phrase)[5] for Hardy's special fictional requirements.

Finally, it may be argued, with some justification, that the distinctive narrative voice, which is heard in varying degree in all Hardy novels, is not that of Hardy the man, but is the voice of an anonymous narrator, representing a dramatized version of Hardy. It is this kind of view which is put forward by J. Hillis Miller, who asserts that 'The narrative voice of Hardy's novels is as much a fictional invention as any other aspect of the story', and, thus, a device for achieving a degree of objectivity. Miller continues:

His goal seems to have been to escape from the dangers of direct involvement in life and to imagine himself in a position where he could safely see life as it is without being seen and could report on that seeing. To protect himself and to play the role of someone who would have unique access to the truth—these motives lie behind Hardy's creation of the narrative voice and point of view which are characteristic of his fiction.[6]

Whether or not we accept Miller's thesis completely, one conclusion is clear: that we should no longer meekly accept the older critical notion that the philosophic comments in *Tess* are mere excrescences. They constitute, in fact, an inalienable element in the narrative, without which the novel would necessarily have been an entirely different kind of book, with an entirely different kind of impact.

[5] Barbara Hardy, *The Appropriate Form*, London, 1964.
[6] *Thomas Hardy: Distance and Desire*, Cambridge, Mass., 1970, pp. 41, 43.

APPENDIX

THE following chart shows the correlation between foliation systems (as used in the B.M. MS. of *Tess*) and chapter divisions (as used in the *Graphic* serial version and in all published editions of *Tess*).

S3 Folio no.	S2 Folio no.	S1 Folio no.	B.M. Folio no.	*Graphic* Chapter no.	Editions Chapter no.
1	1	—	1	1	1
6a	6a	—	7	2	2
15†	15†	—	—	3	3
24	24	—	19	4	4
30	30	—	25	5	[No chapter break]
38	38	—	30	6	5
50	50	—	39	7	6
57†	57†	—	—	8	7
63†	63†	45†	—	9	8
69†	69†	—	52	10	9
77/8	—	63	59	[This material omitted]	10 [Incorporates material used in N.O. sketch]
91	—	76	72	[This material omitted]	11 [Incorporates material used in N.O. sketch]
101†	77†	86†	—	11	12
111	—	96	89	12	13
117	—	110	92	[This material omitted]	14 [Incorporates material used in F.R. sketch]
135	89*	129	103	13	15
139†	93†	133†	—	14	16
149	103	142	112	15	17
160	114	152	122	16	18
171	125	163	133	17	19
182	136	174	143	18	20
187	141	179	148	19	21
196	150	188	157	20	22
200	154	192	161	21	23
210	164	202	171	22	24
216	170	208	177	23	25
221	175	213	182	24	[No chapter break]
229	183	221	190	25	26

S3 Folio no.	S2 Folio no.	S1 Folio no.	B.M. Folio no.	*Graphic* Chapter no.	Editions Chapter no.
238	192	230*	199	26	27
246	200	238	207	27	28
254	208	246	215	28	29
263	217	255	224	29	30
274	228	264	235	30	31
280	234	270	241	31	[No chapter break]
287	241	277	248	32	32
297	251*	287	258	33	33
309	263	299	270	34	34
324	277	—	284	35	35
336	289	—	296	36	36
352	305	—	312	37	37
364	317	—	324	38	38
371	324	—	331	39	39
380	333*	—	340	40	40
390	343	—	350	41	41
401	354	—	361	42	42
408	361	—	368	43	43
424	377	—	384	44	44
438	391	—	398	45	45
450	403	—	410	46	46
465	418	—	425	47	47
477	430	—	437	48	48
485	438*	—	445	49	49
495	448	—	455	50	50
505	458	—	465	51	51
514	467	—	474	52	52
522	475	—	482	53	53
529	482	—	489	54	54
534	487	—	494	55	55
539	492	—	499	56	56
545	498	—	505	57	57
553	506	—	513	58	58
563	516	—	523	59	59

Key: † = missing folio [⅓ of folio 69 is missing].
　　　　* = folio number obscured or omitted.